THE BIBLE SKIT BOOK

VOLUME ONE

52 SERIOUSLY FUNNY BIBLE TEACHING SKITS

BY TOM BOAL

Gospel Light

YOU MAY MAKE COPIES OF THE SKITS IN THIS BOOK IF:

- you (or someone in your organization) are the original purchaser;
- you are using the copies you make for a noncommercial purpose (such as teaching or promoting a ministry) within your church or organization;
- you follow the instruction provided in this book.

HOWEVER, IT IS ILLEGAL FOR YOU TO MAKE COPIES IF:

- you are using the material to promote, advertise or sell a product or service other than for ministry fund-raising;
- you are using the material in or on a product for sale;
- you or your organization are not the original purchaser of this book.

By following these guidelines you help us keep our products affordable.

Thank you.
Gospel Light

CONTENTS

ABOUT THE AUTHOR

Tom Boal lives in Leduc, Alberta, Canada, with his wife, Marilyn, and their two teenage children, Christian and Kelly. Tom writes skits for his fifth and sixth grade Sunday School class as a diversion from his profession of accounting.

EDITORIAL STAFF

Publisher, Billie Baptiste • **Senior Consulting Publisher,** Dr. Elmer L. Towns • **Senior Editor,** Gary S. Greig, Ph.D. • **Senior Consulting Editor,** Wes Haystead, M.S.Ed. • **Managing Editor,** Lynnette Pennings • **Contributing Editors,** Sheryl Haystead, C. A. Hoffman, Linda Mattia • **Designer,** Curtis Dawson

Using This Book

BRING BIBLE STORIES TO LIFE!

Drama activities in a classroom are valuable learning opportunities because of the *process* group members experience, not because of the quality of the final performance. Bible stories come alive when acted out, and Bible truth is seen to be relevant when applied to contemporary situations. In addition:

- Acting out a situation will push group members to think about the application of Bible truth to a real life circumstance.
- Dramatic activities provide a unique opportunity to briefly step into another person's shoes and experience some of his or her attitudes and feelings.

COPIES OF THE SKITS

Purchase of this book includes the right to make copies of the skits for those who will be involved in putting on the skits.

SKIT FEATURES

The skits contain the following features to help you prepare:
Scripture, suggested topics, Bible background, performance tips, discussion questions, characters list and a **pronunciation guide** for those tough biblical names. Optional props are often suggested, but any real prop can be replaced by an imaginary one simply by miming accordingly.

CHOOSING A SKIT

The skits may be used in a variety of ways:

- to **summarize** a Bible story;
- to **illustrate** a concept or topic;
- to **introduce** a Bible character;
- to **reinforce** a Bible story or life application.

The skits will be enjoyed in a variety of settings by students **ages eleven through adult:**

- Sunday School, churchtime or midweek programs;
- large or small groups;
- special events.

To help you find a skit that matches a topic or Bible story you will be studying, indexes list:

- **Scripture references** (p. 225);
- **Topics** (p. 229);
- **Bible characters** (p. 222);
- **Gospel Light Junior Curriculum, Year A** (p. 220).

GETTING READY

After you've chosen and reproduced copies of the skit for the participants, here are some tips for preparing to lead the group:

- Read the Scripture passage. Familiarize yourself with the corresponding Bible story, if applicable.
- Read the skit, noting any vocabulary or pronunciation help you will need to give your group.
- Adapt the script if needed by reducing or increasing the number of characters, adding a scene, etc.
- Take note of the discussion questions. Decide which ones will be most appropriate for your group.
- Collect props.

PRACTICAL TIPS

One of the nicest things about skits is that they are easy to prepare. Skits are not big Broadway-type productions. They can be informal and spontaneous. They can be primped and polished to the hilt when the mood strikes. A lot or a little—it all depends on how you want to do it. Here are the basic steps to go on:

- Good acting is a plus, but it's not essential in order to have a positive experience. What *is* essential is that the lines are heard by the audience. The performers need to speak slowly and clearly—with their mouths directed at the audience.
- It is not necessary for performers to memorize the script. Reading works just as well. Provide several highlighter pens for performers to mark their parts. You may give out the script ahead of time for the performer to practice. However, if you hand out the scripts ahead of time, bring extra copies on performance day, because someone will undoubtedly forget his or her copy.
- Practicing the skits ahead of time will be most important for younger groups and groups for whom English is a second language.

Using the Skits with Gospel Light Junior Curriculum

Each skit in this book corresponds with a lesson in Gospel Light Junior Curriculum, Year A, and can be used to enhance understanding and interest. Vary the way in which the skits are used:

- to replace a **Bible Readiness** choice;
- to present the **Bible story**;
- to expand the **Life Application**;
- to provide an additional **Bible Learning Activity**;
- to supplement **Bible Sharing** activities.

The information given in the Bible Background section and the Discussion Questions in each skit will help you expand the curriculum.

Using Skits with Poor Readers

If your group includes students with poor reading skills or learning disabilities, or those for whom English is a second language, don't lose heart! With a little planning and some TLC, you can help poor readers gain badly needed confidence and self-esteem *and* liven up your classroom with Bible skits.

The following list of ideas can be adapted for use in any setting. Choose the techniques that best suit your group and resources.

FOR INFORMAL PRESENTATIONS AND READ-THROUGHS:

- Highlight each character's lines on a separate copy of the script and add pronunciation pointers as needed.
- Have the entire group read through the skit in pairs or small groups before presenting the skit to the whole group.
- Give everyone in the group a script to follow as selected readers read aloud. Receiving information through more than one sense makes the drama more accessible. This technique also assists students who are better visual than aural learners. It can also ease performers' nerves a bit by providing something other than the readers on which to focus.
- Use lots of visual aids and props.
- If a skit is particularly long or has long speeches, the teacher or leader can summarize a portion of

the skit. Never feel obligated to perform a skit in its entirety; use only as much as your group can handle.

- Use a "jump-in" technique that gives readers control over how much they want to read: When a volunteer has read as much as he or she wants, another volunteer jumps in and continues reading. Or, let each reader choose a helper to consult whenever necessary.
- On an overhead projector or chalkboard, post a word bank or key with pronunciations and/or definitions to words the group might have trouble with. Before the group reading, review the words and locate them in the script with the group.

FOR MORE FORMAL PRESENTATIONS AND PERFORMANCES:

- Assign a "drama coach" to each reader to provide one-on-one help in interpreting and learning lines. Coaches may be other students or an adult.
- The leader may read aloud all character parts before they're assigned. The leader should also discuss the tone of the skit, pronunciation and meaning of difficult words, and make suggestions for changes and word substitutions.
- Students practice reading their parts into a cassette recorder. To provide extra help, the leader may record each character part on a separate cassette to distribute to readers. Record each part twice, the first time speaking slowly and distinctly with no dramatic flair, the second time with dramatic flair so students hear how the lines should be delivered.
- For struggling readers, write out each sentence on a separate index card; this technique makes the job look smaller, and each line is an accomplishment.
- Hand out the script well in advance of the performance date; call and have the student read his or her part to you over the phone to practice.
- Give permission to improvise. Students who understand the sense of a speech, and whose verbal skills exceed their reading skills, may communicate better if allowed to paraphrase.

This Is the Law

SCRIPTURE: Deuteronomy 30:11—31:13; 2 Kings 22:1—23:3; 2 Chronicles 34:1-15

SUGGESTED TOPICS: Obedience to God's Word; following God's instructions; importance of Bible reading

BIBLE BACKGROUND

The people of Israel had demanded a king. Saul, David and then Solomon ruled over the kingdom. Solomon's son, Rehoboam, saw the kingdom divided into the nations of Israel and Judah, each having its own king. Almost from the beginning, the worship of the true God was forgotten in both kingdoms. From time to time a king would remember God, but most of the kings worshiped idols. Some three hundred years after the kingdom split, Josiah ascended to the throne of Judah. Jerusalem was immersed in idolatry, and the Temple of God had deteriorated badly.

PERFORMANCE TIPS

1. Suggested props: a crown for Josiah, an old book to represent the Book of the Law.
2. Have Shaphan read Deuteronomy 28:58-68 when Josiah tells Shaphan to read the book.
3. After the skit, summarize Deuteronomy 30:15-20 to explain why Josiah was so worried.

DISCUSSION QUESTIONS

1. Why was Josiah so worried?
2. Why is it important to read the Bible?
3. Why should you obey God? What good things come from obeying God's law?
4. How can you learn God's law and promises?

This Is the Law

CHARACTERS

JOSIAH (jo-ZI-ah)
HILKIAH (hil-KI-ah)
NARRATOR
GUARD
SHAPHAN (SHAY-fan)
HULDAH

SCENE ONE

JOSIAH: Hilkiah, good of you to come.

HILKIAH: When the king requests an audience, even the high priest must obey.

JOSIAH: True enough. Hilkiah, how long have I been king?

HILKIAH: Eight years, my King. Half of your young life.

JOSIAH: And in those eight years, I have been given advice by many people.

HILKIAH: True, my King.

JOSIAH: However, some advice was better than others. Some was downright terrible.

HILKIAH: Unfortunately true, my King. Although you may fill a man with all the spices of the world, his advice still may not be sage.

JOSIAH: What? Oh. Another proverb. And true. But I have always found your advice trust worthy. *(Pause.)* Now, I have a problem. Many gods are worshiped in Jerusalem.

HILKIAH: Unfortunately, also true.

JOSIAH: But your advice has always been good and true. So I ask you—if I am to give allegiance to one of the gods worshiped in Jerusalem, which one should it be?

HILKIAH: That is simple, my King. Worship the true God, for there is only one.

JOSIAH: And you know this god?

HILKIAH: Of course, my King. I am His chief priest.

JOSIAH: Then teach me about Him, that I may know Him, too.

NARRATOR: For the next four years, Josiah learned about the God of Abraham, Isaac and Jacob from Hilkiah. Then, when he was twenty years old, in his twelfth year as king...

JOSIAH: Hilkiah, I have learned much about Jehovah from you in the past four years.

HILKIAH: All of which is the truth, my King.

JOSIAH: I believe you. Your conduct, your advice—all these things point toward your worshiping the one true God. But one thing you said puzzles me. You said Jehovah wants His people to worship only Him.

HILKIAH: Why should this puzzle you, my King? When people worship false gods, they obey false gods. They follow bad advice and live evil lives. Jehovah wants His people to have the best. To follow what is good and to truly live.

JOSIAH: Guard! *(GUARD enters.)*

GUARD: You screamed, oh King?

JOSIAH: I want you to take this hastily written decree...

GUARD: Most hastily, oh King.

JOSIAH: ...to the scribes. Have it copied many times and posted throughout Jerusalem...

GUARD: On every corner, oh King.

JOSIAH: I don't need THAT many. But post it so that all the citizens of Jerusalem can read it and obey it.

GUARD: It is already done, oh King.

JOSIAH: And then, I want a messenger to ride into every town in Judah to read the decree to all the citizens of my kingdom.

GUARD: This will take one man many years, oh King.

JOSIAH: Use as many messengers as are required. All of the kingdom of Judah must hear this decree immediately.

GUARD: Even as you speak, it is done, oh King.

JOSIAH: Then go! Do it! *(GUARD exits.)*

NARRATOR: What a decree this was. It contained instructions to rid Judah of all false gods. It ordered the destruction of the high places, the groves and wood and metal images. All were broken down into powder and scattered on the graves of those who had sacrificed to the false gods. He even burned the bones of the false priests on their own altars and then tore down the altars. Satisfied that all had been accomplished according to his will, Josiah returned to Jerusalem.

JOSIAH: There. It took six years, but I am certain that all has been put right. All the false gods have been pulverized. I can rest, knowing only Jehovah will be worshiped in Judah. All will come to His beautiful Temple—the TEMPLE! For years it has been in ruins. It must be restored.

NARRATOR: And what a job THAT was. The Levites gathered offerings from the people to begin the task of restoration. The rubble that had accumulated for decades had to be removed. Old stones that had chipped and broken had to be carefully removed from the walls and new ones put in their place. Old rotting timbers had to be replaced with new ones. And in the midst of the work...

(HILKIAH sifts through rubble while SHAPHAN watches.)

HILKIAH: Look what I have found. *(He holds out an old book.)* The king must know of this immediately. Where is Shaphan? The scribe must take this to the king at once. Shaphan! Shaphan!

SHAPHAN: Not so loud. I'm right behind you.

HILKIAH: I have found a treasure that must be taken to the king.

SHAPHAN: Then give it to one of the laborers to carry. I'm a scribe, not a porter.

HILKIAH: But this is a special treasure. One that a scribe would appreciate.

SHAPHAN: *(Gazes at Hilkiah's treasure.)* I see what you mean! I will take it to the king immediately. *(Exits the Temple.)*

SCENE TWO

GUARD: Oh King, may you live forever. There is one here who wishes an audience with Your Most Blessed Majesty.

JOSIAH: I told you I was busy. No visitors today.

SHAPHAN: *(Enters.)* Forgive me, my King, but Hilkiah instructed me to deliver this most important treasure to you immediately.

JOSIAH: Shaphan! Of course I have time to see the one who is overseeing the restoration of the Temple. How does the work progress?

SHAPHAN: Well, my King. The money collected by the Levites has been paid to the workmen. But Hilkiah found this treasure in the midst of the rubble. *(He offers the book to JOSIAH.)*

JOSIAH: Treasure? It looks like nothing more than an old book.

SHAPHAN: It is an ancient manuscript, my King. But it is far more than that. When Hilkiah was instructing you in the ways of Jehovah, he spoke from memory. That which had been passed down from his father and his grandfather, he passed along to you. But now—*(pause)* the Book written by Moses, lost for many years, has been found.

JOSIAH: I may be young, but I wasn't born yesterday. Moses died centuries ago. Such a book would have rotted away by now.

SHAPHAN: Of course, my King. This is the last copy. The one that was faithfully copied from the one before, as has always been the custom in Judah. This is the Book of the Law, the very instructions that Jehovah gave to Moses.

JOSIAH: Then sit down, Shaphan, and read me the book.

NARRATOR: Shaphan did as the king ordered. He read to the king all the words of the Law, from Genesis to Deuteronomy.

JOSIAH: Is this true? Are these words that will come to pass for all in Judah and also in Israel? It cannot be! It MUST not be! *(He tears his clothes.)*

SHAPHAN: Why does the King cry out so? And why does the King rend his garment?

JOSIAH: You read the words! You heard the promises! Did you not also hear the curses? Were you deaf to what you read?

GUARD: I wouldn't worry about it. It's an old book, written in old language. It probably doesn't apply to life today. The words probably don't have the same meaning now.

JOSIAH: Which is why you are a guard and not an advisor. Shaphan, take some men and find someone who can inquire of the Lord—for me and for those left in Israel and in Judah—about the words of this Book. For great is the wrath of the Lord, poured out upon us, because our fathers have not kept the Lord's word.

NARRATOR: So the four men sought out Huldah, a prophetess of the Lord.

HULDAH: Thus says the Lord: "I will bring evil upon this place and upon its inhabitants, all of the curses written in the book that was read to the king of Judah, because they have forgotten me and have worshiped other gods. But say this to the king of Judah. Because your heart was tender and you humbled yourself before God, and wept and rent your clothes when you heard my words, you will not see my wrath in your lifetime."

NARRATOR: When Huldah's prophecy was reported to Josiah, he made a covenant before God to walk in His ways all the days of his life, and he commanded the people of Judah to also agree to the covenant. Josiah honored his promise and served God for the rest of his life, until his death when he was thirty-nine.

THE ROBOT

SCRIPTURE: Psalm 19:7,8

SUGGESTED TOPICS: Following instructions; obedience to God's Word; living according to God's plan

BIBLE BACKGROUND

The Bible is far more than a record of past events. While filled with intriguing stories of many people, it is also a living blueprint for each of our lives, the instruction manual for how to live as God's people in this world. If we only study the Bible to discover insights about the ancient world, we miss the real purpose for which it was given. The psalmist celebrated the exciting realization that "Your word is a lamp to my feet and a light for my path" (Psalm 119:105).

PERFORMANCE TIPS

1. Suggested props: a large cardboard box; an assortment of nuts, bolts, screws and tools; a remote control unit for Lee to use as he tries to start the robot.
2. Ask one person to play the robot. He or she should stand completely still during the skit.

DISCUSSION QUESTIONS

1. Have you ever used a kit to build a model? Was it hard or easy? How did the model turn out?
2. If you planned to build something complicated, what's the first thing you would do? Why?
3. Sometimes it's hard to know the right choices to make. When do you read God's instructions for your life? What are some instructions from the Bible you remember?

THE ROBOT

CHARACTERS

KIM
LEE

KIM: Hi, Lee. What are you doing?

LEE: Hi, Kim. I'm building a robot.

KIM: A robot! Where did you learn how to build a robot?

LEE: Oh, it's easy. I bought a kit. Everything's in it.

KIM: That's a neat robot. What will it do?

LEE: I'm not sure yet. But I think that it'll do almost anything I want it to.

KIM: Wow! It sure looks great! How soon will you be finished?

LEE: I'm just putting on the final touches now. One more screw to tighten. There! Finito!

KIM: Great! How about a demo?

LEE: Sure. What do you want it to do?

KIM: I don't know. Surprise me. Make it do anything.

LEE: OK. Watch this! *(Pushes button.)*

KIM: I'm watching. What's happening?

LEE: Nothing! Must be a malfunction in this remote control. Just let me check it a minute. Aha! The red wire is where the green wire should be. There! Now watch!

KIM: I'm watching. I don't see anything.

LEE: Why doesn't this stupid thing work? People shouldn't be allowed to sell defective merchandise like this. I worked so hard on this thing and all for nothing. They didn't put the right things in the package.

KIM: Are you sure you put it together right?

LEE: Of course I'm sure! What do you think I am? A two-year-old who can't build things?

KIM: Well, no. But there sure are a lot of parts lying around outside of the robot. Maybe you didn't put something in that you should have.

LEE: Those are just extra parts. Whenever you have a model, there's always extra parts so you can build it different ways if you want to. Boy, when I get my hands on the guy who sold me this piece of junk, I'll hit him so hard he won't know up from down.

KIM: I think before you punch somebody's lights out, you should check your work first. You know, go over the instructions one more time and be absolutely certain that you didn't make a mistake.

LEE: What do you mean, "Go over the instructions one more time?" I didn't read them the first time.

KIM: Are you telling me that you tried to build something as complicated as a robot with out reading the instructions so you would know what you were doing?

LEE: Of course not! I've built lots of things before, and I didn't have time to waste. I wanted to get this thing built so I could have fun with it. Get it to do things, like cleaning up my room, taking out the garbage—things I don't like to do myself. But now I can't. All because somebody at the factory was too lazy to make sure that all the right parts were in the box.

KIM *(softly)***:** Or because somebody was too lazy to read instructions.

LEE: What's that? Did you say something?

KIM: No. Nothing.

LEE: Well, I'm going to take this tin man back to the store and give that salesperson a piece of my mind.

KIM *(softly)***:** Are you sure you have any to spare?

LEE: Huh? Did you say something?

KIM: Nothing important.

LEE: Help me pack up this box again, would you? I don't want them telling me the store can't take it back because I kept some of the extra parts. Boy, when I get through with them....

Ocean Front Property

SCRIPTURE: Luke 6:46-49

SUGGESTED TOPICS: God's Word as foundation; putting it into practice

BIBLE BACKGROUND

Of all the questions Jesus asked—and He asked many—perhaps none is more penetrating and convicting than this one: "Why do you call me, 'Lord, Lord,' and do not do what I say?" Jesus' famous story about the wise and foolish builders was told to illustrate the crucial difference between the person who obeys the Word of God and the person who hears but does not obey. The story assumes that both types of person have the same information and ability; but one chooses to do what God says while the other chooses another path. Ignoring God's way seems to have gone satisfactorily for the foolish man until he hit a crisis. Then, his lack of a solid foundation for life was his undoing.

PERFORMANCE TIPS

1. Suggested props: several blueprints for Wise Mann to carry, a glass of lemonade for Don Key.
2. Before the skit, read Luke 6:46,47. Explain that these verses tell Jesus' introduction to the story in the skit.
3. After the skit, read Luke 6:48,49.

DISCUSSION QUESTIONS

1. In the skit, we are told that both men read the building code. Did reading the code help both men? Why or why not?
2. How do we build a strong foundation for our lives? What happens if we do not build a strong foundation?

OCEAN FRONT PROPERTY

CHARACTERS

NARRATOR
WISE MANN
DON KEY

NARRATOR: Once upon a time, there were two men: Wisenthorpe Mann, known to his friends as Wise, and Donald Key. Both men decided to build a new house with an ocean view. Each man carefully studied the building codes and planned his new home.

WISE MANN: Hello. You must be my new neighbor. My name's Wisenthorpe Mann, but you can call me Wise, for short.

DON KEY: Donald Key. Don to my friends. You got your house all planned?

WISE MANN: I sure have. I'm going to lay the foundation next week. You see that spot back near those trees? Just in front. That way, I can save the trees, have a beautiful view out the back window, and have the ocean front view from the front window.

DON KEY: Are you crazy? Way back there? Why, you're going to have to walk forever to enjoy the water. Now me, I'm going to build my house right here. Big deck all around. I could practically dive off the deck into the ocean any time I want.

WISE MANN: Do you think that's a good idea? Look how high the tide comes in.

DON KEY: No sweat. I'm building it on stilts. That way, even if the tide comes in higher than expected, I'm still sitting high and dry.

WISE MANN: I have my doubts. But I guess you've read the charts and know what you're doing.

DON KEY: Darn tootin'. Got it planned to the last detail. How about you?

WISE MANN: Of course. First, I'm driving pylons way down deep into the bedrock.

DON KEY: Pylons into bedrock. Are you nuts? What a waste!

WISE MANN: What do you mean?

DON KEY: Look. You got about eight feet of sand before you get down to the rock, right? You plan to drill through a bunch of rock and plant pylons that deep? A waste of money. All you got to do is what I'm doing. Twelve stilts driven down six feet, connected with a series of triangles. Solid! Couldn't move it if you wanted to. Then, with the money you save, you can build an extra room or finish the walls with better materials. Put your money where it shows, I say.

WISE MANN *(slowly)*: I don't know. I read the building code and it suggests...

DON KEY: Code, schmode. Written by some guy who owns a lumber store. Just wants more business for himself. Take my word for it, my way's best.

WISE MANN: If you say so. But for me, I think I'll stick to what the code says and put in the pylons. Lay a firm foundation.

DON KEY: Suit yourself. Must be nice having money to throw away. I'm putting my money where it shows.

NARRATOR: So the two men went to work. While Wise Mann was still laying his foundation, Don Key had finished all the framing. While Wise Mann was putting up his exterior walls, Don Key had finished paneling his interior walls with the finest wood that money could buy. While Wise Mann was working to complete the interior—not as lavishly as Don Key's home, but stylishly and comfortably—Don Key was relaxing on his deck with a big glass of lemonade. One day, Wise Mann decided to take a short break from construction and go for a dip in the ocean.

DON KEY: Howdy, neighbor. How goes the house?

WISE MANN: Very well, thanks. Just a few more days and it'll be finished.

DON KEY: Now ain't that just hunky-dory. C'mon up and have some lemonade. I've been watching you, slaving away day and night, while my house was being enjoyed. Look at this deck. Know how much this wood cost? Probably nearly as much as your whole house. Finest material known to man. Specially treated to last a hundred years before it needs any work. Ah, yes. This is the life.

WISE MANN: Well, it sure is beautiful. But I'm happy with my home. When it's finished, it will suit me for the rest of my life.

DON KEY: Sure. When it's finished. Meantime, I've been enjoying my house for weeks while you've been slaving away.

WISE MANN: Well, to each his own. Thanks for the lemonade. I'm going for a quick swim and then, back to work.

DON KEY: Go ahead. I'm just going to sit here and relax.

NARRATOR: And so, Wise Mann finished his house, built to the specifications of the building code. Every morning he awoke, looked out his bedroom window to the trees behind the house, looked out the front window at the ocean and Don Key's house. Then, one morning, after a particularly heavy wind the night before...

WISE MANN: What a beautiful morning. Look at those gorgeous trees. And look at that beautiful beach and ocean. Nothing but sand and ocean as far as the eye can see. *(Pause.)* Wait a minute. Something's missing. Don's house. It's not there! I wonder what he did with it? I wonder where he moved it?

TAKE A LETTER

SCRIPTURE: Selected Epistles; Philemon

SUGGESTED TOPICS: Encouragement toward obedience; guidance through God's Word

BIBLE BACKGROUND

Paul's missionary journeys were instrumental in founding the early churches throughout the Mediterranean region. However, the time Paul could spend with these fledgling churches was not enough. Each church had its own problems which needed to be addressed. In order to instruct, edify, and correct the churches and the church leaders, Paul wrote letters which were often shared among those early churches.

Let's consider a few of the problems which beset the New Testament churches and which Paul addressed in his letters:

1. Misunderstanding the relationship between the Law and the grace of God (see Romans, Galatians, Philippians);
2. Divisions and immorality within the church (see 1 Corinthians);
3. Distrust of church authority (see 2 Corinthians);
4. Lack of knowledge about God's purpose for the church (see Ephesians);
5. Threat of new and curious teaching (see Colossians);
6. Questions about the Lord's return (see 1 and 2 Thessalonians);

Obviously, two thousand years have not improved mankind to any noticeable degree. Imperfect people run the church, therefore, the church is not perfect. How gracious of our Lord to provide us with a mirror in which we can see our faults and discover the guidance we need to help us correct those faults.

PERFORMANCE TIPS

1. After Paul tells Stephen to "take a letter," read 1 Corinthians 10:1,2,6,7,11,12. Point out that Paul used a familiar story from the Old Testament to show that we need to learn from the past.
2. Consider reading the whole letter to Philemon. If there are sufficient Bibles for your group, have each person read a verse. Stop from time to time to explain what is happening in case anyone in the group has difficulty understanding the letter.

DISCUSSION QUESTIONS

1. Why do you think Paul wrote letters to the churches and the church leaders?
2. How did Paul use the letters to help the early Christians?
3. How can Paul's letters help us today?
4. What other ways can we receive help to obey God? How can we help others to obey God?

TAKE A LETTER

CHARACTERS

TIMOTHY

PAUL

ONESIMUS (oh-NEH-sih-mus)

SCENE ONE

TIMOTHY: Paul, I think we have a problem.

PAUL: What seems to be the trouble, Timothy?

TIMOTHY: It's the Romans.

PAUL: We always knew we would have trouble from the authorities.

TIMOTHY: Not THOSE Romans. I mean the CHRISTIANS in Rome. They don't seem to understand the basics of what it means to be a Christian. And what can we do for them when we're here, in Corinth?

PAUL: No problem. *(Calls offstage.)* Tertius, take a letter. "Paul, a servant of Christ Jesus, called to be an apostle..."

SCENE TWO

TIMOTHY: Paul, I think we have a problem.

PAUL: What seems to be the trouble, Timothy?

TIMOTHY: It's the Corinthians.

PAUL: Well, we always knew that those who work evil in Corinth would attack our work there.

TIMOTHY: Not THOSE Corinthians. The CHRISTIANS in Corinth. They seem to have for gotten Jesus' love. Instead of showing love for each other, they are showing all the evil traits of that ungodly city. For example, the rich don't give to the poor—it's terrible. But what can we do when we're here, in Ephesus?

PAUL: No problem. *(Calls offstage.)* Stephen, take a letter. "Paul, called to be an apostle of Jesus Christ by the will of God..."

SCENE THREE

TIMOTHY: Paul, I think we have a problem.

PAUL: What seems to be the trouble, Timothy?

TIMOTHY: It's the Corinthians again.

PAUL: What's happening this time?

TIMOTHY: Same as always. But now, some even question your authority.

PAUL: No problem. *(Calls offstage.)* Titus, take a letter. "Paul, an apostle of Jesus Christ by the will of God, and Timothy our brother, to the church of God in Corinth..."

SCENE FOUR

TIMOTHY: Paul, I think we have a problem.

PAUL: What seems to be the trouble, Timothy?

TIMOTHY: It's the Galatians.

PAUL: What are the unbelievers in Galatia doing to the church?

TIMOTHY: It's not that. It's the believers. The Jewish believers are fighting with the Gentile believers. And what can we do about it when we're hundreds of miles away?

PAUL: No problem. Timothy, take a letter. On second thought, I'll write this one myself. Let's see,"Paul, an apostle—sent not from men, nor by man, but by Jesus Christ and God the Father, who raised Him from the dead—"

SCENE FIVE

TIMOTHY: Paul, I think we have a problem.

PAUL: What seems to be the trouble, Timothy?

TIMOTHY: It's the Ephesians.

PAUL: What seems to be their problem?

TIMOTHY: What ISN'T their problem? They seem to have forgotten the great love of Christ, that they were saved by His grace. They're no longer unified, but are fighting amongst themselves—you name it, they're doing it. And here we are, stuck in Rome.

PAUL: No problem. *(Calls offstage.)* Tychicus, take a letter. "Paul, an apostle of Christ Jesus by the will of God, to the saints in Ephesus, the faithful in Christ Jesus..."

SCENE SIX

PAUL: Onesimus, we have a problem.

ONESIMUS: What is the problem, my teacher?

PAUL: The problem is that you are not where you belong.

ONESIMUS: My teacher, you know that I would return to my owner, but I cannot. You know the punishment for a runaway slave. If I could return, I would. But I fear for my life.

PAUL: No problem. Onesimus, take a letter. And I mean, not only write it down but take it to Philemon, personally. "Paul, a prisoner of Christ Jesus, and Timothy our brother, to Philemon our dear friend and fellow worker...."

THE BIBLE SKIT BOOK VOLUME ONE

Make a Deal

SCRIPTURE: Joshua 2

SUGGESTED TOPICS: Godly vs. worldly values; trusting in God's guidance

BIBLE BACKGROUND

For forty years, the Israelites had wandered through the wilderness. Everyone (except for Caleb and Joshua) who was older than twenty years when Israel first saw the Promised Land had perished during the years of wandering. At last God said it was time for Israel to enter the land. In preparation for crossing the Jordan River, Joshua assigned two men to spy out the walled city of Jericho.

We know little of what they discovered about the city's military situation. Instead, the sacred writer focused on the prostitute, Rahab. We learn of her assistance to the spies and their promise of protection in the coming battle. Why so little attention to the major issues of strategy and policy? Why this emphasis on one woman? Perhaps it is to illustrate God's concern for each individual, no matter how seemingly insignificant or unworthy. Perhaps it is to honor Rahab's remarkable confession of faith in the God of Israel (see Joshua 2:8-11; Hebrews 11:31; James 2:25). And perhaps it is because Rahab became part of the lineage of King David and ultimately of Jesus Christ (see Matthew 1:5). Compared with matters such as those, military strategy seems insignificant.

PERFORMANCE TIPS

1. Suggested props: play money for Mammon to give to participants.
2. Most of your group will be familiar with the format of game shows. Both the announcer and Mammon should speak excitedly.
3. The entire group can participate as the audience. Determine a signal to prompt the audience to yell, "Make a deal!"

DISCUSSION QUESTIONS

1. How valuable did the scarlet cord turn out to be to Rahab?
2. How valuable was the bunch of flax to the Israelite spies?
3. Which is more important, God's directions or money? Why?
4. What are some situations in which people need God's guidance?
5. How does God guide you?

Make a Deal

CHARACTERS

ANNOUNCER
AUDIENCE
MAMMON (MAA-mon)
RAHAB (RAY-hab)
SPY ONE
SPY TWO
KING

ANNOUNCER: It's time, once again, for Jericho's favorite game show—

AUDIENCE: MAKE A DEAL!

ANNOUNCER: And now, here's everybody's favorite host, the host with the most, Mammon, the Man Who Can—

AUDIENCE: MAKE A DEAL!

MAMMON: Thank you, thank you, thank you. You're beautiful. You, the lovely lady right here, I'll give you two shekels if you can show me a piece of scarlet cord.

RAHAB: I have one. Right here.

MAMMON: She has one! I like that cord. Tell you what. I'll give you five more shekels if you'll give me the cord.

RAHAB: No. I'd like to keep the cord.

MAMMON: You drive a hard bargain. Ten shekels.

RAHAB: No. I'll keep the cord.

MAMMON: Last chance. One full talent....

AUDIENCE: *(Gasps.)*

MAMMON: That's right. One full talent for that scarlet cord.

RAHAB: No. I prefer to keep the cord. I might need it for something.

MAMMON: OK. You've got your two shekels and the cord. Let's see if we can find someone else who wants to—

AUDIENCE: MAKE A DEAL!

MAMMON: You two. I love those costumes. You almost look like Israelites. But what would Israelites be doing in Jericho? You're going to have to tell me. What are you two supposed to be?

SPY ONE: Uh, spies?

SPY TWO: That's it. Spies. We're pretending to be Israelite spies who are trying to look like they belong in Jericho.

MAMMON: Well, you're doing great. You even have the accent. Here's the deal. Just because I like you, I'm going to give you each ten shekels. And because your accents are so well done, I'm going to throw in five more shekels.

BOTH SPIES: Wow!

MAMMON: You like the deal so far?

SPY ONE: Great!

SPY TWO: Terrific!

MAMMON: But—

BOTH SPIES: But what?

MAMMON: Because I like you, I'm going to give you a chance to—

AUDIENCE: MAKE A DEAL!

MAMMON: That's right. You can keep your fifteen shekels or you can take what's behind the curtain. But you have to agree. So what will it be, fifteen shekels or the curtain? *(SPIES mutter between each other.)*

MAMMON: OK. Time's up. What will it be?

SPIES: We're going to take what's behind the curtain, Mammon.

MAMMON: OK. Open up the curtain and let's see what's there.

ANNOUNCER: It's...flax. That's right. Stalks of flax. Great for processing and turning into linen table cloths. All you need is the flax we're giving you, another five bushels, lots of skilled weavers, and you too can have a fine linen table cloth. Retail value of this prize, one shekel.

MAMMON: Too bad. But what can Israelite spies expect in Jericho? Now, I need someone who has a crown. Does anyone in the audience have a crown? You, sir.

KING: That's sire.

MAMMON: What a great costume. You look just like the king.

KING: I am the king.

MAMMON: And you sound like him, too. Same pompous attitude. Are you ready to—

AUDIENCE: MAKE A DEAL!

KING: I am always ready to make a deal that will benefit Jericho. Except, of course, with the Israelites. I would never make a deal with them.

MAMMON: OK. If you can show me a royal seal, I'll give you two talents of gold. Can you show me a royal seal?

KING: Of course I can. I never go anywhere without my seal, in case I need to make an important proclamation. There. See? Right there on my finger.

MAMMON: And here are your two talents of gold. Now you can keep the money, or you can trade it for whatever's behind the curtain.

KING: What a decision. This is a lot of money.

MAMMON: Time's running. What will it be? The money or the curtain?

KING: I think, I'll keep...no, wait! I'll trade...no, uh, I'll...trade.

MAMMON: A tough decision. Is it the right one? What's behind the curtain?

ANNOUNCER: It's a network of stool pigeons, spies and informants. Yes, know what's happening in your country or household by keeping up-to-date on all the latest developments. Three hundred men, guaranteed to snoop around, stick their noses in where they don't belong, and then come tell you everything they've seen. A prize fit for a king. Retail value of this prize...four talents!

MAMMON: Well, we're almost out of time. It's time for the big final gamble. Let's see if any of our winners want to—

AUDIENCE: MAKE A DEAL!

MAMMON: Our king made the best deal so far. What about it, king? Do you want to keep your deal or gamble it on something better?

KING: I'm happy with my deal. I'll keep it.

MAMMON: Rahab. You made the next best deal. Do you want to keep your two shekels or gamble them on a final deal?

RAHAB: I'll trade, Mammon.

MAMMON: All right, Rahab! Come on over here. Give me the shekels and choose. Do you want Door Number One, Door Number Two or Door Number Three?

RAHAB: Oh, it's so hard. I want Door Number...

MAMMON: Which one? One, Two or Three?

RAHAB: Door Number...Three.

ANNOUNCER: It's...amnesty! Yes, Rahab. You have received the gift of amnesty. In the event the Israelites attack and destroy Jericho, you and all who are with you and your family will be saved!

MAMMON: Hard to tell if you made a good deal or not. But we'd better get approval from the Israelites. Where are those spies?

BOTH SPIES: Here, Mammon.

MAMMON: To seal the deal, you two should make a covenant with Rahab.

SPY ONE: But what is the covenant to be?

RAHAB: Let's see. If you are spying out the land and some of the king's informers should happen to see you, I promise that you can find sanctuary in my house. I will hide you and keep you safe from the king and all others who would seek to kill you. For I know that the Lord has given you this land.

SPY TWO: Our life for yours. If you do not speak of hiding us and seeing us...

SPY ONE: ...then when the Lord gives us this land, we will deal kindly with you.

SPY TWO: You may bring your father, your mother, your brothers and sisters and all your father's household into your house.

SPY ONE: Any who remain in your house will be spared.

SPY TWO: But any who leave your house to venture onto the street will not be protected.

SPY ONE: To be certain that all Israel will recognize your house and honor this covenant...

SPY TWO: ...take a scarlet cord and hang it from your window.

RAHAB: Let it be according to your words.

MAMMON: Just to seal this covenant, something should change hands. How about you boys give her the flax. She can keep it on her roof. Now then, I have a shekel for anyone who can show me an idol. Does anyone have an idol with him? Any kind of an idol, and you can—

AUDIENCE: MAKE A DEAL!

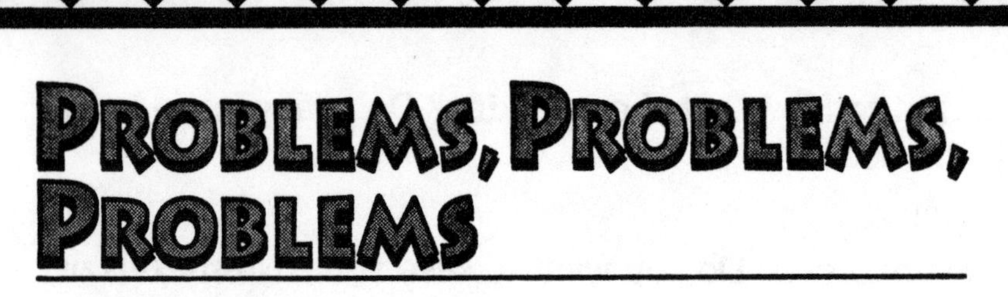

Problems, Problems, Problems

SCRIPTURE: Joshua 3; 4

SUGGESTED TOPICS: Trusting in God's guidance; obedience resulting from trust

BIBLE BACKGROUND

Forty years previously, the Israelites had been challenged to cross the Jordan River into the Promised Land. They had been dissuaded then by reports of giants in the land (see Numbers 13,14). After forty years, the giants were still in their fortified cities. However, this time, the Israelites elected to follow God and to cross the river.

Both groups of Israelites had witnessed God's power to do what seemed impossible. The earlier generation had seen Pharaoh agree to release two million slaves, ultimately begging Israel to leave Egypt. The latter generation had lived for forty years in the desert with God's provision of food and water for the wandering multitude. Whether the Israelites had really learned to trust God's promises or they had simply had all they could take of life in the desert, they finally were willing to step forward, following the priests who carried the Ark of the Covenant into the waters of the Jordan.

A considerable body of false information concerning the Ark of the Covenant has arisen over the years. The Bible is clear concerning the nature of this object. It was a wooden box, overlaid with gold, having rings through which poles were placed to carry the box (see Exodus 25:10-22). It was not a radio transmitter, it did not shoot bolts of lightning, it was never an artifact of magic. It was always a physical symbol of the reality of God's presence among His people.

PERFORMANCE TIPS

1. Suggested props: twelve rocks stacked in a mound.

2. Set the scene for your group. Indicate an area of the room to represent the swollen river which separated the land from the people.

3. Before the skit, ask, "If you were the Israelites' leader, Joshua, how would you bring two million people across a river where there is no bridge? Remember—babies, grandmothers and grandfathers are part of the crowd."

DISCUSSION QUESTIONS

1. Do you have a friend you trust? Why do you trust that friend?

2. What kinds of problems do you have in your life?

3. Think of one particular problem. How might God help you with that problem? Why can you trust God?

4. How can God guide you today? What methods might He use?

PROBLEMS, PROBLEMS, PROBLEMS

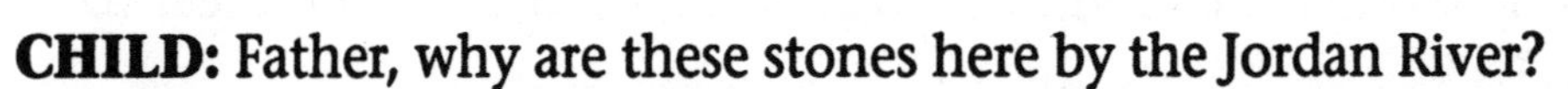

CHARACTERS

CHILD
FATHER
BENJAMIN
ADAM
JOSHUA

CHILD: Father, why are these stones here by the Jordan River?

FATHER: Interesting that you should ask. They were put here when I was about your age, as a sign and a remembrance.

CHILD: What kind of a sign? You mean like a stop sign or a warning?

FATHER: No. More like a joyful occasion. Like candles on a birthday cake.

CHILD: This was to celebrate someone's birthday?

FATHER: No, child. I see I am not explaining this very well. Let me start at the beginning. When I was a boy, we were preparing to enter into the Promised Land...

(FATHER and CHILD exit or freeze. BENJAMIN and ADAM enter.)

BENJAMIN: Father, what's everybody so excited for?

ADAM: We have been given the order to go into the Promised Land.

BENJAMIN: But, Father, the Promised Land is on the other side of the river!

ADAM: The Jordan. A magnificent river. Look how fast the current flows. At this time of year, the river is flooded. It is so deep, so wide, so treacherous.

BENJAMIN: How will we get across? Will Joshua build an ark, like Noah did?

ADAM: I don't know how we will cross. We have been told to follow the priests—those who bear the Ark of the Covenant.

BENJAMIN: But that ark is only a small box.

ADAM: No, Son. It is much more than that.

BENJAMIN: You mean, it's magic?

ADAM: No, my son. Not magic. True, it is a wooden box, overlaid with gold, but it is more than that. It is a symbol, God's promise to us that we are His people and that He will work His plan for His people.

BENJAMIN: But how will all the people get across the river? All the old people and the little babies. They can't swim across the river.

ADAM: And you can, my son?

BENJAMIN: Well...I could swim farther than Grandma.

ADAM: But you would still not be able to swim the full distance. You would be swept away and drowned, the same as the old people and the babies.

BENJAMIN: Then God brought us to the river to die?

ADAM: No, Son. God brought us to the Promised Land to show us that He is our God and we should trust and obey Him.

BENJAMIN: But if we all die in the river...

ADAM: We will not die, my son. God will protect us. You'll see. Are you frightened?

BENJAMIN: Of course not. I'm ten years old, and I'm not frightened of anything.

ADAM: Then I have not taught you well. There are many things to fear.

BENJAMIN: Are you afraid, Father?

ADAM: Yes. But in spite of my fear, I will obey. When Joshua calls us, I will follow.

BENJAMIN: But isn't being afraid the same as not having faith?

ADAM: No, my son. Faith is following God, even when you are afraid. Many years ago, our fathers were preparing to enter the Promised Land. But they allowed their fear to stop them from obeying God.

BENJAMIN: But if they were here, why are we only now entering the Promised Land? Why are we not already in our new home?

ADAM: Because our fathers did not obey God. This will not be an easy task, conquering this new land. God knows the difficulties that lie ahead. He knows that if we are not ready to obey Him, we will fail. That is why we have spent the last forty years in the wilderness. We have been learning to trust and to obey God.

BENJAMIN: How have we been doing that?

ADAM: By watching what God does. When we were in the wilderness, how did we eat?

BENJAMIN: We gathered manna. How else does anybody eat?

ADAM: No other people gather manna. God knew that when we were traveling in the wilderness, we would need food. He solved the problem by sending manna for us to eat. When we obeyed Him, we had enough for the day. But when we disobeyed and gathered more than we needed, the excess became moldy and not fit to eat.

BENJAMIN: So we learned that God would provide food for us?

ADAM: True. And where does one find water in the desert?

BENJAMIN: You just go to where it is.

ADAM: But where is it? Most places in the desert do not have water. Nobody knew where there was water. So we had another problem. But God led Moses to water. Once again, God solved our problem.

BENJAMIN: And now we have another problem.

ADAM: Right. We have to cross a river that nobody could possibly cross. So even though we are afraid, we will remember what God has done. We will trust and follow Him.

(JOSHUA enters.)

JOSHUA: Priests, raise up the Ark of the Covenant.

ADAM: Now, Benjamin, we will obey and see God work.

JOSHUA: Priests, walk into the waters of the Jordan.

BENJAMIN: Father! Look! The river is standing up!

ADAM: It looks that way, does it not? All the waters flowing down have made a huge wall!

JOSHUA: People of Israel, move across the river and into the land that God promised to Abraham. One man from each tribe will be chosen to pick up a rock from the bed of the Jordan and carry it to shore. Adam, will you represent your tribe?

ADAM: I would be honored, Joshua.

BENJAMIN: Father, shouldn't the river bed be all muddy?

ADAM: Yes, my son, it should be.

BENJAMIN: But it isn't. It's dry ground!

ADAM: Very true. Ah, here is a good rock. I will take this one.

JOSHUA: Is everybody across the river? Priests! Come across!

ADAM: You see, Son. I told you we would be safe.

BENJAMIN: Father! Look! When the priests left the river bed, the river rushed back along its course. That Ark of the Covenant MUST be magic.

ADAM: No, Son. What you saw was not magic. It was God's power. God simply used the Ark to remind the people that He was at work here.

JOSHUA: People of Israel, you see the stones taken from the waters of the Jordan where the priests held the Ark of the Covenant. These stones are a sign to you, so that in days to come, when children ask their fathers, "Why are these stones here?" you will be able to tell them all that happened here today. These stones will be a memorial to you...

(BENJAMIN, ADAM and JOSHUA freeze or exit. FATHER and CHILD enter or unfreeze.)

FATHER: ...a symbol of all that God has done for us.

CHILD: So when we have problems, we can remember that God loves us and cares about us?

FATHER: That's right. We can remember what He has done in the past and know that He will help us with our problems today. And that is the meaning of these stones along the river.

Such Sound

SCRIPTURE: Joshua 6:1-21

SUGGESTED TOPICS: Trusting in God's guidance; following instructions; obedience resulting from trust

BIBLE BACKGROUND

The Israelites crossed the Jordan River, ready to begin their conquest of the Promised Land. Joshua began the campaign by circumcising the soldiers, effectively putting the entire army out of commission for a few days. He then faced the task of conquering Jericho. How to attack a city fortified with a double wall all around? There was no way; Jericho would never be defeated by human means. But with God, all things are possible.

Scholars disagree concerning the timing of the forty years of wandering in the wilderness. Some say the Israelites entered Canaan forty years after leaving Egypt; others, forty years after seeing the Promised Land but not entering for fear of giants. The skit chooses the latter view.

PERFORMANCE TIPS

1. Suggested props: microphone for VJ, kazoos or rolled-up pieces of paper as trumpets for the priests to play, large cardboard boxes or blocks to represent the walls of Jericho.

2. Select a few members of the group to be priests. If you have "trumpets," have the priests "play" a familiar tune, such as "When the Saints Go Marching In," as they lead the Israelites in marching around the room.

3. Designate one side of the room as Jericho. Have the Israelite camp on the other side of the room.

DISCUSSION QUESTIONS

1. What made the walls of Jericho fall? What do you think would have happened if Joshua had not followed God's plan?

2. God gives everyone instructions. How do you find out God's instructions?

3. Why should you follow God's instructions?

4. What can you do to pay better attention to God's instructions?

SUCH SOUND

CHARACTERS

GROUP OF ISRAELITES
VJ
JOSHUA

VJ: Hi and welcome to the nation's music video station, "Such Sound." Today we have a special treat: the Israelites' new music video. We all remember their last video—still a classic—the "Song of Moses." Now, some forty-two years later, we have the group's second video. Of course, in forty-two years, some changes have occurred. Lead singer, Moses, has been replaced by Joshua. Only two members of the original band are still playing with the Israelites: Joshua and Caleb. As an extra treat today, Joshua is with us in the studio. Welcome, Joshua.

JOSHUA: Thank you, Zophar. Always a pleasure to be here.

VJ: Tell us about this new song. First, the time span. Forty-two years between records. Why the long wait?

JOSHUA: Well, you might say that the last forty-two years have been a dry period for the group. We were reviewing our situation, deciding who to follow. Strengthening the band for our current status.

VJ: Tell us about the group's development. I understand that some major changes have taken place over the years.

JOSHUA: That's true. We were planning to release this record forty years ago, but there was some disagreement as to how we should go about making it.

VJ: So, there was dissension in the group?

JOSHUA: That's right. Caleb and I were ready to begin recording, but the others were afraid that the giants from the other labels might hear of our plans and retaliate. Destroy us.

VJ: But you and Caleb thought otherwise?

JOSHUA: Yes. We knew that God wanted us to proceed with the record, but fear won out. We wandered in the wilderness for forty years, learning again that God was the one we should follow. Finally, when only Caleb and myself were still alive out of the original group, God told us it was time.

VJ: And now, we have the new video. Tell us about the song itself. Is this video going to be as spectacular as your last? I'm thinking particularly of the special effects: the parting of the Red Sea, drowning the Egyptian army, the pillar of fire. Will we see more of this?

JOSHUA: Not exactly. But there will be some surprises.

VJ: Don't want to give it away, right? OK. Let's take a look at the Israelites' latest video, "Jericho, Bye Bye." It's a long one, seven parts, so we'll watch each part separately. Here goes "Jericho, Bye Bye," Part One.

(ISRAELITES quietly march around the room and return to their seats.)

VJ: Well, as Joshua said, there were some surprises. I don't recall seeing anything quite like this before. I like the trumpet music, but can you explain the lack of lyrics, Joshua?

JOSHUA: I can't say that I truly understand it myself. I only know that God instructed us to march quietly around Jericho and then to return to our camp.

VJ: OK. A mystery that will probably never be solved. Let's continue and see what surprises Part Two has in store.

(ISRAELITES quietly march around the room and return to their seats.)

VJ: Interesting concept. Two parts, identical in all respects. Would it be fair to say that you are symbolically showing that God is always the same? I notice that the trumpeters are all priests. The music is the same, the movement is the same, the only sound comes from the priests' trumpets. God is the same. That's the symbolism, right?

JOSHUA: I never thought about that. I only know that God instructed us to quietly march around Jericho and then return to our camp.

VJ: Another mystery. This will have music historians scratching their heads for years to come. Let's continue now with "Jericho, Bye Bye," Part Three.

(ISRAELITES quietly march around the room and return to their seats.)

VJ: I think I'm beginning to understand. Your first video was filled with all those spectacular special effects. That pillar of fire was especially impressive. Now you're showing that even though there has been flash in the lives of the Israelites, they're really ordinary people, no different from anybody else. They commute to work, return home. A remarkable insight into the everyday existence of everyday people.

JOSHUA: I never thought about that. I only know that God instructed us to quietly march around Jericho and then return to our camp.

VJ: For the lead singer, you know remarkably little about your own video. Oh, well. Let's continue with "Jericho, Bye Bye," Part Four.

(ISRAELITES quietly march around the room and return to their seats.)

VJ: It is amazing. Four parts, all the same. And every time I see it, I see something that I had previously missed. Take, for example, that big wooden box carried by the priests that come right behind the priests with the trumpets.

JOSHUA: The Ark of the Covenant.

VJ: Is that what it's called? Angels on top of it, one on each end with their wings touching. This must indicate that the Israelites are a united people. The two angels probably represent men and women. Or possibly, old and young. Or, being angels, perhaps they represent all things that are opposites in people and show that, in the case of the Israelites, they join together. Differences united into similarity. That's what this video is all about, right?

JOSHUA: I never thought about that. I only know that God instructed us to quietly march around Jericho and then return to our camp.

VJ: Give me some help here, Joshua. You want this video to be a hit, and I'm doing my best, but there's only so much that can be said about a long hike with priests playing the same trumpet tune over and over. There is something hidden in here that we have to dig out. Maybe Part Five will give us the missing clue. "Jericho, Bye Bye," Part Five.

(ISRAELITES quietly march around the room and return to their seats.)

VJ: It's beginning to make sense. I notice that all the men of war precede all the other people of Israel. War first, followed by peace, obviously indicating that people should be peace-loving, for war does not solve our problems. By having the long walk, with war in front, you are showing that problems can be eventually solved only by noncombatants The women of the land and the children, not yet grown.

JOSHUA: I never thought about that. I only know that God instructed us to quietly march around Jericho and then return to our camp.

VJ: Well, in spite of your inability to assist us in uncovering the deep meanings contained within this work, I think that we're beginning to see the light. Part Six is bound to add to the total picture. "Jericho, Bye Bye," Part Six.

(ISRAELITES quietly march around the room and return to their seats.)

VJ: What a masterful stroke of symbolism. How did I miss it before?

JOSHUA: What's that?

VJ: The city itself. Look at the cold, grey, lifeless walls. Gates completely shut up. Nobody coming or going. Symbolically showing that if people shut themselves out, not allowing others to enter or get close, they become as cold and lifeless as the stone walls of Jericho. And then, in all this bleakness, we see the scarlet cord hanging down against the grey stone, showing that even though the exterior is grey and dead, there is life inside. The scarlet cord symbolizes the life blood that flows through living creatures. Life is not lost; there is hope. Masterful!

JOSHUA: I never thought about that. I only know that God instructed us to quietly march around Jericho and then return to our camp.

VJ: I'm excited about this video, now. In spite of no special effects, in spite of its length, this video will go down as one of the great videos of all time. Let's tie up all the loose ends now with "Jericho, Bye Bye," Part Seven.

(ISRAELITES quietly march around Jericho seven times, then JOSHUA cries, "Shout; for the Lord has given you the city!" *and all the ISRAELITES shout.)*

VJ: Wow! Look at those special effects! Look how the walls of the city fell away! I knew that Part Seven would bring everything into the light! Your song clearly says that God tears down the stone of our lives to let in the light. This has to be the most exciting video in the last hundred years. Congratulations, Joshua! That one burst of lyric has more meaning than all the songs ever written. We will have to watch this again and again.

JOSHUA: Actually, I believe that the video is saying that you should follow and obey the Lord.

VJ: Nonsense. Don't try to belittle the great work that you've done to unravel the human condition. We're out of time, but be sure to stay tuned for Elah's Comedy Hour, next on the nation's music video station, "Such Sound."

SCRIPTURE: Joshua 6:19; 7:1-4

SUGGESTED TOPICS: Sin hurts others; consequences of disobedience; following God's instructions

BIBLE BACKGROUND

Mighty Jericho had fallen. The power of God caused the city's walls to tumble down. Jericho was destroyed, never to return to her former glory. Next on the campaign trail was Ai, a much smaller city in the central hills of Palestine. The Israelites were confident, the Canaanites worried. If Jericho fell, how could Ai stand?

The Bible does not tell us whether Achan went or stayed behind when the Israelites went to battle Ai. Perhaps he went, wanting to be able to haul out his booty from Jericho under the guise of the spoils of the battle of Ai. Perhaps he would have gone because he was afraid he would be branded a coward if he did not volunteer to fight. The skit chooses to show Achan as avaricious in the extreme, wanting to stay back and admire what he took from Jericho.

PERFORMANCE TIPS

After the skit, tell the story of the battle at Ai (see Joshua 7:2-5). Read Joshua 7:20,21 to find out Achan's actions.

DISCUSSION QUESTIONS

1. What was Achan's sin? What happened because of his sin?
2. In what ways do you sometimes not follow God's instructions?
3. This story shows how sin hurts others. In what ways can your sins hurt other people?

Ai!

CHARACTERS

JOSHUA
FIRST SOLDIER
SECOND SOLDIER
THIRD SOLDIER
ACHAN (AY-ken)

PRONUNCIATION GUIDE

Ai (AY-eye)
Canaan (KAY-nun)

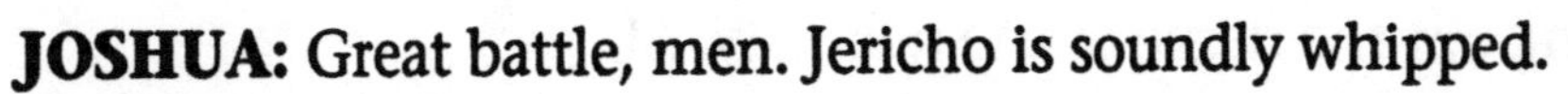

JOSHUA: Great battle, men. Jericho is soundly whipped.

SOLDIERS: Three cheers for us. Hip, hip, hooray! Hip, hip...

JOSHUA: Sorry to break up your celebration, boys, but we still have the rest of Canaan to conquer.

SOLDIERS: No problem. We're tough. We're rough. We'll beat 'em, thump em...

JOSHUA: Let's not forget that the Lord is with us. He really won the battle.

SOLDIERS: Oh, yeah. Right. Forgot about that.

JOSHUA: Now, let's review our previous strategy.

FIRST SOLDIER: We march...

SECOND SOLDIER: Silently...

THIRD SOLDIER: Around the city seven times...

SOLDIERS: Then blow the trumpets, shout and watch the walls fall down.

JOSHUA: And then...

SOLDIERS: Then?

ACHAN: I know, I know.

JOSHUA: Yes, Achan.

ACHAN: We burn everything and don't keep any plunder for ourselves.

JOSHUA: Right. Those were the Lord's instructions that we all obeyed. Right?

FIRST SOLDIER: Right!

SECOND SOLDIER: Right!

THIRD SOLDIER: Right!

ACHAN: Uh, *(pause)* right.

JOSHUA: That was the previous battle. From now on, we behave more like soldiers and fight our battles according to military strategy.

SOLDIERS: And we get to keep the spoils of our victories?

JOSHUA: Right.

SOLDIERS: Three cheers for Joshua. Hip, hip...

JOSHUA: Those are the Lord's commands, not mine. I don't need any cheers. Now, come closer. We need to make plans to conquer the next city.

FIRST SOLDIER: Ai!

JOSHUA: What's wrong?

FIRST SOLDIER: Nothing. Why do you ask?

JOSHUA: I thought you screamed. I must have been mistaken. Now, the next city...

SECOND SOLDIER: Ai!

JOSHUA: What's wrong?

SECOND SOLDIER: Nothing. Why do you ask?

JOSHUA: I thought you screamed. I must have been mistaken. Now, the next city...

THIRD SOLDIER: Ai!

JOSHUA: OK, what's the deal here? Every time I talk about going to the next battle, you scream. Are you cowards, or what?

SOLDIERS: No! We're just calling out the name of the next city. Ai.

JOSHUA: Oh. OK. Let's plan our strategy for conquering Ai.

FIRST SOLDIER: No problem.

SECOND SOLDIER: It's a tiny, little place up in the hills.

THIRD SOLDIER: We won't need the whole army.

JOSHUA: You're suggesting that some of the army stay here, in camp?

ACHAN: I'll volunteer to stay. I have, uh, things to do here in camp.

JOSHUA: Why not send the entire army? End the battle quickly?

FIRST SOLDIER: We've spied out the place.

SECOND SOLDIER: It doesn't have great defenses.

THIRD SOLDIER: Not many men defending it.

ACHAN: No sense in tiring the whole army on a march to such a little city. Why, it couldn't have much to offer in booty—I mean, be difficult to conquer.

JOSHUA: How many men should be sent to fight the battle?

FIRST SOLDIER: No more than a few thousand.

SECOND SOLDIER: How about three thousand? I've always liked the number three.

THIRD SOLDIER: Sure. That'll be plenty.

JOSHUA: What do you think, Achan?

ACHAN: Three thousand. I like it. Has a nice ring to it.

JOSHUA: Right. Then gather three thousand soldiers...

FIRST SOLDIER: I can get one thousand.

SECOND SOLDIER: I can get another thousand.

THIRD SOLDIER: I can get the third thousand.

ACHAN: And I'll be in my tent, counting gold—I mean, planning our next attack.

JOSHUA: It's good to know the Lord has men like you, ready to do His will when we go into battle. Go! And may the Lord be with you.

CANAAN TV NEWS

SCRIPTURE: Judges 4; 5

SUGGESTED TOPICS: Prejudice; disobedience vs. obedience

BIBLE BACKGROUND

The Israelites had conquered Canaan. However, contrary to God's command, not all the former inhabitants had been driven out (see Judges 1). The result of this incomplete victory was a vicious cycle that continually repeated itself for centuries: Israel would worship God and prosper; then Israel would be drawn away from the worship of God and would eventually be oppressed by its neighbors; finally, God would raise up a judge to call Israel back to the worship of the true God. Othniel, Ehud and Shamgar were the first of the judges to deliver Israel. However, for twenty years Israel was cruelly dominated by Jabin, the king of Canaan, seeking to restore Canaanite rule which had been ended by Joshua (see Joshua 11:1,10). Jabin may have been the name of a dynasty of Canaanite kings. During this bleak period Deborah, a prophetess, became Israel's next judge.

PERFORMANCE TIPS

1. Suggested props: one or more microphones for newscasters; large, potted palm tree to represent "Deborah's Palm"; sheet of paper for Barke.
2. This skit is best used with older groups. Younger groups may find the skit long and difficult to follow.
3. Distribute the skit in advance. Do not attempt to have the group perform it without practice.
4. Introduce the skit by saying, "We're about to see TV news from long ago. Watch closely and see if you can understand all that happened." After the skit, ask the group to tell you the story based on what they saw. Be prepared to supplement information they might have missed.
5. The commercials are just for fun. If you have creative participants who would enjoy the challenge, ask them to write their own commercials.
6. If your church is having a special event, you might use the commercial time to advertise it.

DISCUSSION QUESTIONS

1. What were the religious beliefs of the newscasters? How might the newscast have been different if they had been Jewish?
2. Were the Israelites in Canaan intolerant? Is intolerance always bad? When might intolerance be good and when might it be bad?
3. How should you treat people with beliefs different from yours?
4. Why do you believe Christianity is true?

Canaan TV News

CHARACTERS

ZAMAN (ZAY-mun)
ZORAH (ZOH-ruh)
HAMATH (HAY-muth)
TEREZ (teh-REZ)
TABOR (TAY-bur)
BARKE (BAR-keh)
ANNOUNCER

Amalek (AM-uh-lek)
Barak (bah-RAHK)
Kishon (KEE-shon)
Manasseh (muh-NAA-suh)
Naphtali (NAF-tuh-lye)
Phoenicia (foe-NEE-sha)
Sisera (SIS-er-ah)
Zebulon (ZEH-byoo-lun)

ZAMAN: Good evening. I'm Zaman...

ZORAH: And I'm Zorah....

ZAMAN: And this is the twelfth-hour Canaan TV news.

ZORAH: Tonight's top story: Deborah is missing! But first, this message.

ANNOUNCER: After a long, hard day, do you find that your feet feel like they have wandered forty years in the wilderness? There's probably nothing wrong with your feet! It's your sandals! Yes! End aching feet forever with a pair of Dr. Samuel's sensational sandals! Your feet will love you for it!

ZAMAN: Welcome back to the news. Our feature story tonight: one of Canaan's true characters, Deborah, the judge and prophet of the Israelites. As everyone in Israel knows, Deborah spends most days sitting under a palm tree. However, for the past few days she has not been at her usual location. For an on-the-spot report, we go to Hamath at the palm tree. Hamath?

HAMATH: Thank you, Zaman. Today, Deborah did not appear at the palm at her appointed time. Hard-nosed investigation has revealed that she has not been here for several days. Unusual, to say the least. What has happened to her? Is she the victim of foul play?

ZAMAN: Have there been rumors about the cause of her absence?

HAMATH: There certainly have! Some of Deborah's critics suggests that she has run off with Barak, captain of Israel's army. When we went to her home and questioned her husband, Lappidoth, he became unreasonably upset, a reaction that leads some to suspect the rumor may be true.

ZAMAN: Thank you for your in-depth analysis, Hamath. Another fine job of reporting. Zorah?

ZORAH: Racial intolerance has once again reared its ugly head in our fair land. With us tonight is Professor Terez of Jezreel University. Welcome to the program, Professor.

TEREZ: Thank you, Zorah. It's a pleasure to be here.

ZORAH: Professor, can you shed any light on this latest round of racial prejudice?

TEREZ: Certainly, Zorah. For centuries there was never any racial strife in Canaan. Oh, we had our little squabbles and disputes, the same as anybody else, but basically, we got along pretty well. If your neighbor chose to worship a rock while you worshiped a tree, fine. Nobody worried about it. If you chose to sacrifice your children to Baal while I chose to sacrifice mine to Molech, what was the big deal? Everyone was happy. Content.

ZORAH: What happened to change this, Professor?

TEREZ: The Israelites arrived. Naturally, the people already here were concerned about the new arrivals. But it was expected that after a few years, the Israelites would come to accept our ways as reasonable. After all, everybody else who moved in had.

ZORAH: You're saying this has not been the case with Israel?

TEREZ: It certainly was not! Do you remember the name Joshua?

ZORAH: Only too well, Professor. The Scourge of Canaan, I believe he is called in the history scrolls.

TEREZ: Joshua, as you remember, led the first Israelites here, and as soon as he did, there was war. Every day, another city was being attacked by the Israelites. Jericho, Ai, the list is almost endless.

ZORAH: Why was Joshua so intent on destroying Canaan, Professor?

TEREZ: The man was obviously imbalanced. He claimed something about the land being promised to them by God. His rallying cry to his troops was, "Drive out those God has cursed!" That kind of thing.

ZORAH: What I don't understand, Professor, is why people were afraid of someone who claimed to be obeying a god. After all, aren't all gods just about the same?

TEREZ: The Israelites have always claimed to have a different god than everybody else. They say things like, "Remember the God of Abraham, Isaac and Jacob." I know this sounds peculiar to anybody with an ounce of sense, but they actually believe there is only one god.

ZORAH: In this enlightened age, doesn't everyone accept that everything around us is a god and that everyone has his own god to help him? Why don't the Israelites understand something that simple?

TEREZ: Well, over the years, the Israelites realized that trying to worship one god was ridiculous. Most of them accepted the gods of the people living around them. Life actually became peaceful.

ZORAH: Then why do the Israelites always seem responsible when racial—and I suppose, religious—prejudices crop up?

TEREZ: About every forty years or so, some Israelite claims to be a messenger from God and calls the Israelites to forsake the gods of Canaan. When that happens, look out. The Israelites forget the reasonableness of many gods and go back to only one god. When THAT happens, the only possible outcome is war.

ZORAH: Are you suggesting that we might have another conflict in Canaan?

TEREZ: I'm afraid it's a very real possibility. That's the problem with intolerance. It always leads to violence.

ZORAH: Thank you again for being our guest, Professor.

TEREZ: Any time, Zorah.

ZORAH: There you have it. It appears that we could be in for more unnecessary violence in our fair land. Zaman.

ZAMAN: Our last story tonight also involves the Israelites. Eyewitnesses report a mass migration of Israelites, something on the order of ten thousand men, moving from the north country into the south. It's a well-known fact that Israelites tend to be home-bodies. Sounds as though something strange is brewing up north. Stay tuned. Tabor will be right back with the weather.

ANNOUNCER: Is your camel getting old? Do you find yourself having to add water at every oasis along the way? Are you getting fewer miles per pound of grain? Then it's time to trade up, and now is the time to deal! Ahab can't afford to haggle! He's over stocked! Get down to Ahab's today! Make your best deal and ride away on the camel of your choice! Single hump, double hump, compact, full-size—whatever you need, Ahab has it!

ZAMAN: And now, here's Tabor with the weather.

TABOR: Thank you, Zaman. Before tonight's weather, I want to apologize to all of you. I told you that the weather would be sunny and warm. As you know now, I was wrong. Somewhere out in the Great Sea, the wind god and the cloud god got into some kind of big argument. That caused hundreds of bushels of water to pour down, especially around Kishon Valley.

Things are looking up for tomorrow, however. I consulted the priests of the weather gods, and they say all have made peace with one another. So tomorrow, we should have the pleasant weather we expected today. Get outside and enjoy yourselves, because who knows when the gods will begin fighting again. Good night and good weather.

ZAMAN: Thanks for that report, Tabor. We'll be back with sports after this word from our sponsor.

ANNOUNCER: Has all this bad weather from the gods given you a nasty cough, aching throat, runny nose? Well, don't worry! Bothersome colds can now be a thing of the past with Zadok's new Elixir of Health. Approved by the god of health, this elixir will give you health, wealth, happiness—everything that makes life worth living! Order yours today. This special TV offer cannot be found in stores. Send seven drachmas for each bottle to Elixir, Box 7750, Station A, Beth-Shan. Don't wait! Do it now!

ZORAH: Welcome back. And now, here's Barke with the sports.

BARKE: Thank you, Zorah. Well, it's been a big day in sports. Let's review what happened around the leagues.

Egypt was a big loser against Amalek, and that's what we've come to expect. Egypt is no longer a great powerhouse since it has lost the leadership of Rameses II. A close game between Ammon and Midian saw Ammon squeaking out the narrowest of victories. Moab beat the Philistines in overtime.

Today's big game went on at Megiddo Stadium in the Kishon Valley. Weather conditions were not ideal. Rain, thunder, lightning—you name it, we had it. And we had some other surprises, as well. Coach Jabin had his team ready. You could see it in the eyes of his captain, Sisera. The home team was well prepared and well equipped. They had the best chariots, horses and weapons that money could buy. Nine hundred chariots! And Sisera was ready to use them.

The visiting Israelites fielded an amazingly large team for them: approximately ten thousand men. However, they were poorly equipped and poorly trained. Their captain, Barak, made a surprise change in personnel for this game. Everyone in the know was certain he would select his team from the tribe of Manasseh, men who live in the area and know the terrain. But in an unprecedented move, he chose his entire team from the tribes of Naphtali and Zebulon. What's more, he had a woman on the sidelines with him. Nobody seems to know just who she was, but she seemed to be in on the decision making during the game.

Anyway, back to the game itself. Sisera had his game planned out for a dry afternoon, but you know what happened. The gods fought in the heavens and dumped water all over the field. Sisera's chariots were stuck in mud and couldn't move. Instead of being an asset, they were a liability. And the gods, not content with simple rain, threw in blinding flashes of lightning and ear-splitting thunder. The war horses reared up in terror, throwing their riders and running in panic. Coach Jabin's team was totally confused, even the experienced Captain Sisera. To make a long story short, Sisera was thumped by Barak and the unknown woman. *(BARKE is handed a sheet of paper.)*

This late-breaking story just in. It seems that Sisera, having fled the field at Megiddo, sought shelter at the tent of Heber. Heber wasn't home but his wife, Jael, let Sisera in anyway. Bad move on Sisera's part. We don't know Jael's motive—maybe she dropped a bundle betting on the game—but when Sisera was asleep, Jael drove a tent spike through his head. This is a sad day for sports, indeed. One of Canaan's great players, Sisera, first defeated and now dead at the hands of women. One hardly knows what the far-reaching effects of this development will be, but I expect that Jabin will no longer be the force he once was. For now, that's all in sports.

ZORAH: Another development just in. It seems that Deborah has returned home. Her disappearance was nothing more than a little trip to watch a sporting contest. We're glad you're home safe and sound, Deborah. That's all for tonight. Until tomorrow, I'm Zorah—

ZAMAN: And I'm Zaman—

ZORAH: Good night.

THE CALL OF GIDEON

SCRIPTURE: Judges 6

SUGGESTED TOPICS: Handling fear; trusting God in spite of fear

BIBLE BACKGROUND

Forty years after Deborah's term as judge, the Israelites again fell away from God. As a result of their disobedience, they were conquered by the Midianites (see Judges 6:1), a nomadic people who formed alliances with the Amalekites and Moabites. Most of the crops Israel grew were taken by the Midianites, leaving Israel impoverished. In their anguish, the Israelites cried out to God. In His mercy, God responded by raising up another judge.

Gideon heard God's call, but did not believe at first (see Judges 6:17). Even Gideon's own family had built, and probably maintained, an altar to Baal. In spite of Gideon's disbelief and his family's acceptance of idol worship, the Lord used him to redeem Israel.

Purah, Gideon's servant, has been included as the second character in the skit because, other than Gideon's father, Purah is the only other name mentioned in the biblical account. Although the Bible does not specifically say he was among the ten servants who took part in tearing down the idol of Baal, the skit assumes he did because of his close position to Gideon.

PERFORMANCE TIPS

Introduce the skit by setting the scene: "Often in the history of the Israelite people, we see a pattern develop. The Israelites started out by obeying God, but then gradually began to worship false gods. As a result, God withdrew His protection, and the enemies of the Israelites caused trouble for them. Then the Israelites cried to the one, true God for help. Because God loved the Israelites, He answered their cries and sent them a strong leader. This skit tells the story of one of God's greatest leaders, Gideon."

DISCUSSION QUESTIONS

1. Why was Gideon afraid? How do you think he felt when the other Israelites tried to kill him for tearing down Baal's altar?

2. Are you ever afraid? What sort of things scare you?

3. Does trusting God mean you will never be afraid again? Why or why not?

4. What should you do when you feel afraid?

THE CALL OF GIDEON

CHARACTERS

PURAH (POO-rah)
GIDEON (GID-ee-un)

PRONUNCIATION GUIDE

Manasseh (muh-NAA-suh)
Naphtali (NAF-tuh-lye)
Zebulon (ZEH-byoo-lun)

PURAH: May I ask you a question, Gideon?

GIDEON: Yes, but that's already a question.

PURAH: Quit clowning around. You know what I mean.

GIDEON: What's the question?

PURAH: Could you please tell me how you know we're supposed to fight the Midianites?

GIDEON: Purah! You're my servant! I'm the boss. You're supposed to do what I say without asking a lot of questions.

PURAH: I know. But I'd feel better if you could tell me why we're going to do this.

GIDEON: *(Sighs.)* OK. If it will make you feel better. I was threshing wheat in the winepress...

PURAH: How come?

GIDEON: Because if you don't thresh it, you get a lot of dirt in with the grain.

PURAH: I mean, how come you were threshing wheat in a winepress? Wouldn't it be easier to thresh it outside?

GIDEON: Of course it would! But if I threshed it out in the open, then the Midianites would have come and taken it away. Remember the Midianites? They're the enemy.

PURAH: You don't have to be sarcastic. So, you were threshing wheat...

GIDEON: In the winepress. Then, suddenly, I heard a voice. Was I ever scared!

PURAH: Why? There's nothing illegal about threshing wheat in a winepress. It's a little strange, maybe, but not illegal.

GIDEON: I wasn't afraid of breaking any law. I thought the Midianites had found me and that they would take away all the wheat.

PURAH: Oh, Gideon! Don't let them take away your wheat! If you do, your family will starve to death and I won't ever see you again...

GIDEON: Purah.

PURAH: ...and we won't ever be together again...

GIDEON: Purah.

PURAH: ...and I'll be all alone and so unhappy...

GIDEON: Purah!

PURAH: Yes?

GIDEON: I'm telling a story. There are no Midianites here. And I couldn't change the story anyway. So be quiet and listen.

PURAH: I'm listening.

GIDEON: Good. As I said, I was scared. I heard the voice, but I hadn't really heard what it said. You know what I mean?

PURAH: Sure. Because it was talking in a foreign language.

GIDEON: No! Not like that. I understood the language. But I was so afraid that I didn't hear the words. My brain was so busy thinking the Midianites had found me, it wouldn't decipher the words I was hearing.

PURAH: Oh. Then how did you finally know what it was saying?

GIDEON: My brain finally figured out that the voice was not a Midianite. Then I stopped to think about what it had said.

PURAH: And what did the voice say?

GIDEON: It said, "The Lord is with you, oh mighty man of valor."

PURAH: That's funny, Gideon.

GIDEON: What's funny?

PURAH: You were quaking in your boots and somebody says, "Hey there, you're a tough soldier, a brave fighter..."

GIDEON: Do you want to hear the story, or not?

PURAH: Sorry. But I still think it's funny.

GIDEON: Anyway, I peeked out from the winepress, and I saw an angel.

PURAH: An angel?

GIDEON: Right.

PURAH: With wings and a shiny halo?

GIDEON: No! Angels don't look like that.

PURAH: Then what did it look like?

GIDEON: It looked kind of like a man...

PURAH: Then how did you know it was an angel? Did it walk around and say, "Behold, mighty quaking-in-your-boots man of valor! I am an angel. Listen to what I say..."

GIDEON: You're making fun again.

PURAH: Look, Gideon. I'm your main servant, right? But I have trouble believing that you saw an angel. Angels don't exist! They're like boogeymen. Only nicer.

GIDEON: I'm telling you what happened. If you don't believe it...

PURAH: Go ahead. I'll pretend to believe it for now.

GIDEON: OK. Well, I saw this angel. And I had trouble believing what it had said about the Lord being with me.

PURAH: And you're giving me a hard time about not believing?

GIDEON: OK, OK. But I said to the angel, "If the Lord is with us, then where are all the miracles that our fathers told us about? If the Lord is with us, why are we oppressed by the Midianites?"

PURAH: Hah! That's telling him. By the way, are angels hims?

GIDEON: I don't know. I guess so.

PURAH: Doesn't matter. You sure told him a thing or two. Hah, angel. *(Pause.)* But, Gideon, if that was an angel, should you have been speaking to it that way?

GIDEON: No. But I didn't know at the time that it was an angel.

PURAH: But you said you saw an angel.

GIDEON: Yes. I saw an angel, only I thought it was a man at the time. That's why I wasn't afraid to be a little bit rude.

PURAH: So how did you figure out that it was an angel?

GIDEON: When it touched the bread with its staff, and it all burned up.

PURAH: What bread?

GIDEON: The bread that was with the meat.

PURAH: What meat?

GIDEON: The meat that I served the angel.

PURAH: Do angels eat bread and meat?

GIDEON: No.

PURAH: Then why did you serve the angel bread and meat?

GIDEON: Because I didn't know that it was an angel! How about if I tell the story in its proper order? Then you might understand everything.

PURAH: Good idea. Go for it.

GIDEON: This angel that I thought was just a man said, "Go and save Israel from the Midianites. I am sending you."

PURAH: And you believed him?

GIDEON: Not right away. But I thought that maybe he was a prophet and he had got the wrong person. So I told him, "You've got the wrong guy. My family isn't important. We're poor. And I'm the youngest. Who is it that you're looking for? Maybe I can give you directions to his house."

PURAH: That makes sense. Israel needs a leader we can all look up to...

GIDEON: I'm telling this.

PURAH: Sorry. But you're not the kind of guy who looks like a leader, you know?

GIDEON: Well...you're right. Anyway, the angel that I thought was maybe a prophet said, "I will be with you. And you will strike down the Midianites as if they were only one man."

PURAH: That's weird.

GIDEON: What's weird?

PURAH: Some guy tells you that the two of you are going to fight the Midianites and you'll outnumber them two to one.

GIDEON: You don't understand the way prophets speak. What he meant was God would be fighting beside me and so the Midianites would be destroyed because they cannot stand up to God.

PURAH: So, prophets talk weird. What did you do?

GIDEON: I thought if he was a prophet he could do something to show me that he meant what he said. So I asked him to show me a sign that he really meant me. But I thought I should try to make up for being rude earlier, so I asked him to wait while I got him something to eat.

PURAH: But angels don't eat.

GIDEON: But I thought that he was a man.

PURAH: Right. I forgot.

GIDEON: So I brought him some bread and meat.

PURAH: I bet your mom was mad at you. Giving the family supper to a stranger.

GIDEON: You'd be surprised at my parents. They're pretty cool. Anyway, that was when he touched the meat and bread with his staff and it all just burned up.

PURAH: You should have known better than to put it on something flammable. These sudden fires have happened before, you know.

GIDEON: I didn't put it on something flammable. I put it on a rock. When fire came up out of the rock, I realized I had been talking to an angel. And that's when I got really scared. I was sure that I was going to die.

PURAH: So what happened? Did you die?

GIDEON: Look at me. Do I look dead?

PURAH: To tell you the truth, you have looked better. You're a little pale...

GIDEON: No! I didn't die. But God told me to do something.

PURAH: God told you to do something?

GIDEON: Right, He told...

PURAH: First an angel, now God. Are you sure you're feeling alright, Gideon?

GIDEON: I never felt better. Anyway, God told me to do something.

PURAH: And...

GIDEON: I did it.

PURAH: What?

GIDEON: What God told me.

PURAH: Which was?

GIDEON: I thought you knew. You were there. When we tore down the idol of Baal.

PURAH: Oh, that! I thought that was some kind of Halloween joke.

GIDEON: It was no joke. And Halloween hasn't been invented yet.

PURAH: I thought we were goners the next day. That was some lynch mob.

GIDEON: But Dad stood up for us.

PURAH: Yeah. Even after he found out you'd killed his bull. If it had been my dad, we'd be dead meat by now.

GIDEON: Back to the story. That was when the Midianites joined with the Amalekites and brought a huge army up to the Valley of Jezreel. God told me to gather an army from the tribes of Manasseh, Asher, Zebulon and Naphtali.

PURAH: God spoke to you again?

GIDEON: Right.

PURAH: And you jumped right to it?

GIDEON: Well...not right away. I wanted to be sure that I hadn't misunderstood.

PURAH: Good thinking. Might have just been a dream.

GIDEON: So I laid a fleece out all night.

PURAH: That's it? You put a sheepskin on the ground?

GIDEON: And what do you think happened?

PURAH: The Midianites came in the night and stole it?

GIDEON: No! The next morning, I wrung a bowlful of water out of the fleece.

PURAH: And...

GIDEON: And what?

PURAH: You were getting a sign. What happened to the water? Did it turn red, or did fish appear in it, or what?

GIDEON: Nothing else happened to the water.

PURAH: Then what was the sign?

GIDEON: The water was the sign.

PURAH: The water.

GIDEON: Right. The water.

PURAH: You know, Gideon. This may come as a bit of a surprise to you, but on a summer's eve in Israel when you leave something out overnight, it always gets wet. It's called dew, Gideon. The fleece got wet because of dew.

GIDEON: But the ground around it was dry. Bone dry. Still, I was not certain myself. So I asked for another sign.

PURAH: Good idea. Showers of gold or something like that?

GIDEON: No. I laid the fleece out again.

PURAH: And it got wet again. You've got no imagination, Gideon.

GIDEON: That's just it. This time, the ground all around the fleece was wet, but the fleece itself was as dry as dust.

PURAH: OK. I'll admit it. That was a good trick. So now what?

GIDEON: So now we're going to meet the army that I've gathered.

PURAH: To fight the Midianites?

GIDEON: Right.

PURAH: Have you told them your story yet?

GIDEON: Not yet.

PURAH: A word of advice, then.

GIDEON: Which is?

PURAH: When you do, go easy on the angel and the talking with God and the sheepskin. If you tell them those parts, you're not going to have much of an army left.

GIDEON'S ARMY

SCRIPTURE: Judges 7

SUGGESTED TOPICS: Trusting God when outmatched; obedience resulting from trust

BIBLE BACKGROUND

For seven years, the Midianites had viciously oppressed the Israelites. The Midianites had the technology for processing iron and, consequently, had the latest in military hardware. They formed a powerful coalition with Amalek and other nearby nations. Judges 7:12 records that together they were like a swarm of locusts in number—unable to be counted. Against these odds, Gideon was to take an army which had access to only very primitive weapons. The Israelites were still working with wood and stone. Even so, when the Israelites assembled to fight the Midianites, most must have expected some form of military protocol to be followed. What must have been the reaction to Gideon's seemingly offhand method of breaking every rule of war found in the military handbook?

Every army has its sergeants; surely Gideon's army was no different—one man cannot possibly hope to give orders to thirty-two thousand men without some help. Since no other name is mentioned in the biblical account, Gideon's servant, Purah, has been chosen to be one of the sergeants in this skit. Although Purah is presented as a comic character, consider how much loyalty a man must have to follow a leader who, from a worldly viewpoint, is going about things all wrong.

PERFORMANCE TIPS

1. Suggested props: several rocks and thick, wooden sticks for troops to carry.

2. Before the skit, describe the military strength of the Midianites. (See Bible Background.) Make certain the group understands the hopelessness of the Israelites in their fight against Midian.

3. The skit ends before Gideon and Purah travel to the enemy camp. Tell the rest of the story to the group, emphasizing how God encouraged Gideon in the face of insurmountable odds.

4. In Gideon's time, fighting at night was not common. It was too easy to kill your own soldiers. Help the class understand that the strategy God gave to Gideon worked because of the confusion caused by a nighttime battle.

DISCUSSION QUESTIONS

1. Have you ever seen a swarm of grasshoppers? What are other phrases that would describe a group of people too large to be counted?

2. There is a very fine line between being foolish and being brave. Was Gideon brave or foolish? Why?

3. How would you feel if you were Purah? The Bible tells us that Purah went with Gideon to the Midianites' camp before the battle started. Would you be ready to fight the Midianites if you were Purah? Was Purah brave or foolish? Why?

4. How can the story of Gideon help us today? When have you faced a situation in which it was difficult to obey God? How can God help you when you are afraid to obey Him?

GIDEON'S ARMY

CHARACTERS

PURAH (POO-rah)
GIDEON (GID-ee-un)
ISRAELITE TROOPS

PURAH: OK, men. You know why you're here. We have come together as the great nation of Israel to fight the Midianites. Led by our great and noble leader, Gideon, we will fight the good fight, which will be long remembered in Jewish history...

GIDEON: Purah.

PURAH: Our children will sing songs of our gallant bravery! They will sing of our memory! Those who bravely die in battle...

GIDEON: Purah.

PURAH: Their exploits will be remembered long after their bodies are rotting in the grave. As their souls cry out in Sheol...

GIDEON: Purah!

PURAH: No! Their souls will not cry out, "Purah!" Who said that?

GIDEON: I did.

PURAH: Why are you making fun of me in front of the men, Gideon?

GIDEON: I didn't make fun of you, Purah.

PURAH: You certainly did. When I was giving my stirring speech to the troops, you said the souls in Sheol would cry out, "Purah!"

GIDEON: No I didn't. I was calling out your name to get your attention.

PURAH: Oh. Just a minute then. OK, men! Take five! Smoke if you have them!

GIDEON: What does that mean?

PURAH: I have no idea. But sergeants always yell that to the troops.

GIDEON: In the future, I think you should know what you're saying before you say it.

PURAH: OK. You're the boss. You wanted to see me about something?

GIDEON: Yes. I'm going off to pray, to ask God's guidance...

PURAH: Shh!

GIDEON: What? Did you hear something?

PURAH: No. But you should hold back on that talking to God stuff in front of the men. They might think you're a few bricks short of a load and go home. There'll be nobody left to fight the Midianites except you and me.

GIDEON: You're worrying for nothing. These are brave men, the finest in all of Israel. They won't desert us. And they SHOULD know that God is our leader, not me.

PURAH: Don't say that, Gideon! The men need somebody to follow that they can see.

GIDEON: No they don't. It's always better to follow God than to follow a person. Anyway, while I'm off praying, I want you to check out our weapons situation.

PURAH: Right! You've got it, boss. OK men! Fall in!

TROOPS: Fall in what?

PURAH: That's army talk. It means, "Get over here, now!" Now then. How many of you men brought weapons with you? How many brought a sword? Anybody? *(Pause.)* No. OK then. We have no swords. How about spears with iron tips? How many of you have spears with you? Anybody? *(Pause.)* Hmm. No spears. Shields! We do have shields, right? How many of you have shields? *(Pause.)* None? You must have brought something! Pointed sticks? How many have pointed sticks?

TROOPS: Yo!

PURAH: OK. Now we're cooking. How about rocks? Did anybody bring rocks with him?

TROOPS: Yo!

PURAH: Alright! Pointed sticks and rocks! How about wooden clubs?

TROOPS: Yo!

PURAH: Great! We have sticks and rocks and clubs. Everything an army could want.

GIDEON: How are things going, Purah?

PURAH: Terrific! Couldn't be better. Every man here has at least one weapon. Some have pointed sticks, some have rocks, some have wooden clubs...

GIDEON: Men, I would like to speak to you.

PURAH: OK you jokers! The general's about to speak! Listen up!

GIDEON: Thank you, Purah.

PURAH: Don't mention it.

GIDEON: Men, I have been talking with God.

PURAH *(whining)*: Gideon. Ixnay on the odgay stuff.

GIDEON: It has been brought to my attention that although you are willing to fight, some of you are afraid. If you have any fears at all, please feel free to go home. Nobody will think less of you if you decide to leave now.

PURAH: Hold it! Don't nobody go nowhere! Gideon, could I talk to you, please?

GIDEON: Certainly, Purah. *(They step away from troops.)*

PURAH: Gideon, are you out of your ever-lovin' mind?

GIDEON: What do you mean, Purah?

PURAH: Do you know how many men we have here?

GIDEON: At a guess, maybe thirty-one or thirty-two thousand.

PURAH: Right! And how many men do the Midianites have?

GIDEON: Hard to say. They're like a swarm of locusts. There's so many of them that they're impossible to count.

PURAH: Right! And what kind of weapons do they have?

GIDEON: Swords, shields, spears, suits of armor. The usual stuff.

PURAH: Right! So we're hopelessly out-manned, hopelessly out-armed, and you want to send some of our soldiers home.

GIDEON: That's right.

PURAH: But why?

GIDEON: Because God told me to.

PURAH: Why would God do that? I thought He wanted us to win.

GIDEON: He does. But He wants us to realize that it's His victory, not ours. If we go into battle with thirty-two thousand men and win, Israel will boast that its soldiers are such great fighters that we can defeat anybody. God wants us to realize we won because He won the battle for us.

PURAH: It still doesn't make sense to me, but if you say so. At least we won't have as many casualties as we would if everyone stayed. Men! You heard our illustrious leader! If you're chicken-livered, yellow-bellied cowards...

GIDEON: Purah!

PURAH: If any of you have any doubts as to the wisdom of your being here, feel free to go home. But leave your sticks and rocks and clubs for the real soldiers.

GIDEON: Purah! I said they would not be criticized, and I meant it.

PURAH: Look at them all leaving! Most of them are splitting! Two thirds or more! Gideon, there's only going to be about ten thousand men left.

GIDEON: I'm going to pray again. While I'm gone, you can redistribute the weapons.

PURAH: OK! We've got lots of weapons now! Everybody should have at least one rock, one stick and one club. If you have an extra club, tie it to your waist as a spare, in case you break the first one.

GIDEON: Purah.

PURAH: Yes, Gideon.

GIDEON: Have the men go down to the spring.

PURAH: Good idea. We shouldn't go into battle thirsty. Are any of you men thirsty?

TROOPS: Yo!

PURAH: OK then! Everybody to the spring. Drink lots, because there won't be any time for drinking while the Midianites are slaughtering...I mean, while we're fighting the enemy.

(TROOPS move to spring. GIDEON and PURAH observe them.)

GIDEON: Do you notice how the men have different styles of drinking, Purah?

PURAH: They're not drinking Purah. They're drinking water. I think maybe you've been standing outside in the sun a little long, Gideon.

GIDEON: I didn't say they were drinking Purah. I was calling you by name, again.

PURAH: Oh. What was the question again?

GIDEON: Do you notice the different drinking styles that the men use?

PURAH: Yeah. Some of them are kneeling, scooping up a little bit of water in their hands. They can't get a decent mouthful that way. But most of them bend right over and get their faces down near the water. That's the way to get a good drink.

GIDEON: Men. I'd like to have a word with you.

PURAH: OK you mangy dogs! Listen up! The general's talking!

GIDEON: Thank you, Purah.

PURAH: Don't mention it.

GIDEON: I was speaking with God, again...

PURAH *(whining)*: Gideon.

GIDEON: I want to thank all of you for being willing to risk your lives in the service of your country, but God wants a somewhat smaller army than we currently have. So all you men who drank directly from the stream may go home.

PURAH: Hold it! Don't nobody go nowhere! May I talk to you again, Gideon?

GIDEON: Certainly, Purah. What is it?

PURAH: I don't want you to think that I'm trying to undermine you, Gideon...

GIDEON: I wouldn't think that, Purah.

PURAH: But are you sure you heard God right?

GIDEON: Yes, I'm sure. He said ten thousand men was too many, and Israel would boast of its greatness if an army of ten thousand defeated the Midianites. He told me we need to have a smaller army.

PURAH: But our army will be down to only about three hundred men if you send home the others.

GIDEON: That's right. God is going to win the victory. We just have to be there.

PURAH: OK. If you say so. Listen up, men! You guys who drank from out of your hands, stay! The rest of you can go home! But leave your weapons behind. We need all the help we can get now!

GIDEON: I'm going to pray one more time. Redistribute the weapons while I'm gone.

PURAH: OK! We've got lots of weapons now! Everybody carry as many clubs and pointed sticks as you can! If the rocks are too heavy, you can leave those behind! We can find more! Everybody got that?

TROOPS: Yo!

GIDEON: Purah.

PURAH: Yo! I mean, yes, Gideon?

GIDEON: Give every man a torch, a pitcher and a trumpet.

PURAH: But, Gideon. If they're carrying that stuff, how are they going to carry their weapons?

GIDEON: They won't.

PURAH: They won't what?

GIDEON: They won't be carrying weapons.

PURAH: Let me get this straight. We're going to fight a superior force...

GIDEON: Right.

PURAH: An army that has superior weapons...

GIDEON: Right.

PURAH: And we're going into battle without weapons...

GIDEON: Right.

PURAH: And you expect to win.

GIDEON: Right.

PURAH: And how will this miracle take place?

GIDEON: At last. You understand!

SAMSON: THE EARLY YEARS

SCRIPTURE: Judges 13; 14

SUGGESTED TOPICS: Talents and abilities; consequences of disobedience; wisdom

BIBLE BACKGROUND

After Gideon came Abimelech, Tola, Jair, Jephthah, Ibzan, Elan and Abdon. After Abdon's death, the Israelites again did evil in God's sight. Consequently, they were delivered into the hands of the Philistines for forty years (see Judges 13:1). Once again, the Israelites cried out to God and God raised up the thirteenth judge, Samson.

Samson is one of the most difficult biblical characters to understand. He did not seem to have much consideration for the laws of God, respect for his parents or even common sense. In spite of these shortcomings, God used Samson as a hero of the faith (see Hebrews 11:32).

In the skit, Samson is portrayed as being totally self-centered. What he wants matters; nothing else does. He is shown as breaking every part of his Nazarite vow with the exception of cutting his hair (see Numbers 6:1-21). The Bible does not indicate that he drank wine or ate grapes but this is assumed as having happened from observing his other actions.

PERFORMANCE TIPS

1. Suggested props: chair and newspaper for Manoah, jar of honey for Samson.
2. If you have a large group, the Philistine man can be played by three or four men who follow Samson around and talk among themselves.
3. For comic effect, have the Philistine man (or group of men) follow right on Samson's heels just prior to his introduction.
4. Before the skit, read Numbers 6:2-6 to find out about the Nazarite vow.

DISCUSSION QUESTIONS

1. How did Samson use his great strength to obey God? How did he use it to disobey God?
2. What happened when Samson obeyed God? What happened when he didn't?
3. God gives everybody some kind of special ability or abilities. What special abilities do you have?
4. How can you use your abilities to obey God?

SAMSON: THE EARLY YEARS

CHARACTERS

MANOAH'S WIFE
MANOAH
SAMSON
SAMSON'S BRIDE
MAN
NARRATOR

PRONUNCIATION GUIDE

Nazarite (NAA-zer-ite)
Philistine (FIL-ih-steen)

WIFE: Manoah, will you please put your paper down? I have something very important to discuss with you.

MANOAH: What is it, my dear?

WIFE: I don't know if you've noticed or not, but we don't have any children.

MANOAH: It would be hard not to notice. Is there a point to your comment?

WIFE: Yes. We are going to have a son very soon.

MANOAH: You sound very sure of yourself. Are you absolutely certain about this? Not the child part. I know you can be certain about that. But what makes you think it will be a boy? People have girl babies, too, you know.

WIFE: An angel of the Lord appeared to me and said I would have a son. I am one hundred percent certain that the angel would not lie to me.

MANOAH: Do me a favor, please. Don't tell the neighbors you were speaking to an angel. I mean, why would an angel speak to you, or to me for that matter? We are not famous, like Moses or Joshua or even Gideon. Angels don't speak to nobodies.

WIFE: But those three you just mentioned were nobodies. They are famous because God or His angels spoke to them.

MANOAH: You have a point there. OK, I believe that an angel spoke to you. Did he tell you anything special about our son?

WIFE: He said that our son would deliver Israel from the Philistines and that he is to be a Nazarite.

MANOAH: Now I have a problem with what the angel told you. We're from the tribe of Dan and don't live anywhere near Nazareth. How can our son be a Nazarite?

WIFE: You're thinking of Nazarene. Our son is to take the Nazarite vow from birth. You know. The vow in the Law.

MANOAH: Oh, right! That vow! Maybe you could refresh my memory a little.

WIFE: Remember? A person devotes himself entirely to the Lord. He doesn't drink wine...

MANOAH: I could stand my son not being a drunkard.

WIFE: And he is not to approach any dead body...

MANOAH: If we want a decent funeral, we better have more children.

WIFE: And a razor is never to touch his hair.

MANOAH: Hold on, now! I don't know that I like that part. I mean, what's he going to look like in twenty years? Hair all over the place! How long is this Nazarite vow supposed to last?

WIFE: All of his life.

MANOAH: I don't know. I would like to meet this angel and make sure that you got all the instructions straight. Maybe I will ask God to have the angel come again so that I could ask some questions.

NARRATOR: A son was born to Manoah and his wife, just as the angel said. Years pass, and one day the young man, whose name is Samson, came to his parents...

SAMSON: Mom! Dad! Guess what? I met the girl of my dreams and I'm going to marry her!

WIFE: Isn't this lovely, Manoah? Our little boy is all grown up and is going to get married. Who's the girl? Is she pretty? Does she come from a good family?

MANOAH: Yes. That is important. Where does she live and when can we meet her and her family?

SAMSON: She lives in Timnah. And you can come with me tonight and meet her family.

MANOAH: That's a strange place for an Israelite family to live.

WIFE: Isn't Timnah a Philistine city? Why would an Israelite family live there.

SAMSON: Who said she's an Israelite?

WIFE: You mean you're planning to marry a Philistine? Oh, my son! How can you do this to your father and me? Can you not find a nice Israelite girl to marry? Surely there are many who would love to be your wife.

SAMSON: Maybe so. But there aren't any that I want to marry! I want to marry this Philistine girl. And nothing you can say will make me change my mind. I'm going to see her now. If you don't want to come along, that's fine with me! Good-bye! Don't wait up. I'll probably be quite late.

NARRATOR: Samson leaves his parents to go to Timnah. But on the way...

SAMSON: My parents. What a couple of relics from the dark ages. I guess they mean well, but what a drag they are sometimes. This Nazarite vow thing is a perfect example. Not cutting my hair and my beard is OK. That's kind of a status symbol. But not drinking any wine? How can you have a decent party without a little wine? And if that's not bad enough, I'm not even supposed to have any grapes. Well, really! Is it any wonder that I prefer to visit in another city where nobody knows I have a restricted diet? Boy, sometimes my parents really make me mad! Do this! Don't do that! I wish there was something I could tear to pieces! There's never a phone book around when you need one. Wait a minute. What's that lion doing? It thinks it's going to have me for supper. I'll show it a thing or two. Take that, lion! Ha! That was no tougher than beating up a baby goat. Well, that's one less lion for the shepherds to worry about.

NARRATOR: Meanwhile, in Timnah...

BRIDE: Oh, this is the happiest day of my life. Not only am I getting married soon, but to the strongest man in the entire country. The only problem is that his father has not come to see my father yet. Oh well, that's minor. Still, it will be a whole lot easier to make all the wedding plans if the two fathers would get together and finalize every thing. Really! How difficult can it be? I am so beautiful and he is so strong that it's easy to see we were made for each other. His hair is a bit of a problem, but maybe I can convince him to get it cut for the wedding. Here he comes now. Hello, Sammy!

SAMSON: Greetings, my beauty, my love. Did you miss me while I was gone?

BRIDE: I miss you every minute you're not near me. Did you talk to your parents?

SAMSON: Of course I did. I said I would.

BRIDE: How did they take the news?

SAMSON: Oh, like typical parents. You know how parents are. "She's not good enough for you." All that kind of stuff. But they'll come around. Don't worry. The wedding will come off as planned.

NARRATOR: Samson continued to visit his Philistine love, and one day, while returning home...

SAMSON: Look at this. Here's the carcass of that lion I killed a few days ago. There seems to be a lot of activity around it. Lots of buzzing. I think I'll go over and have a look. Well, I'll be! Look at that! A swarm of bees has taken over the body for a nest and has already started to make honey. I think I'll take some home for Mom and Dad.

WIFE: Manoah. Our boy is coming home. And it looks like he's carrying something.

MANOAH: How can you call him "our boy"? Planning on marrying a Philistine girl. I'm thinking of disowning him.

SAMSON: Mom! Dad! I'm home. Look, I brought you a present. Some nice, fresh honey, straight from the hive.

WIFE: That's so sweet of you, Son. Wasn't that thoughtful of him, Manoah? Where did you find it?

SAMSON: Oh...it was just...lying around.

MANOAH: So, have you given this marriage business any more thought? Like maybe deciding to call it off?

SAMSON: Yes, I have given it more thought. And no, I'm not going to call it off. At least come and meet her, OK? You'll see that she's a very nice girl. Much nicer than the Israelite girls.

MANOAH: Alright. I guess there's nothing I can do to stop the wedding anyway.

NARRATOR: So Samson's father met Samson's intended. And Samson made plans for a great feast....

BRIDE: Oh, Sammy! Isn't this nice? Look at all the people who stop us on the street to congratulate us. Just think, in seven days, I will be your wife. Isn't that wonderful?

SAMSON: I'm sure looking forward to it. Say! Who are these thirty men who keep following us around?

BRIDE: They're your groomsmen. You don't think I'm going to have the smallest wedding in Canaan, do you? I'm having one of the largest bridal parties you've ever seen, and how many of your Israelite friends are going to come? So Daddy arranged for some of the local boys to come out to be your groomsmen.

SAMSON: I'm glad to meet you fellows. Say! Do you like riddles?

MAN: Sure. Who doesn't?

SAMSON: Well, I've got a good one. You'll never guess it in a million years.

MAN: What will you give us if we guess it?

SAMSON: Well, let's see. There are thirty of you. If you guess it, I will give each of you a complete change of clothes and a linen sheet. But if you fail, each one of you will give me a change of clothes and a linen sheet. How about it?

MAN: I don't know. What do you think, guys? We're pretty good at solving riddles. Let's take the bet. OK, you're on. What's the riddle?

BRIDE: Oh, this is so exciting! Already Sammy is making friends in my town. We'll be able to live next door to Mommy and Daddy and we'll live happily ever after.

SAMSON: This is the riddle. Out of the eater came something to eat. Out of the strong came something sweet. Now! Solve it.

MAN: How long do we have to work on this? Because it's a tough riddle. We shouldn't have to solve it this minute.

SAMSON: Until the seventh day of the wedding feast. That'll give you fourteen days.

MAN: That sounds fair enough. Let's see...out of the eater....What is an eater? A wolf! But we don't eat wolves. Tigers, lions, bears? Same problem. Sheep and cattle, we do eat. But we don't get sweet things from them....This is tough! But we'll have it solved in fourteen days, don't you worry about that.

SAMSON: I'm not worried. I know the answer and you don't. And I'm sure that you'll never guess it.

BRIDE: Oh, my Sammy! Not only is he brave and strong but he's smart enough to think of clever riddles, too.

NARRATOR: For three days the Philistines tried to think of the answer....

MAN: We've been working on this riddle for days now, and we're no closer to solving it than we were on the day we first heard it. I think we better get some inside help on this.

BRIDE: Hi, guys. What are you doing here? I thought you would be working on Sammy's riddle.

MAN: We are working on it. That's why we're here. You're going to help us solve the riddle.

BRIDE: Oh, I'm not very good at riddles. I wouldn't be any help to you at all.

MAN: You don't understand. You're going to get the answer from that Israelite boyfriend of yours and then you're going to tell us the answer.

BRIDE: Oh, I would never do that! Why do you think I would do that to my Sammy?

MAN: Because if you don't, we're going to burn down your father's house, with you and your family inside.

BRIDE: Well, if you put it that way, I'll see what I can do. We wouldn't want an Israelite to appear smarter than a Philistine, would we?

NARRATOR: So, every day until the final day of the feast, Samson's sweetheart wept in front of him and begged him to tell her the answer to the riddle.

BRIDE: If you really loved me, you would tell me the answer to the riddle. Come on. Be a sport. Tell me the answer. Husbands and wives shouldn't have secrets from each other.

SAMSON: I haven't even told the answer to my parents. Why should I tell you the answer? You'll learn the answer later today.

BRIDE: But I don't want to know the answer later. I want to know it before anybody else. Please! Pretty please! Let me know the answer.

SAMSON: Woman, you've pestered me almost to death for nearly a week now. OK, I'll tell you the answer. I killed a lion and some bees made honey in the carcass of the lion. That's the answer to the riddle. Hey! Where are you going in such a hurry?

BRIDE: Oh...I just thought of some last minute things that need to be done. See you at supper tonight.

SAMSON: I don't think I'll ever understand women. Well, well, well. Here comes my wedding party. Coming to outfit me for my honeymoon with thirty new suits, no doubt. Hello, fellows! How goes the riddle solving?

MAN: We think we've got it solved. Now. What's the strongest eating animal around? Obviously, the lion. And as for the sweet part, what could possibly be sweeter than honey? We think you found a lion that was killed that had a hive of bees making honey in it. How about it? Is that the correct answer?

SAMSON: The only way you could have known that was if my woman had told you. Well, I didn't say you couldn't use her help in solving the riddle. You wait here, and I'll go and get your new clothes. But if you see that woman I was supposed to marry, tell her the wedding's off!

MAN: But you can't just leave her at the altar. She's all set to get married today. What's she going to do?

SAMSON: Tell her to marry the best man who'll have her.

MAN: What's that? Did he say let his best man marry her? Well, I don't see any problem with that, do you fellows? Let's go and finish off what's left of the food and celebrate this new wedding.

Samson's Downfall

SCRIPTURE: Judges 15; 16

SUGGESTED TOPICS: Talents and abilities; consequences of disobedience; wisdom

BIBLE BACKGROUND

Samson had left Timnah angrily after killing thirty Philistines to pay off his bet. Later he relented and returned to claim his bride.

Wedding customs were substantially different from what they are today. Samson was legally married to the Philistine girl on the first day of the feast. However, his walking away on the seventh day of the feast was sufficient to constitute a legal divorce under the Philistine law. From their viewpoint, she was free to remarry.

Israelite women in biblical times had a considerably exalted status in comparison to the women of neighboring countries. Mosaic law required a certificate of divorce to be given to a woman if a marriage broke up; a man could not just walk away from her and later walk back and claim nothing had happened. If she had not been given the certificate, the man was responsible to meet her needs as his wife. Samson, by walking away from the marriage and then trying to take his wife back, again shows his disregard for both God's law and the customs of human society.

The fact that the Philistines wanted to know the secret of Samson's strength suggests that Samson did not have a substantially different physique from that of most other men. If he had massive muscles, would the source of his strength not be obvious to the most casual observer? To learn the source of Samson's strength, the Philistine leaders approached Samson's latest flame, Delilah. Although Delilah proved herself faithless on three different occasions, Samson finally gave in and revealed the secret.

PERFORMANCE TIPS

1. Suggested props: several chairs placed together to represent the couch at Delilah's house, ropes to loosely tie around Samson's wrists.

2. Older Samson is the narrator. If your room has enough space, have Samson slowly walk in a circle (as though grinding the Philistines' grain) as he speaks.

3. During the final scene, have someone lead Samson around the room. Let Samson bump into walls and objects to indicate his blindness.

DISCUSSION QUESTIONS

1. Read Colossians 3:23,24. God calls us to do things with all our heart. What does the phrase "with all our heart" mean?

2. How does doing things with all your heart show that you love and obey God?

3. What was Samson's job? How would you evaluate his performance?

4. What jobs do you have in your daily life? How can you do them to show that you love and obey God?

SAMSON'S DOWNFALL

CHARACTERS

OLDER SAMSON
YOUNG SAMSON
FIRST PHILISTINE
SECOND PHILISTINE
ISRAELITE
DELILAH

SCENE ONE

OLDER SAMSON: Oh, what disgrace. Here am I, the mighty Samson, formerly the scourge of the Philistines, now blinded and their slave. How could this happen? How could such a strong man be brought so low? Because of my own foolishness, that's how! Why didn't I listen to my parents? Why didn't I listen to God? Why did I have to hang out with the Philistines? Why am I talking to myself, now? Why not? I'm the only one who will listen to me anymore. I guess my downfall began when I went back to Timnah to be reconciled with my bride....

YOUNG SAMSON: Hey there, father-in-law. It is I, Samson, the best son any father could ever hope for. I've decided to forgive my bride. I'll just go into her room and surprise her. What's that? You gave her to my best man to marry? Why did you do something stupid like that? You thought I hated her? Why would I hate her? I married her, didn't I? You'll just have to call off the second marriage. What do you mean, you can't do that? It's simple. Just tell her she's married to me and the other marriage doesn't count. No! I don't want to marry her younger sister! I want my wife! You won't let me have her? Then forget it! But don't blame me for what happens. Blame yourself!

OLDER SAMSON: I was angry. And when I was angry, I did rash things....

FIRST PHILISTINE: Isn't it great to be a Philistine? Just look at all these beautiful wheat fields. Plenty to last all winter. Maybe even into next harvest.

SECOND PHILISTINE: It sure is great! And you're right about the wheat, too. But don't forget, if we don't have enough, we can always take some from the Israelites. Now that's something I wouldn't want to be, an Israelite. Except maybe to be that Samson fellow.

FIRST PHILISTINE: I know what you mean. He's the one man in Canaan who does whatever he wants, goes wherever he wants and never has to worry about what other people think. Nobody wants to get into a fight with him. If he gets mad at you, look out!

SECOND PHILISTINE: I'll say. You've heard the talk around the Israelites that he was supposed to be their next savior, haven't you? I'm sure glad he hasn't tried to fill that role, yet.

FIRST PHILISTINE: You and me, both. If he ever decided to wipe out the Philistines, you wouldn't be able to find enough of us to form a crowd at a...hey! What's going on in that wheat field?

SECOND PHILISTINE: It looks like a bunch of foxes running through the field. And their tails are on fire! No, that's not exactly it...

FIRST PHILISTINE: There must be three hundred foxes. In pairs. With their tails tied together. And a firebrand tied to their tails. They're setting the fields on fire! We better go get some help to put out the fire or we'll lose the entire crop!

OLDER SAMSON: But they were too late. Not only all their wheat was destroyed but, also their corn, grapes and olives.

SECOND PHILISTINE: Who would do this to us? Foxes don't tie their own tails together with firebrands. I suspect we're the victims of foul play.

FIRST PHILISTINE: I was talking to that old man over there. The one that was going to be Samson's father-in-law. He says Samson was here earlier today, and get this—the old man threw Samson out on his ear. He told Samson that his daughter was married to somebody else and Samson couldn't have her. He says Samson went away mad!

SECOND PHILISTINE: So this old man caused all our trouble. Well, we'll fix him. Our crops were all burned. Put the old man and his daughter in their house, and we'll burn it down. Let's see what he thinks of fire.

(PHILISTINES exit. YOUNG SAMSON enters.)

YOUNG SAMSON: Boy! Was that fun! Catching those foxes and setting that fire. What a blaze! I bet it goes down in history as the most famous fire ever. Hey! There's a guy I know. What did you think of the great Philistine blaze? What do you mean, which one? No, I didn't hear about the one in Timnah. Tell me about it. *(Exits.)*

OLDER SAMSON: And once again, my anger was kindled. To avenge the death of my wife and father-in-law, I went into Philistine territory and slaughtered many Philistines.

(PHILISTINES enter.)

FIRST PHILISTINE: OK! That does it! I've had it up to here with Samson! He's only a man. Get as many men together as you can. We're going to teach that boy a lesson in manners!

SECOND PHILISTINE: We've got a whole army here. What are we going to do?

FIRST PHILISTINE: We're going to march into Israelite territory and demand that they turn him over to us! After tying him up, of course.

SECOND PHILISTINE: How will that help us? Nobody can tie up Samson if he doesn't want to be tied up.

FIRST PHILISTINE: Oh, it will work just fine. Samson may be a jerk, but he does have a soft spot when it comes to other Israelites. You'll notice he's never hurt any of them. He'll have to let them tie him up because if he doesn't, we'll destroy Israel.

SECOND PHILISTINE: Alright! I like this plan. I won't be afraid of a Samson who is securely tied.

FIRST PHILISTINE: Well, here we are. You there! Israelites! We want Samson and we want him now! Take some men, go tie him up securely, and bring him here to us! If you don't, we wipe out Israel! Well, what are you standing there for? Go get him!

SECOND PHILISTINE: That's telling them. *(PHILISTINES exit.)*

YOUNG SAMSON: Well, well, well. Look at this. There's a party of men, all Israelites, I'd say. There must be three thousand men there. It looks like they're coming to see me. Hi, guys. What's happening?

ISRAELITE: Hi, Samson. We have a little favor to ask of you.

YOUNG SAMSON: Well, go ahead and ask. Have I ever turned you down before?

ISRAELITE: No. But we've never asked for a favor before.

YOUNG SAMSON: That's true. But there's always a first time, right? Now, what's the little favor you want?

ISRAELITE: I'm not sure how to word this...

YOUNG SAMSON: Take your time. Get the words all straight. I'll play with these two new ropes you brought. Do you want to see a neat rope trick? You take two cords, like these, tie a special knot in them...

ISRAELITE: We didn't bring the ropes for you to do tricks with. OK, I'll put it to you straight. There's a bunch of angry Philistines down in the valley. If we don't tie you up and take you down to them, they say they will destroy all of Israel. We have to ask you to let us tie you up and take you to them.

YOUNG SAMSON: What do they want with me?

ISRAELITE: They didn't say, exactly. But the word barbecue did come up in their conversation once or twice.

YOUNG SAMSON: So I'm supposed to let you tie me up. Then you'll take me as a prisoner and hand me over to the Philistines. Have I got this straight?

ISRAELITE: That's pretty much it.

YOUNG SAMSON: There's nothing fancy in this idea, is there? Nothing like you planning to kill me yourselves?

ISRAELITE: No. We just tie you up and take you to the Philistines. Just between you and me, I think if we delivered your dead body to them, they would be madder than they are now. I think they want the pleasure—sorry, wrong word...uh, honor of killing you themselves.

YOUNG SAMSON: If all you want to do is to tie me up, go ahead. No problem. Make sure that you've got some good, solid knots there. If there's one thing I can't stand, it's shoddy workmanship. *(ISRAELITES begin tying.)* That's good! You fellows really tie some fine knots....

OLDER SAMSON: Samson's finest hour! That's what it should have been called. There I was. All tied up, waiting for the wrath of the Philistines to be cast upon me. But that's not the way the scene played. When I got to the Philistine camp, I saw the bones of a donkey lying on the ground. Just the bones, you understand. The donkey was long gone. Well, the Philistines shouted at me, called me all sorts of mean, nasty, ugly names. They told me what they were going to do to me, things that shouldn't be repeated in mixed company. But the Spirit of the Lord came upon me, and I broke those strong, new ropes as if they were fire-weakened flax. Then, I picked up that donkey's jawbone and used it as a mighty war club. I killed more than a thousand Philistines that day. I must say, it was a fitting weapon. A jackass using a jackass's jawbone to destroy his enemies. You would think I would have learned by then that God wanted to use me to destroy the Philistines. But no! Samson is too smart! He doesn't need anybody to tell him what to do. I continued to associate with the Philistines. They kept making plans to kill me, and I kept outwitting them. Then, I met Delilah....

SCENE TWO

FIRST PHILISTINE: Delilah, we've got a job for you.

DELILAH: Oh, yeah? What?

SECOND PHILISTINE: Nothing tough. You've heard of Samson, right?

DELILAH: He comes around from time to time. So what?

FIRST PHILISTINE: You know that he's a pretty strong boy.

DELILAH: One of history's great understatements. So what?

SECOND PHILISTINE: You've probably heard about the time we had him trapped in Gaza one night. And how we surrounded the city, knowing he couldn't leave until morning, but then he ripped the gates off the city wall and walked away with them...

DELILAH: I've heard the stories. Do you have a point to make or not?

FIRST PHILISTINE: We're getting there. The point is, the reason Samson is such a nuisance to us is because of his great strength...

DELILAH: All that buildup for such a simple statement. Samson is stronger than all of the Philistines put together. Again I say, so what?

SECOND PHILISTINE: So, we remember a time, some years ago, when Samson had a secret. He wouldn't reveal the answer to anybody, except for the woman he was planning to marry...

FIRST PHILISTINE: And Samson is pretty close to you...

SECOND PHILISTINE: And will tell you things he wouldn't tell anybody else...

FIRST PHILISTINE: So you could learn the secret of his great strength...

SECOND PHILISTINE: Then we fix it so that he isn't strong any more...

FIRST PHILISTINE: And capture him.

DELILAH *(bored)*: Terrific. What's in it for me?

SECOND PHILISTINE: The knowledge of a job well done.

DELILAH *(sarcastically)*: How wonderful.

FIRST PHILISTINE: The gratitude of Philistines everywhere.

DELILAH *(more sarcastically)*: Marvelous.

SECOND PHILISTINE: And eleven hundred pieces of silver from every Philistine lord.

DELILAH *(enthusiastically)*: Now you're talking my language! Look! Here he comes now. Go out the back way. I'll learn his secret and tell it to you tomorrow.

YOUNG SAMSON: Hi there, Delilah. You got anything to eat here?

DELILAH: All kinds of things. You know, Samson, I was thinking. If we're going to be good friends, we should know things about each other. You go first.

YOUNG SAMSON: Did I ever tell you about the time I killed a lion?

DELILAH: Often.

YOUNG SAMSON: How about the great fire?

DELILAH: I've heard it.

YOUNG SAMSON: How about the time I killed a thousand men...

DELILAH: With the jawbone of a donkey. Heard it. I was thinking of something a little more personal. Take your great strength, as an example. What makes you so strong? You don't look different from any other man. Why can't anything be used to bind you? C'mon. Be a sport. Tell me. Is there anything that could be used to tie you up?

YOUNG SAMSON: You promise not to tell anybody?

DELILAH: Cross my heart and hope to...well, cross my heart.

YOUNG SAMSON: You know those really thin branches on vines? The ones that can be tied. If I were tied up with seven of them, then I'd be as helpless as a newborn lamb.

DELILAH: I'd love for you to stay and talk, but I've got a lot of things to do. You go now, and I'll see you tomorrow night.

YOUNG SAMSON: But we didn't talk about you.

DELILAH: That's alright. You're more interesting than me, anyway.

YOUNG SAMSON: That's true. OK, I'll see you tomorrow. Good-bye.

OLDER SAMSON: The next day...

FIRST PHILISTINE: Seven green branches from the vine. You're sure of this?

SECOND PHILISTINE: It sounds too easy to me.

DELILAH: Has anybody tried it before?

SECOND PHILISTINE: No, but it still sounds too easy.

DELILAH: Trust me. You have some men hiding in the back room at my place and when Samson is powerless, grab him!

FIRST PHILISTINE: They'll be there. You just be sure he's tied up.

OLDER SAMSON: Later, that evening...

YOUNG SAMSON: Hi there, Delilah. What's happening?

DELILAH: Nothing much. How about coming in and lying down? You look a little tired.

YOUNG SAMSON: Food and sleep. Everything a man could want. *(He lies down and sleeps, while Delilah ties him up.)*

DELILAH: He's finally drifted off and he's tied up. All that money is as good as mine. Here goes nothing. Samson! Wake up! The Philistines are coming to capture you!

YOUNG SAMSON: *(Breaks the vines.)* Huh? Who? What? Where?

DELILAH: Samson! You lied to me! You told me that seven green branches would secure you and look what happened. You broke them as if they were a piece of string stretched across a fire. If we're going to have any kind of relationship, we have to be honest with each other. So tell me the truth. Isn't there anything that could make you weak?

YOUNG SAMSON: OK. So you caught on to my little joke. There's nothing special about my strength that new ropes that have never been used before wouldn't cure.

DELILAH: That's it? Just use new ropes?

YOUNG SAMSON: Sure. Nothing to it. Now, where's something to eat?

DELILAH: You'll have to find something at home. I just remembered some things I need.

OLDER SAMSON: The next day...

FIRST PHILISTINE: You're sure about it, this time? We have to use brand new ropes. There's nothing tricky about the knots or anything?

SECOND PHILISTINE: Didn't those Israelites use new ropes when we tried to capture him before?

FIRST PHILISTINE: They said they did. But you can't trust Israelites for anything. They were probably making it up just to impress us.

SECOND PHILISTINE: Are you sure he's not kidding you again, Delilah?

DELILAH: Why would he? He knows I tested him last time. Even Samson isn't stupid enough to lie to me again.

FIRST PHILISTINE: OK. The men will bring the ropes when they come to your place. You get Samson tied up and we'll have him.

OLDER SAMSON: Later, that evening...

DELILAH: Well, I've got him trussed up like a Thanksgiving turkey. What will I buy with all that money that will soon be mine? I'd better test this before I call those men in here. Samson! Wake up! The Philistines!

YOUNG SAMSON: *(Breaks the ropes.)* Huh? Who? What? Where?

DELILAH: I can't believe it! You lied to me again! Those were some of the best ropes money could buy, and you've ruined them. This joke of yours is getting tiresome, Samson. Are you going to tell me what makes you stronger than other men or not?

YOUNG SAMSON: Women! They've got no sense of humor. A guy tries to make a little joke and they get all huffy. Maybe I'll tell you and maybe I won't.

DELILAH *(sweetly)***:** I'm sorry that I yelled at you. I just don't want there to be any secrets between us. C'mon. Tell me the secret of your strength.

YOUNG SAMSON: OK. It has to do with my hair. If you were to weave the seven locks of my hair together, I would be as helpless as the proverbial kitten up a tree.

DELILAH: There. That wasn't so hard, was it? You go back to sleep now. I have some weaving to do. *(She begins braiding his hair.)* Weaving. That's it! Clothes! That's what I'll do with all that beautiful Philistine money. New clothes. There. I'm finished. Now. Let's try it. Samson! The Philistines!

YOUNG SAMSON: Huh? Who? What? Where?

DELILAH: OK! That does it, buddy! We're through! You want to come here again, you tell me the real secret! If you tell me another lie, I'll never speak to you again! You got that?

OLDER SAMSON: So I told her the real secret. And while I was asleep with my head in her lap, she called in a barber. He shaved me as bald as an egg. No more hair. No more beard. I really was helpless then. The Lord was no longer with me. I had completely violated my Nazarite vow. The Philistines blinded me, put me in brass fetters and have been using me as a slave to grind their grain. But nobody seems to notice that my hair has been growing again. And with it, I can feel my strength returning. Wait! Somebody's calling me. Oh, it's only the jailer. What's that? *(Pause.)* The Philistine lords and their ladies are in Dagon's temple. Who cares? Let them worship their god, Dagon, if they want to. What do they want me there for? Probably to laugh at. That's about all I'm good for, now. Yeah, keep your shirt on. I'm coming. But somebody will have to lead me there. Oh. There's a boy here to be my guide. Right. Lead on, MacDuff. There's a lot of noise in this place. How many people are here? No kidding. Three thousand? Where's the pillars that support this place? Lead me over to them, would you? I'm tired and I need to lean on something to rest. Hey, kid! Do you like riddles? Here's one for you. What do you call a Nazarite whose hair has grown back? You don't know? Well, listen close. Because the answer to this one is going to bring the house down.

THE SAVIOR

SCRIPTURE: Genesis 3; Isaiah 9:6,7; 53:3-6; Jeremiah 23:5,6; Micah 5:2-4; Romans 5:12,17-19

SUGGESTED TOPICS: The Savior; prophecies about Christ; witnessing; God's plan of salvation

BIBLE BACKGROUND

The history of humanity tells of people living their lives according to their own wisdom and desires, rather than obeying and loving God. As a result, they drove a wedge between themselves and God. Throughout those years, God repeatedly chose men and women to call people back to Himself. Also, He repeatedly promised to send a Savior to reconcile people to Himself.

Who is this Savior? Many expected a political or military leader. Others were sure God would send someone who was part of the established religious order. However, careful study of the prophetic messages clearly shows both the character and the mission of the Savior: He is God in human flesh, God who loves us so much that He willingly took our sin on Himself.

PERFORMANCE TIPS

1. Suggested props: two telephones for Tony and Kelly to use in their conversation. (Adjust opening lines accordingly.)

2. Introduce the skit by asking, "How would you summarize God's plan for the world?" After group responds say, "Compare your answers to those in this skit."

DISCUSSION QUESTIONS

1. What is sin? What has happened in the world because of sin?

2. What sins do you think are most common?

3. People often rate sins: this one isn't too bad, this one is much worse. Do you think God rates different sins? Why or why not?

4. Because of sin, what did God do?

5. Are you a member of God's family? What would you like to know about Jesus, the Savior?

THE SAVIOR

CHARACTERS

KELLY
TONY

KELLY: Hi, Tony. Where are you going?

TONY: Sunday School. Wanna come?

KELLY: No way! I go to school all week. Why would I want to go on Sunday, too?

TONY: Sunday School isn't like regular school, Kelly. We have lots of fun.

KELLY: I doubt it. My mom made me go for years. I hated it.

TONY: Bummer! We do all kinds of interesting stuff and learn fascinating things from the Bible.

KELLY: Oh yeah? Like what?

TONY: Right now we're studying about Jesus.

KELLY: Well then, I sure don't need to go—I know all that stuff. The manger, the shepherds, the wise men, the Cross. I don't need to hear it again.

TONY: OK, smart aleck. If you know it all, then you know when Jesus was first mentioned in the Bible, right?

KELLY: Sure. Let's see...Matthew. That's it. You thought I didn't know, didn't you?

TONY: Yeah, I thought you didn't know. Now I KNOW that you don't know.

KELLY: Oh, yeah? Well if you're so smart, when WAS Jesus first mentioned?

TONY: In Genesis.

KELLY: Yeah, right. This must be some kind of brilliant Sunday School class you go to. Jesus doesn't come around until the New Testament.

TONY: Have you ever heard of Adam and Eve?

KELLY: What is this, kindergarten? Everyone's heard of Adam and Eve.

TONY: Then you remember that God made a perfect world, and He created Adam and Eve to live in it.

KELLY: Yeah. And Eve ate the apple because the snake told her to...

TONY: This would probably go faster if you wouldn't interrupt. Who said Eve ate an apple?

KELLY: Everybody knows Eve ate an apple and then God zapped her for it.

TONY: Well, maybe everybody is wrong. The Bible doesn't say anything about an apple.

KELLY: OK, so maybe it wasn't an apple. Maybe it was a peach. Who cares? The point is, what does that have to do with Jesus?

TONY: It has everything to do with Jesus. Remember that Adam and Eve only had one rule to obey in their perfect world...

KELLY: That doesn't sound perfect to me. Perfect would be NO rules.

TONY: Have you ever tried to play a game where there were no rules?

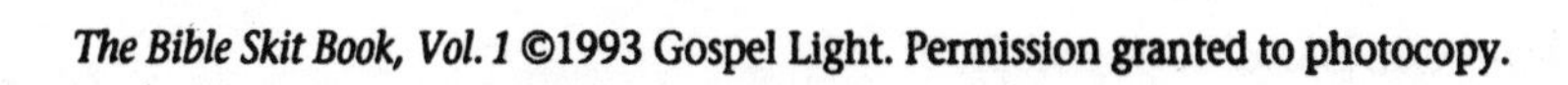

KELLY: No. Let me think about it. *(Pause.)* If there are no rules, then everyone does what ever he wants to do. That might be pretty confusing.

TONY: All right! You're beginning to get it. So God gave them lots of privileges and one rule: Don't eat the fruit of the tree of knowledge that was in the middle of the garden.

KELLY: This is the part about the snake. You don't really believe that Eve was out talking to a snake, do you? That's just a fairy tale.

TONY: Yes, I do believe it. The Bible says that the snake was Satan in disguise. And Satan told Eve that God made the rule because He was afraid if people ate from that tree, God would have some competition. But that was a lie that Satan told her just to make her sin. Once she and Adam ate the fruit, the world wasn't perfect any more.

KELLY: You told me all this had something to do with Jesus. I haven't heard His name yet.

TONY: I'm almost there. God made plans for correcting the damage that Adam and Eve did. He promised that the seed of woman would bruise the head of the serpent and the serpent would bruise the heel of the woman's seed.

KELLY: So? What's that supposed to mean?

TONY: That's Genesis 3:15. That's God's promise that a Savior would come into the world and Satan would hurt Him a little, but the Savior would destroy Satan. That Savior is Jesus. The name Jesus isn't used, but that's who the passage is talking about.

KELLY: OK. So Jesus is mentioned in Genesis. So what?

TONY: It's not the only time Jesus is mentioned. The Old Testament is filled with references about Him. And it's important, because it shows how much God loves us.

KELLY: Because He's going to send a Savior? Why didn't He just stop Adam and Eve from sinning in the first place?

TONY: If He had stopped Adam and Eve, then we'd be robots, not people. God wants us to do right because we want to, not because He forced us to. So, God not only promised to send us a Savior, but He told us what the Savior would be like, and how we could recognize Him. God sent lots of prophets to tell different things about the promised Savior.

KELLY: You mean like those people on TV who tell what's going to happen next year.

TONY: No, not at all. If God's prophets said that something would happen, it had to happen exactly the way they said. That's how we know we can trust the things they have to say about the future. Do you want to know what the prophets had to say about the Savior?

KELLY: OK, I'm curious. What did they have to say about the Savior?

TONY: Well, God told the prophets whose earthly family the Savior would belong to. Jeremiah prophesied that the Savior would come from the family of King David.

KELLY: That's the guy who killed Goliath, right?

TONY: That's right. Another prophet, Isaiah, told us what some of His titles would be. Isaiah said the Savior would be called Wonderful, Counselor, the Mighty God, the Everlasting Father and the Prince of Peace.

KELLY: I've heard some of those before. What else did the prophets say?

TONY: Another prophet, Micah, told where the Savior would be born. Micah said that even though Bethlehem was one of the smallest places in Judah, God's chosen Savior would be born there.

KELLY: Anything else?

TONY: Yes. In Isaiah, chapter fifty-three, God tells why the Savior is coming.

KELLY: A savior comes to save. You need a whole chapter to say that?

TONY: But remember, God wanted us to know for certain who the Savior would be. God said, through Isaiah, that people are like sheep who go straying off, and God would put all of our wrong on the Savior. The Savior would take the punishment we deserve for the wrong things we've done.

KELLY: But that's not fair! Why would somebody want to be punished for something that somebody else did? I got in trouble at school because someone else was goofing off and the teacher thought it was me. That really made me mad. Why would God make somebody else suffer because I did something wrong? Why doesn't He punish the ones who do wrong and leave the others alone?

TONY: God didn't MAKE anyone suffer for other people's sins. Jesus willingly took the punishment that everyone else deserved. Romans chapter five, says that one man's disobedience made many sinners. Do you know who that's talking about?

KELLY: Adam, I guess. That's when everything stopped being perfect.

TONY: That's right. It also says that by the obedience of one, many shall be made righteous.

KELLY: I guess that's talking about Jesus. But why didn't everyone pay for their own sins? Then Jesus wouldn't have had to die on the cross.

TONY: Because the payment for sin is separation from God, and God wants us to be united with Him, not separated. Because Jesus was perfect, He could pay the price for our sins and only be separated from God the Father for a short time. If we had to pay for our own sins, we would be separated from God forever.

KELLY: But what about people who don't sin? Aren't they being treated unfairly?

TONY: But that's just it! Everybody sins! Sinning doesn't just mean doing horrible things like committing murder. Sinning just means not being perfect. Do you know anybody who is perfect?

KELLY: Well...no.

TONY: OK. So Jesus came to pay the price for the sins of everybody who ever lived and everybody who ever will live. That way, we ALL can have our sins forgiven and be able to live with God forever.

KELLY: I guess maybe I don't know as much as I thought I did. I mean, if Jesus did so much for me, maybe I should learn more about it. Is that invitation still open?

TONY: It sure is.

The Birth of John

SCRIPTURE: Matthew 1:18-25; Luke 1:5-45,57-66

SUGGESTED TOPICS: The Savior; responding to God's Word

BIBLE BACKGROUND

The time for the Savior's birth was almost at hand. But first, God had a few necessary announcements.

God does nothing on the sly. If something is important for us to know, God ensures we will have access to the knowledge. The birth of the Savior was the beginning of the most important series of events in the history of mankind. God did not want this to be misunderstood. Among the things God wanted understood at the Savior's birth were the prophecies which were being fulfilled.

For example, prophets had foretold that Elijah must return (see Malachi 4:5,6). John the Baptist was a partial fulfillment of this prophecy—not that John was Elijah, but his ministry and spirit was so like Elijah's it was correct to say, "Elijah has come and will come" (Matthew 17:10-12).

To further fulfill prophecy, the Savior must be born of a virgin (see Isaiah 7:14). God wanted the people involved to understand God's plan and their roles in it. Since people do not have God's understanding, He sent His messengers to tell Zechariah, Mary and Joseph what they must do.

PERFORMANCE TIPS

1. Suggested props: a slate and chalk or paper and felt pen for Zechariah. (Have Zechariah write in large letters "His name is John" as directed in the skit.)

2. During the skit Zechariah is struck mute. The person playing the part of Zechariah should be prepared to pantomime a need for writing materials.

3. The skit is written with Mary as an off-stage character. If desired, Mary could be visible but without spoken lines. Or, write lines for Mary to use in response to the angel and to Elizabeth. Refer to Luke 1:26-45.

DISCUSSION QUESTIONS

1. Girls, suppose you were Mary. How would you feel if you learned you would have a baby before you were married?

2. Boys, suppose you were Joseph. Would you have believed Mary's story about the angel? Why or why not?

3. Why did God send angels to speak to Zechariah, Mary and Joseph?

4. What are some ways God speaks to you today? When might it be hard to believe God's messages?

THE BIRTH OF JOHN

CHARACTERS

ZECHARIAH (zek-uh-RYE-uh)
ANGEL
ELIZABETH
NARRATOR

ZECHARIAH: Here I am in the Temple. What an honor to serve God in this way. I just wish Elizabeth and I had some children who could continue as priests before the Lord. But, I guess you can't have everything. Now then, where is that incense? Ah! There it is. Wait a minute! Who are you?

ANGEL: I am an angel of the Lord, Zechariah. I have come to deliver a message to you from God.

ZECHARIAH: You know, just the other day, I was telling Elizabeth that we lived in a boring village where nothing ever happened. Now, I come into the Temple, and I meet a crazy person.

ANGEL: I am not a crazy person, Zechariah. I am an angel of the Lord. I repeat, I have a message for you from God. Do you want to hear it or not?

ZECHARIAH: I might as well. I have nothing to lose. Go ahead crazy person—I mean, angel. What's the message?

ANGEL: The Lord has heard the prayer that you and your wife, Elizabeth, have been praying for many years. God is going to give you a son.

ZECHARIAH: Hold it! You don't need to go any farther. I know you're not an angel. That bit's been done before.

ANGEL: I beg your pardon?

ZECHARIAH: Does the name Abraham mean anything to you? He was very old and so was Sarah, but God promised to give them a son.

ANGEL: So? What's your problem?

ZECHARIAH: Well now. That's called a miracle. Do you know what a miracle is? It's something that only happens once. God already did that one. So now I'm SURE you're a crazy person.

ANGEL: What makes you think a miracle can only happen once?

ZECHARIAH: Well, if something happens again and again, it's hardly unusual. It's natural. And miracles are supernatural.

ANGEL: How long ago did this miracle happen to Abraham?

ZECHARIAH: Well, I'm not sure. About two thousand years ago?

ANGEL: Do you call something that happens once every two thousand years commonplace?

ZECHARIAH: Well, no...

ANGEL: Then please stop interrupting me and let me get on with the message. *(Formally.)* You will have a son and you will name him John. He will never drink wine nor strong drink. From the time he is conceived, he will be filled with the Holy Spirit of God. Because of him, many of the children of Israel will turn back to God. He will speak with the spirit and the power of Elijah to prepare the people to meet the Lord.

ZECHARIAH: *(Pause.)* I must admit, that is some message. My son—a great prophet and preacher. But there is still the problem of my age, and Elizabeth's. How can I be sure you are an angel? What happens if I run out and tell everybody an angel told me I'll have a son, and three years later, nothing? People will tap their heads when they see me and say, "There goes crazy, old Zechariah who talks to angels." So, if you don't mind, I'll hold off on the birth announcements for a while.

ANGEL: Zechariah! I am Gabriel, who stands in the presence of God. I was sent to speak to you. But don't worry—you will not be making any birth announcements. As a sign to you that what I say is, indeed, a message from God, from this moment until all these things have happened, you will not be able to speak.

NARRATOR: And at that very moment, Zechariah became mute. He could not utter a word, not even when he left Jerusalem and returned home....

ELIZABETH: Hello, my husband. Welcome home. Did you have a nice time in Jerusalem? What's the matter? *(ZECHARIAH pretends to write something.)* Wait! A game! We're going to play a guessing game. OK, give me a clue. You're writing something. A book. This is the name of a book. No? A writer. That's it. You're a writer. No? You're not very good at this game. You just do the same thing over and over. Wait! *(Pause.)* This ISN'T a guessing game. You want to write something and you need a pen and paper. Well, why didn't you say so? Speak up, man. What is it? *(Pause.)* You want some paper and pen.

NARRATOR: The angel Gabriel visited others besides Zechariah.

ANGEL: Fear not, Mary, for you have found great favor with God. I am the angel, Gabriel, and have been sent to bring you this good news. You will bear a child and shall call His name Jesus. *(Pause.)* Yes, I am well aware you have never been with a man. But the Spirit of God will come upon you, and the Holy Child born of you shall be called the Son of God.

NARRATOR: Bubbling with excitement, Mary went to visit her elderly relative, Elizabeth.

ELIZABETH: Hello, Mary. Why, you look positively radiant. What brings you all this way to visit? Not that I'm complaining, mind you. That husband of mine hasn't said a word since he came back from Jerusalem six months ago. But you don't have to tell me why you're here. I know you're going to have a baby, too. A baby specially blessed by God. And, Mary, the baby inside me jumped for joy when I heard your voice. But I'm hurt. Why didn't you invite us to the wedding? *(Pause.)* What do you mean, there hasn't been a wedding yet? But you and Joseph—NOT you and Joseph? Does Joseph know about this? Come into the house. We have a lot of catching up to do. When are you planning to tell Joseph about it? Do you think he'll believe you?

NARRATOR: Mary stayed with Elizabeth for about three months. In the meantime, God was making SURE that Joseph would believe what Mary told him.

ANGEL: Joseph! I am an angel of the Lord. Do not be afraid to take Mary to be your wife. The child inside her is from the Holy Spirit. This baby will be a boy, and you shall name Him Jesus, for He will save His people from their sins.

NARRATOR: Soon, Elizabeth's child was born.

ELIZABETH: *(Talks to someone offstage.)* Yes, we're excited and so pleased. Just think. Already he is eight days old. *(Pause.)* We're going to name him John. *(Pause.)* I know that no one in our family has ever had that name. But John will be his name. You'll have to ask his father. *(Sighs.)* Zechariah, our friends think it's strange that you haven't spoken since you got back from Jerusalem, nine months ago. They think it's even stranger that we're naming the baby John. Please tell them, Zechariah. *(Sighs again.)* I mean, write for them. Everyone look. *(She points over Zechariah's shoulder as he writes.)* He's writing, "His...name...is...John."

ZECHARIAH: At last! I can speak again! Praise God! It's just as the angel said it would be! God is sending us a Savior, and this child will prepare His way! Oh, praise be to God in the highest...

ELIZABETH: *(Shrugs.)* Well, there goes the peace and quiet.

HEROD

SCRIPTURE: Matthew 2

SUGGESTED TOPICS: The Savior; God's protection

BIBLE BACKGROUND

The fullness of time had come. The Savior was born in a small stable in an insignificant town in a conquered country. Rejoicing was heard throughout the heavens and in a few selected places in the world.

God sent His Son to save the world. All the world should have rejoiced; however, not everyone was excited about the good news. Herod was so concerned about the possibility he would lose prestige or power, that he feared the coming of Jesus, the Messiah. He was not prepared to change his ways, to surrender control of his life. To Herod, the good news was the worst news.

PERFORMANCE TIPS

1. Suggested props: crown for Herod, overcoats and sunglasses for spies.
2. Herod is an angry character and should speak loudly and forcefully.
3. If time permits, ask your group to work together to write a preamble to the skit. The wise men could discuss what they will need to bring for the long journey. Or, write dialog for Herod's meeting with the wise men.
4. After the skit, finish the story. Describe how God protected His Son or read Matthew 2:13-23.

DISCUSSION QUESTIONS

1. Read Micah 5:2. What does this verse tell about Bethlehem?
2. How many wise men came to see Jesus? Read Matthew 2:1,2 to check your answer.
3. What was Herod's response to the birth of Jesus? What was the response of the wise men? What is your response?
4. How can you show love and praise to God for His gift of Jesus?

HEROD

CHARACTERS

HEROD
SPY ONE
SPY TWO
SPY THREE

SCENE ONE

HEROD: Spies! Get in here! On the double!

SPY ONE: With the greatest of haste.

SPY TWO: Never wasting a second.

SPY THREE: At the instant of your command,

SPIES *(together)*: Your Highness.

HEROD: What's going on here?

SPY ONE: Concerning...

SPY TWO: ...what...

SPY THREE: ...matter...

SPIES *(together)*: Your Highness?

HEROD: What do you mean, concerning what matter? All of Jerusalem is in an uproar. I can hear it from here, through the palace windows. What's going on out there? Has Caesar declared a holiday that nobody told me about? Because if that's happened, heads will roll!

SPY ONE: We can assure you...

SPY TWO: ...no holiday has been declared...

SPY THREE: ...behind your most majestic back,

SPIES *(together)*: Your Highness.

HEROD: Then what's all the ruckus about?

SPY ONE: Wise men from the East...

SPY TWO: ...here, in Jerusalem...

SPY THREE: ...camels and donkeys carrying great wealth...

SPIES *(together)*: Your Highness.

HEROD: Wise men from the East. Hmm. Carrying great wealth. Hmm. They probably want to consult me about an important matter and brought me a few little gifts, as befits my great station in life. Find out what it is they want.

SPY ONE: With the greatest of haste.

SPY TWO: Never wasting a second.

SPY THREE: At the instant of your command,

SPIES *(together)*: Your Highness. *(Spies exit.)*

SCENE TWO

HEROD: This is most disconcerting, most distressing, most annoying! Spies, get in here!

SPY ONE: With the greatest of haste.

SPY TWO: Never wasting a second.

SPY THREE: At the instant of your command,

SPIES *(together)***:** Your Highness.

HEROD: Why are those wise men asking, "Where is He, born King of the Jews?"

SPY ONE: Interrogative...

SPY TWO: ...requesting information...

SPY THREE: ...concerning the birth of the King of the Jews,

SPIES *(together)***:** Your Highness.

HEROD: I know that! But I'M the king of the Jews!

SPIES *(together)***:** Oh, yeah. We forgot.

HEROD: Well DON'T forget it! Or heads will roll! Well? What did they mean by that crack about king of the Jews?

SPY ONE: Perhaps they wish to know the date of your birth...

SPY TWO: ...to celebrate it with a great feast...

SPY THREE: ...and honor you with great riches,

SPIES *(together)***:** Your Highness.

HEROD: Yeah! That's it. They do want to give me presents. No! That's not it! They didn't ask about MY birthday. They asked, "WHERE is He born King of the Jews?" They KNOW where I live. EVERYONE knows where I live. What other king could they be talking about? I must know! If there is somebody else claiming to be king, and if you're hiding him from me, heads will roll!

SPY ONE: Never in the world...

SPY TWO: ...would we do such a thing.

SPY THREE: That would be treason,

SPIES *(together)***:** Your Highness.

HEROD: Then WHO is this king they're talking about?

SPIES *(softly, together)***:** The Messiah.

HEROD: The who? Quit mumbling! Speak up, or heads will roll!

SPY ONE: There has been much talk lately...

SPY TWO: ...of one to be born from the family of David...

SPY THREE: ...to rule over Israel and save her from her enemies,

SPIES *(together)***:** Your Highness.

HEROD: Well, nobody like that was born in THIS palace.

SPY ONE: Truer words...

SPY TWO: ...were never...

SPY THREE: ...spoken before,

SPIES *(together)*: Your Highness.

HEROD: Messiah, huh? Well, I'll show Him a thing or two about being king. I just have to find Him. If He wasn't born here, where was He born? Messiah—religion! Bring the chief priests and scribes to see me!

SPY ONE: With the greatest of haste.

SPY TWO: Never wasting a second.

SPY THREE: At the instant of your command,

SPIES *(together)*: Your Highness. *(Spies exit.)*

HEROD: That's why I'm king—because I'm smarter than anybody else. I'll tell those wisemen to search for the child so I can worship Him, too. And when they report back, I'll send my troops to find this King. And one head will roll.

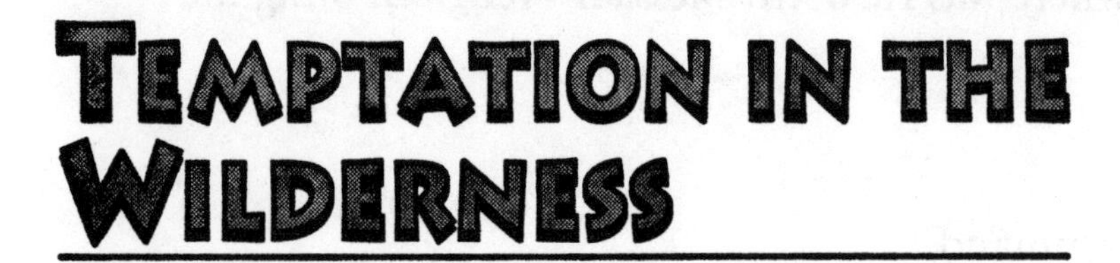

Temptation in the Wilderness

SCRIPTURE: Matthew 4:1-11; Luke 4:1-3

SUGGESTED TOPICS: Temptation; handling conflict; wisdom

BIBLE BACKGROUND

Near the age of thirty, Jesus was baptized by John, and was almost ready to start His ministry. First, the Holy Spirit led Him into the wilderness to be alone with His Father for forty days.

Jesus knew His ministry on Earth was to reconcile people to God. In order to have this happen, men and women had to listen to Him and then recognize their sin. How was He to accomplish this?

Satan had many suggestions. Recognizing Jesus' great hunger after forty days of fasting, Satan proposed that Jesus make bread to satisfy His need. But Jesus knew that "man does not live by bread alone." So Satan had another idea. Dazzle the populace with stunts like leaping from the Temple. But Jesus knew thrill-seekers would only follow so long as new thrills could be found. Then, Satan offered political power. Take over the world. Accept Satan's power over the affairs of this world. Jesus knew better. People must see themselves as lost sheep, needing to be redeemed through the only possible method, His death.

PERFORMANCE TIPS

1. Suggested props: several rocks.
2. Portraying Jesus may be difficult. To show righteous anger, Jesus should be firm and controlled, but not sarcastic.
3. Satan is a formidable adversary. Do not portray him as foolish.
4. Before the skit, briefly tell the story of Jesus' baptism (see Matthew 3:1-6,13-17). Then say, "After His baptism, Jesus went into the desert to pray for forty days. Here's what happened at the end of the forty days."

DISCUSSION QUESTIONS

1. Is being tempted the same as sinning? Why or why not?
2. In what ways are you tempted? What can you do when you are tempted?
3. Read 1 Corinthians 10:13. How would you say this verse in your own words? What advice does the verse give?

TEMPTATION IN THE WILDERNESS

CHARACTERS

SATAN
JESUS

SATAN: Hello there, young man. This desert is a pretty desolate place. At least there's no traffic. Have you been here very long?

JESUS: I've been here for forty days.

SATAN: My, my. Forty days. Say! Aren't You that fellow who thinks He's the Son of God?

JESUS: I don't think I'm the Son of God.

SATAN: That's strange. You look just like that Jesus of Nazareth fellow.

JESUS: There's a good reason for that. I am Jesus of Nazareth.

SATAN: Well then. You ARE the fellow who thinks He's the Son of God.

JESUS: No, I don't think that. I KNOW that I'm the Son of God.

SATAN: Oh, well, let's not quibble over words. But what are You doing out here in the wilderness? I thought You would be among the people You came to save.

JESUS: I have not yet begun my ministry. I came out to the wilderness to be alone with My Father before I begin.

SATAN: Funny. I don't see anybody else. Where's Your father? I would have thought he would be at home in the carpentry shop.

JESUS: I am referring to My Father in heaven.

SATAN: Forty days is a long time to be alone. You'd need lots of food to last that long out here. What did You carry it in?

JESUS: I didn't bring any food with Me. I have fasted for these forty days.

SATAN: You didn't bring any food? You must be very hungry by now. But I guess if You're the Son of God, You don't get hungry.

JESUS: You know very well that I am hungry.

SATAN: I do? Well then, look at those rocks. They almost look like loaves of bread. If You really are the Son of God, change the rocks to bread and feed Yourself. I bet that any bread God's Son personally made would be the best bread that anyone in the world ever tasted.

JESUS: It is written, "Man does not live on bread alone, but on every word that comes from the mouth of God."

SATAN: Yes, I've heard that. Wait! I want to show You something I think You will find very interesting. Don't move. I want to take You on a little trip. (*Pause, then SATAN stretches out his hand.*) Since You're the Son of God, You must recognize this place.

JESUS: Certainly. The Temple in Jerusalem.

SATAN: Prove that You are indeed the Son of God. Jump off the pinnacle of the Temple. For it is written, "He will command His angels concerning you, and they will lift you up in their hands, so that you will not strike your foot against a stone." *(Smiles.)* I believe that's Psalm 91:11 and 12.

JESUS: But it is also written, "Do not put the Lord your God to the test."

SATAN: Yes, I've heard that, too. *(Pause.)* Let me show You something else, up on that mountain over there. I know. You're hungry and don't feel like walking. You don't have to. I'll take You there. *(Pause, then SATAN stretches out his hand.)* What do You think?

JESUS: It's a very nice view of all the kingdoms of the world. If you have a point to make about them, then make it.

SATAN: Sometimes You can be very impatient. OK, the point is, I'm willing to give all of them to You. All You have to do is worship me. Then, I promise, everything I have in this world will be Yours.

JESUS: Get out of My sight, Satan! For it is written, "You shall worship the Lord, your God. Him only shall you serve."

SATAN: OK, Jesus. But I'm not finished with You. There'll be other times and places. You know me. I won't rest until You are destroyed.

DON'T WORRY

SCRIPTURE: Matthew 6:25-34; 7:7-11; Luke 12:6,7,22-31

SUGGEST TOPICS: Worry; God's love and provision; our value to God; God's guidance

BIBLE BACKGROUND

Jesus chose twelve disciples to follow Him. These twelve left everything—jobs, homes, families—to follow. Along the way, Jesus gave them many lessons in God's love and care for His own.

Jesus wanted His disciples to understand the love of God to be like that of a loving father; and not just any father, but the perfect Father. Would a father on earth trick his child and give a rock instead of bread? Would he give his child something that appeared good but would bring harm, such as a snake or eel in place of a fish? Would a father deliberately give his child a white scorpion curled up and call it an egg? A father who cares for his children would not attempt to harm them, although we sometimes do inadvertently. The perfect Father never harms His children, even unintentionally.

However, not harming and disciplining are two different precepts. Jesus sometimes spoke sharply to His disciples and even more sharply to the Pharisees, who should have known God and His character. Jesus made it clear that we must expect God to correct us when we go astray, not out of vengeful or malicious intent, but out of His deep, abiding love for all who follow His Son.

PERFORMANCE TIPS

1. Suggested props: Bible-times costumes and/or walking sticks.
2. Introduce the skit by saying, "Jesus used stories and word pictures to teach people about God. Listen for the stories and word pictures in this skit."

DISCUSSION QUESTIONS

1. Some people do not feel love from their fathers. The word "father" may carry bad connotations for some people. In discussing the skit, comment, "Jesus said God was like a loving father. How would a perfect father act?"
2. Why do you think people worry? What do you know about God that will help you when you are worried or afraid?
3. How did God show His love for people in the Bible? How has He shown His love for you?
4. What can you do to thank God for His love?

DON'T WORRY

CHARACTERS

JAMES
JOHN
PETER
PHILIP
MATTHEW

JAMES *(whining)*: We sure have to walk a long way. What happens if our sandals wear out? Where are we going to find the money to buy new ones?

JOHN: And what about our cloaks? Each of us has only one. What happens when a cloak gets a hole in it?

PETER: Weren't you Sons of Thunder listening to the Master today? Didn't He tell us not to worry about what we would wear? Didn't He remind us that the flowers of the field don't have to shear sheep or spin wool to weave their yarn into clothes?

PHILIP: That's right. Even Solomon, the richest king Israel has ever known, didn't have clothing as beautiful as the way God clothes the flowers.

PETER: Right. I wish you two would listen to what the Master says instead of always worrying. Besides, if you want to worry about something, worry about food. It's getting late and we're nowhere near any town. How are we going to fill our bellies tonight?

MATTHEW: That's you right to the core, Peter. Always worrying about your belly. When have we ever gone hungry since being with the Master? But you still worry about food. If you're going to be like that, go back to fishing.

PETER: At least I had an honorable profession before joining Jesus. I wasn't a lousy tax gatherer, working for the Romans...

PHILIP: Knock it off, Peter. You may not have been a tax gatherer before you met Jesus, but you weren't the best person in the country. How many fights did you get into over nothing?

JAMES: Besides, you aren't any better than John and me.

JOHN: That's right. You don't listen any better than we do to what the Master says. Didn't He tell us today not to worry about food?

PHILIP: They've got you there, Peter. Remember what He said about birds? God doesn't let them starve. He takes care of them.

MATTHEW: He even talked about how much more valuable we are than those birds. He said, "Five sparrows are sold for a few pennies..."

PETER: Trust a tax collector to know the price of everything.

MATTHEW: Better than only knowing about scaling fish and fixing nets.

PHILIP: Would you two stop bickering? How do you think Jesus would feel if He heard you two? Keep it up and you'll make the Pharisees look good.

PETER: What do you mean?

PHILIP: Don't they say one thing and do another? That makes them hypocrites. You two are acting exactly the same way, saying Jesus is your Master and then behaving the way you do. It's disgusting. Worrying and fighting over every little thing, when the only important thing to worry about is what's going to happen to us and our families—being separated for so long. How will everyone survive? Are we doing the right thing or not?

JAMES *(to John)***:** Maybe Philip needs a taste of his own medicine.

JOHN: A little reminder of the Master's words.

PHILIP: What are you two going on about?

MATTHEW: Should we explain it to him, Peter?

PETER: Sure. You do it. You're the educated man. You know bigger words.

MATTHEW: Anybody could explain this. Remember Jesus asking, "If a child was hungry and asked his father for a piece of bread..."

PETER: "Would that father give the child a stone that looked like bread?"

JAMES: "And if the child asked for a piece of fish..."

JOHN: "Would the father give the child a snake that is not to be eaten?"

PETER: "And if earthly fathers, who sin, are kind to their children..."

MATTHEW: "How much more kind is our Father in heaven, who knows what we need even before we ask for it."

PHILIP: OK, so I'm not perfect either. I guess we all need to stick close to Jesus to understand what He says and put His words into practice.

Lost and Found

SCRIPTURE: Luke 15:1-10

SUGGESTED TOPICS: God's love; our worth to God

BIBLE BACKGROUND

The scribes and Pharisees criticized Jesus for associating with tax collectors and "sinners." Jesus, wanting them to understand God's care and concern for all people, told three parables concerning the lost: the lost sheep, the lost coin and the runaway son.

Jesus described God by using everyday situations people could easily understand. In a heavily agrarian society, everyone understood a shepherd's concern for each member of the flock. Everyone understood a woman's concern for a lost coin. Beyond the monetary value (the drachma was a silver coin worth about a full day's wage), it is likely that the ten coins Jesus' mentioned were part of this woman's headdress, which denoted her marital status and had been given as her dowry. And everyone understood the concern of a parent for a wayward child.

PERFORMANCE TIPS

1. Suggested props: walking stick for shepherd, broom and coin for woman.

2. Explain to the group that Jesus often told stories or parables about everyday situations in Israel. A single sheep or a coin were very valuable to Bible-times people.

3. To set the scene, read Luke 15:1,2. Then say, "Jesus told a story about two people who had lost something."

DISCUSSION QUESTIONS

1. What is something you have lost? What did you do to look for it? If you found it, how did you feel?

2. How is God like the shepherd and the woman in the story? What is God searching for?

3. When we are not members of God's family, we are lost from God. What did God do to show His love for lost people?

4. God loves us and doesn't want us to be lost from Him. That's why He sent Jesus to be our Savior. How can you respond to God's love?

LOST AND FOUND

CHARACTERS

SHEPHERD
WOMAN

SHEPHERD: What a day I had yesterday! Nobody ever had a tougher day.

WOMAN: What do you know about hard days? Out in the fresh air, in the sun...

SHEPHERD: Protecting my flocks from every kind of danger imaginable. What do you do that's so difficult all day? A little sweeping, a little cooking...

WOMAN: Working to keep food on the table for ungrateful men like you. Watching every penny. Having to scrimp for myself so my children and husband can be fed. What do you know about such work?

SHEPHERD: I'll tell you about my day. Then you'll see how easy you have it. I was out in the fields all day. Finding good grass for my flock, finding some still waters so they would have something to drink. Keeping a sharp eye out for wolves, bears, lions. Do you know what a strain it is, never knowing if danger is near?

WOMAN: So you were outside on this nice warm day. Sounds rough.

SHEPHERD: Sweating under the hot sun. Chasing away flies. Lots of fun. But that was the easy part of the day. The hard part came when my day's work was supposed to be done.

WOMAN: Just like a man. *(Mocking.)* "The hard part of my day came when it was finished."

SHEPHERD: I didn't say it was finished. I said day was done. Just before dark, I brought my flock into the safety of the fold. I counted each one to be sure all were there. Sixty-seven, sixty-eight, sixty-nine, and so on.

WOMAN *(sarcastic)***:** Now I understand. Being a man, counting is hard for you.

SHEPHERD: Not the counting. The last few sheep were coming into the fold. Ninety-six, ninety-seven, ninety-eight, ninety-nine. Ninety-nine? But I have one hundred sheep in my flock!

WOMAN: So you counted wrong. Why worry about it?

SHEPHERD: Because they are my sheep. So I counted them again. And again, ninety-nine. Not one hundred—only ninety-nine.

WOMAN: It's only one out of one hundred. Why worry? You have lots in the fold.

SHEPHERD: Spoken like a woman. My sheep was out on the mountainside. Lost. In the dark. I had to find it. So, I got a torch and went back to the mountains to find my lost sheep. All night I searched. Over the rocks, in the valleys, everywhere I could think to look. Finally, just as dawn was breaking, I found him. Caught in some thorns. So I reached in, scratching my arm terribly as you can see, and freed him from the thorns. Poor thing was trembling and bleating. But I calmed him and petted him. Then I hoisted him onto my shoulders and carried him safely home.

WOMAN: So YOU'RE the fool who came into the village this morning shouting, "Rejoice, I have found my sheep which was lost!" Waking up everybody before they had to be out of their beds.

SHEPHERD: I was happy. I had found my sheep. Ah, how can I expect a woman to understand these things? But now you can see how difficult yesterday was. You maybe can understand how tiring a man's work is.

WOMAN: You call that tiring? Let me tell you about the day before yesterday. All day long, I cleaned the house, washed clothes, cooked meals for my husband and children. And one of the children was sick, so I had to spend extra time with that one. Which made my day much later than normal.

SHEPHERD: Inside. Out of the hot sun. Sounds difficult.

WOMAN: Children crying. Husband grumpy because things are late. Well, I didn't finish my cleaning until well into the evening, when you had already finished your supper and were getting ready for bed, no doubt.

SHEPHERD: Sleep. The well-earned reward of the just man.

WOMAN: Well, just as I was about finished, what do I see? One of my ten coins is missing! I say to myself, it's just the dim light. So I pick them all up and count them again. No. One is missing.

SHEPHERD: What are you worried about? Your husband has many coins...

WOMAN: But this is one from my headdress, from my wedding! I had to find the coin. I did not rest. I lit a candle and cleaned the entire house again. I looked in all the corners, under the beds, moved all the pots and pans, took everything from the cupboards. All this, searching for my silver coin by candlelight.

SHEPHERD: You would compare the ease of searching for a lost coin with that of searching for a lost sheep? You only had to search the inside of a house. I had to search the entire mountainside.

WOMAN: And when you called your sheep, it answered you. A coin cannot answer. I was frantic. I had to find my coin. Finally, after cleaning the entire house, I found the coin, right where it had fallen. I was so excited, I ran to my friends and told them.

SHEPHERD: YOU were the woman making that infernal racket in the night, waking men from their sleep? Such foolishness, over a lost coin!

WOMAN: You make such a fuss over a sheep and criticize me. Never will I understand men.

SHEPHERD: Nor will I ever understand women.

Forgive and Forget

SCRIPTURE: Matthew 18:21-35

SUGGESTED TOPICS: Forgiveness; gratitude; God's love

BIBLE BACKGROUND

Peter had a question for the Master: "How often should I forgive someone who sins against me?" Wanting to demonstrate his great patience, Peter suggested a very generous number—seven times.

Jesus' response to Peter was, "Not seven times but seventy-seven times." Jesus' words could also be translated as seventy times seven. In either case, the meaning is clear: keep on forgiving.

To show Peter what He meant, Jesus told the story of the unforgiving servant. Ten thousand talents was a great deal of money, the equivalent of millions of dollars. In the skit, the ten thousand talents has been assumed to be talents of gold, with gold priced at four hundred dollars an ounce. Obviously, Jesus intended to show that the man was hopelessly in debt. In contrast, the second servant owed the first one an insignificant debt in comparison. (The *denarius* was a Roman coin, equivalent to the Greek *drachma*, which was worth about a day's wages.)

Jesus' contrast of the debt the steward owed the king and the debt the other servant owed the steward showed Peter the magnitude of his debt to God compared to others' debts to him. The obvious point of Jesus' answer to Peter is that, if God forgives that which can never be repaid, we must forgive the comparatively tiny amount owed us.

PERFORMANCE TIPS

1. Suggested prop: a large book for use as an account book. (Or fold in half a large black sheet of construction paper.)
2. Before the skit, read Matthew 18:21,22.

DISCUSSION QUESTIONS

1. What does this story tell us about God? How is God like the king?
2. In Matthew 6:12, what does Jesus say about forgiveness?
3. When has someone done something wrong to you? How did you feel? What does God want you to do when this happens?
4. When have you done something wrong to somebody else? What does God want you to do when this happens?
5. How do you know God forgives our sins? How can you thank Him?

FORGIVE AND FORGET

CHARACTERS

KING
STEWARD
SERVANT
GUARD

KING: Steward! Bring me my account books.

STEWARD: Sire, it's late. Why look over the numbers now? Wait for tomorrow.

KING: No. I've decided to go over the accounts now.

STEWARD: Such tiring work. It really is best left until a new day dawns.

KING: No! I want to go over my accounts now. I must see what I owe everybody. And, better yet, what everybody owes me.

STEWARD: Very well. You're the king. Here are the books.

KING: They are very large. My subjects must owe me a great deal of money.

STEWARD: I'm sure you're right. Say, I have an idea. Why don't you go to bed now while I go through the books? And tomorrow, I'll tell you exactly who owes who how much.

KING: That's very kind of you. But I think I will check the accounts myself. *(Begins looking at books.)* My goodness, these books are much more complicated than I remember.

STEWARD: I made a few...improvements in the system. Really, Sire, these things are best left to the professionals. Let me decipher everything for you and let you know exactly where you stand in the morning.

KING: No, I think I'll be able to figure everything out.

STEWARD: Well, if you don't need me at the moment, I think I'll head out of the countr— I mean, off to bed. I'm rather tired...

KING: Wait here, Steward. I might need something explained.

STEWARD: Very well, Sire.

KING: Hmm. Good, good. Ah! Very good. Hmm. Not so good. What? STEWARD!

STEWARD: You bellowed, Sire?

KING: I'm having trouble with this one account.

STEWARD: Which one is that, Sire?

KING: YOUR account, Steward.

STEWARD: Oh. That one works out alright. I'm always careful about the household affairs and the money left in my trust. It's always in perfect balance.

KING: There seems to be a slight discrepancy in your account.

STEWARD: Impossible! Uh, how slight a discrepancy?

KING: TEN THOUSAND TALENTS!

STEWARD: T-t-t-ten....

KING: Just how do you explain that?

STEWARD: It's only ten, Sire. Not all that serious. Not as if it were a hundred thousand talents. It's only ten thousand talents.

KING: Or a few million dollars!

STEWARD: Give or take few pennies here and there.

KING: It's time to settle the account. Give me my ten thousand talents.

STEWARD: Well, we have a slight problem. I've had a few bad investments in the past few weeks and don't have the money right now. But if you could give me a little time to recoup my losses...

KING: WE do not have a problem, YOU have a problem. If you cannot repay the debt, then all you own is forfeit. I hereby take your house, all your possessions, and your family. I will sell every last thing you have and cut my losses.

STEWARD: I beg you, Your Majesty, have mercy on me! Please be patient with me, and I will repay you every penny I owe.

KING: How will you repay me that much money?

STEWARD: I do not know, Your Highness. But please give me a little time. I will find a way.

KING: There is no way you could find to repay so great a debt. But I see you are in great distress for what you have done. So, I have an idea. Give me your pen.

STEWARD: At once, Sire. Here it is.

KING: There. One quick stroke of the pen and the debt is cancelled. Now, you owe me nothing.

STEWARD: Nothing?

KING: Nothing.

STEWARD: Oh, Your Majesty. May your great name be praised forever! May all your enemies fall before your mighty strength! May you live forever! Let all the nations sing your praise...

KING: Enough. We've been at this all night. I think I'll retire while you carry on with your duties.

STEWARD: Of course. Certainly. Good night, I mean, good day, Sire.

KING: Good day, Steward. *(Exits.)*

STEWARD: What luck! I can't believe my ears. I'm free. I still own all my possessions. My family has not been sold as slaves. *(Sees SERVANT.)* This IS my lucky day. Not only am I debt free, but there is that worthless servant who owes me money. Hey, you!

SERVANT: You called, steward of the house.

STEWARD: I sure did. I don't supposed you've forgotten that you owe me...

SERVANT: One hundred denarii. No. I've not forgotten. I certainly appreciate your loaning me the money. I've been saving carefully and have earned almost enough to pay you back...

STEWARD: Enough of that! You've been putting me off with that "I don't have the money right now" stuff. I want my money! I suppose you think that four months' pay is nothing! Well, you're wrong! It's a lot of money, and I want it paid now!

SERVANT: I know it's a lot of money. But I don't have it with me. If you could just wait until next payday, I'm sure I can find a way to pay you back all that I owe.

STEWARD: I've been too patient with you already! Guard! Take this worthless wretch and throw him into prison! *(GUARD and SERVANT exit.)* Let him sit there until he finds some way to pay me! I'll show these scoundrels they can't take advantage of me. *(GUARD enters.)* Well? Have you done what I told you to do?

GUARD: Certainly. But the king wishes to see you.

STEWARD: The king wants to see me? I wonder what he wants? On a lucky day like this one, he probably wants to give me a raise. *(KING enters.)* Your Majesty. You wanted to see me?

KING: I did. I understand you had a servant thrown into prison.

STEWARD: I certainly did. That scoundrel was giving me some kind of song and dance about not being able to pay me the one hundred denarii he owes me. So I decided to teach him a lesson. Let him rot in prison if he can't pay his debts.

KING: You ingrate! You despicable wretch! I forgave you a fortune merely because you begged me to give you a little time to pay. Could you not follow my example and treat your fellow servant with the same kindness? Well, as you have forgiven, so shall you be forgiven. Your debt has been reinstated. Guard! Take this worm and throw him into prison until he has paid me the full debt.

GUARD *(smiling)*: With pleasure, Sire.

THE TALENTS

SCRIPTURE: Matthew 25:14-30

SUGGESTED TOPICS: Talents and abilities; responsibility; stewardship

BIBLE BACKGROUND

Jesus wanted His disciples to understand their responsibility to wisely use all they had been given by God, the great King. To make His point, Jesus told a parable which clearly indicates that God has given all of us something of real value. Along with the gift comes a responsibility—a responsibility which is measured, not in comparison with what others might do, but in proportion to what God has bestowed.

The talents which the man in the story entrusted to his servants were worth more than a thousand dollars each. The term "talent" was used originally to indicate weight (about sixty-five pounds) and gradually came to represent a monetary value.

PERFORMANCE TIPS

1. Suggested props: play money or coins.
2. Before the skit, explain that the word "talent" was a Bible-times word for money. (See Bible Background.)
3. Servants One and Two should speak confidently. Servant Three should whine.

DISCUSSION QUESTIONS

1. Think about the three servants. How did their attitudes affect their actions?
2. God has given abilities to everyone. What abilities or talents has He given to you?
3. How can you use your abilities or the things you enjoy doing to show your love for God?

THE TALENTS

CHARACTERS

MASTER
FIRST SERVANT
SECOND SERVANT
THIRD SERVANT

SCENE ONE

MASTER: Servants! Come here!

FIRST SERVANT: Here I am, Master.

SECOND SERVANT: And I.

THIRD SERVANT: Yo! Did you call?

MASTER: Yes, I did. Good, you're all here. I'm about to leave on a journey.

FIRST SERVANT: May the wind be at your back.

SECOND SERVANT: May all your roads be level.

THIRD SERVANT: Uh, good luck?

MASTER: Thank you. There are many things that need to be done while I'm gone.

FIRST SERVANT: The livestock. The sheep and camels must be watered and fed every day. I'll make certain all your livestock is well cared for.

SECOND SERVANT: Don't forget the crops. If the master is to be gone for a lengthy journey, the harvest might come before he returns. I'll see that the crops are watered and weeded and be sure that the harvesting is done on schedule.

FIRST SERVANT: Let's not forget the house. Think of all the things to be done inside.

SECOND SERVANT: You're right. There's the cleaning, and if something breaks, it will have to be repaired.

FIRST SERVANT: Not to mention general maintenance.

THIRD SERVANT: Uh, mmm, er...eat! We have to eat. Meals need to be prepared.

MASTER: Well, I can see I am leaving everything in capable hands.

FIRST SERVANT: You can count on us.

SECOND SERVANT: We'll look after everything.

THIRD SERVANT: Uh, yeah.

MASTER: However, I'm giving each of you an additional responsibility.

FIRST SERVANT: Anything you say, Master.

SECOND SERVANT: We're ready for any challenge.

THIRD SERVANT: Another one?

MASTER *(Pointing to FIRST SERVANT)***:** I'll begin with you. You have shown many abilities in the past. So I am entrusting five talents to you. Do whatever you think best with them. I'll ask for an accounting when I return.

FIRST SERVANT: Five thousand dollars! I've never seen so much money. I'll do my best, Master.

MASTER: I know you will. You always have in the past. *(Turns to SECOND SERVANT.)* And I'm trusting you with two talents.

SECOND SERVANT: Two thousand dollars! That's a lot of money. You can trust me, Master.

MASTER: I know I can. *(Turns to THIRD SERVANT.)* And you. Here is one talent.

THIRD SERVANT: One thousand dollars! But what am I supposed to do with it?

MASTER: Use it wisely. Remember, I will seek an accounting from all of you when I return. *(Exits.)*

FIRST SERVANT: Good-bye, Master. Have a pleasant journey.

SECOND SERVANT: Good-bye, Master. May everything go well.

THIRD SERVANT: Oh, woe is me. What am I going to do?

FIRST SERVANT: Well, what are you going to do with your money?

SECOND SERVANT: I'm not sure. I've got a few ideas to try out. Old Saul is trying to sell his business. Maybe I could buy it. I think I could do as well as he has, maybe even better. What are you planning to do?

FIRST SERVANT: I don't know, yet. I never planned on having so much money at one time. But I do remember seeing some good bargains in the marketplace. If I search out as many as I can, perhaps I could resell them at a profit. Or maybe land. There's always land available. I wonder if I could make a good real estate deal? I'll have to consider everything carefully. After all, it's not my money. It belongs to the Master.

SECOND SERVANT: True. So we will have to exercise care in our business deals.

FIRST SERVANT *(to THIRD SERVANT)***:** What about you? Have you thought about what you'll do with your talent?

THIRD SERVANT: Oh, woe is me. What will I do? What will I do?

SECOND SERVANT: Don't worry so much. You'll think of something. Well, I'm going to make sure the field hands are looking after the crops and then, off to see how much Saul wants for his business.

FIRST SERVANT: And I'll see that the stable boys are looking after the animals properly. Then I'm off to the market to see what bargains are waiting there.

THIRD SERVANT: Oh, woe is me. Woe is me.

(Skit continues on next page.)

SCENE TWO

MASTER: Servants! Come here!

FIRST SERVANT: Here I am.

SECOND SERVANT: And I.

THIRD SERVANT: Did you call?

MASTER: Yes, I called. I have returned from my journey.

FIRST SERVANT: And a long journey it was. I trust everything met with your approval.

SECOND SERVANT: I trust that all went in your favor.

THIRD SERVANT: Oh, me. It wasn't long enough.

MASTER: I had a marvelous journey. But I'm eager to see how you made out.

FIRST SERVANT: Well, it's kind of a long story. Here are all my records. You can examine them at your leisure in the next few days. The bottom line is, here are your original five thousand dollars. And here is the profit—five thousand more.

MASTER: Well done, good and faithful servant! You have been faithful over the few things I gave you, so I will make you ruler over many things.

FIRST SERVANT: You're too kind, Master. I was only doing my duty.

MASTER: Not at all. You are to be commended. Now, what about you?

SECOND SERVANT: Well, I tried my hand at a little of this and a little of that. Here are all the records of my dealings. But, to make a long story short, here are your original two thousand dollars. And here is your profit—two thousand more.

MASTER: Well done, good and faithful servant! You have been faithful over the little I have given you, so I will make you ruler over many things.

SECOND SERVANT: You're too kind, Master. I was only doing my duty.

MASTER: Not at all. You are to be commended. Now, what about you?

THIRD SERVANT: Me, Master?

MASTER: Yes, you. You're the only other one here. Give me an accounting. What did you do with your thousand dollars?

THIRD SERVANT: I knew you were a hard man, Master.

MASTER: Flattery will get you nowhere. What about the money?

THIRD SERVANT: I knew you take advantage of every opportunity.

MASTER: Sure. I'm a good businessman. The money?

THIRD SERVANT: I was afraid, Master. What if I lost your money? I knew you would be angry. So I kept it safe. I dug a hole and buried it. Here is your one thousand dollars.

MASTER: You did what?

THIRD SERVANT: I hid it. In the ground.

MASTER: You wicked and lazy servant! You knew that I expected some kind of profit! But you hid the money in the ground? You could have at least put it into the bank so it would have earned some interest. But no! You hid it! In the ground! Where it did no good! Give the one thousand dollars to the one who has ten. And then leave. You're fired for being lazy and worthless.

NICODEMUS

SCRIPTURE: John 3:1-21

SUGGESTED TOPICS: Eternal life; God's plan of salvation

BIBLE BACKGROUND

Jesus created a stir wherever He went. He taught with authority, not as the scribes who would only quote what others had written about a topic. Jesus' teaching upset most of the religious hierarchy. But some Pharisees, such as Nicodemus, were deeply interested in what Jesus had to say.

The very quality in Jesus' teaching which attracted Nicodemus also made it hard for him to understand Jesus' words. Nicodemus was used to complicated, scholarly consideration in which the varying positions of respected rabbis were balanced one against the other. In contrast, Jesus spoke directly, even bluntly, causing Nicodemus to ask, "How can this be?"

Some people criticize Nicodemus for his lack of insight. However, Nicodemus deserves a great deal of credit for asking the questions that he did, for continuing to seek understanding. While many people of his day (and ours) reject what they do not immediately grasp, Nicodemus pursued his quest for insight. When other Pharisees were ready to pronounce a curse on anyone who believed in Jesus, Nicodemus courageously raised a question which shows deeper understanding. Then, at the Cross, unashamed of his Savior, Nicodemus accompanied Joseph of Arimathea, bringing enough burial spices for a royal funeral (see John 19:39).

PERFORMANCE TIPS

1. Suggested props: Bible-times costumes.

2. Introduce the skit by saying, "Nicodemus was a Pharisee who was interested in Jesus' teaching. The Bible tells us Nicodemus came by night to talk to Jesus. Nicodemus was puzzled by some of Jesus' words. This skit shows what might have happened if Nicodemus had talked to another Pharisee about Jesus' teachings."

DISCUSSION QUESTIONS

1. Read John 3:5-8,14,19,20 and discuss the other word pictures Jesus used when talking with Nicodemus.

2. Why was Nicodemus afraid to be seen visiting Jesus?

3. Read John 3:16,17. What is the main point of these verses?

3. God offers the gift of eternal life to everyone in the world. What happens if a person does not accept the gift?

4. Have you accepted God's gift of eternal life?

NICODEMUS

CHARACTERS

MATTHIAS (math-EYE-us)
NICODEMUS (nik-uh-DEE-mus)

MATTHIAS: Hey! Watch where you're going. Old men should get glasses if they can't see what's in front of— Oh, Nicodemus. Sorry. I didn't mean to yell at you.

NICODEMUS: I'm sorry I bumped into you, Matthias. But I'm glad I bumped into you, figuratively speaking.

MATTHIAS: You mean, you wanted to see me about something?

NICODEMUS: Yes. You've just graduated from seminary. Maybe some new things are being taught that I don't understand.

MATTHIAS: A man of your intellect? Not understanding something?

NICODEMUS: None of us are too old to have learned everything, I think.

MATTHIAS: Except possibly for yourself and Gamaliel. Not that you're so old, but that you have learned so much.

NICODEMUS: Sometimes a man of thirty can cause a much older man to think. But enough of my musings. The question: What would you say to the phrase, "You must be born again"?

MATTHIAS: A riddle?

NICODEMUS: Possibly.

MATTHIAS: I love riddles. Makes the old mind work a little harder. Now then, "You must be born again."

NICODEMUS: Is this anything new that is being discussed in theology?

MATTHIAS: Ah! A theological riddle. That makes it more interesting.

NICODEMUS: Why?

MATTHIAS: Well, if we were talking a question of nature, the thing is wholly impossible. I mean, really. You can't expect someone or something to be born twice, now can you?

NICODEMUS: Of course not. But you said it's more interesting as a theological riddle.

MATTHIAS: Certainly. Because now we can examine figures of speech, make parallel observations, really have some fun with this.

NICODEMUS: Then you believe it is understandable?

MATTHIAS: Well...maybe. Of course, we would all just be guessing, but that's half the fun. Let's see. Born again, born again. Hah! I've got it! It wasn't "born again." It was "borne again," spelled b-o-r-n-e.

NICODEMUS: That sounds like the same thing to me.

MATTHIAS: No, no, you don't understand. Born without the *e* means you have to be a baby for a second time. But that's obviously not the meaning. Borne with an *e* has to do with carrying something for a second time. Now let's see how this could be...

NICODEMUS: No, I think it means rebirth.

MATTHIAS: Don't interrupt. I think I've got a handle on this. Now, to bear again implies lifting and carrying. A burden. What could be a burden?

NICODEMUS: You weren't listening. The phrase was, "You must be born again," not "You must carry something again."

MATTHIAS: You're sure of that?

NICODEMUS: Positive.

MATTHIAS: Well, that is different. How can I reconcile the word "born," which obviously only happens once in a lifetime, with the word "again"? Wait! Wait! It's coming to me! Yes! I have it!

NICODEMUS: What? You can explain this clearly?

MATTHIAS: Of course. It's so simple that it's profound. "You must be born again" is some kind of comparison with change. So. You must change from the ways of the Gentiles and become a child of Judaism.

NICODEMUS: It's an interesting idea. But what if it was said to a devout Jew—a Pharisee? A rabbi?

MATTHIAS: You mean to somebody like you? Couldn't be. Wouldn't make sense. You already are a part of Judaism. You are just about as perfect as a man can be, as are all we Pharisees. I obviously don't need to change. I really don't see how any of this applies to you or to me, Nicodemus. See you around.

NICODEMUS: Well, I guess I'll just have to visit Jesus again. Maybe if I listen to Him again, He will help me understand what I need to know.

To Trap a Teacher

SCRIPTURE: Matthew 6:5-15

SUGGESTED TOPICS: Prayer

BIBLE BACKGROUND

Jesus' teaching resulted in a variety of reactions. Some listened and believed, some were interested to hear more, others were jealous and listened only to trap Jesus.

Among those who opposed Jesus were men like Saul (later to become Paul), who saw His teaching as blasphemous and needing to be stopped. Others, motivated by nothing more than their possible loss of prestige, also wanted Jesus stopped. Still others who opposed Jesus did so because He came from Galilee—and not only from Galilee, but Nazareth. Nathaniel summed up the prevailing attitude toward Galilee in general and Nazareth in particular when he asked Philip, "Can anything good come out of Nazareth?" (see John 1:46).

The Pharisees were a highly learned group of men. They were not only religious leaders, but also political leaders. For dramatic interest, this skit assumes that at least one member would not have the same intellectual capacity and the same dedication to the Law and his duties as did the others. It also assumes that jokes about Galilee were told by those who considered themselves more educated than those from the north.

PERFORMANCE TIPS

1. Suggested props: notepads and pencils for Matthias and Lynas to use as they take notes about Jesus' teachings.

2. Thomas is portrayed as somewhat hard-of-hearing, not overly diligent and more interested in his comfort than his duty. During the skit Thomas looks around, shuffles his feet, etc. Have the other Pharisees, Matthias and Lynas, look at one spot in the room as though they are paying attention to Jesus.

3. Before the skit, have your group say the Lord's Prayer together or read it from Matthew 6:9-13.

DISCUSSION QUESTIONS

1. Why do you think most of the Pharisees did not believe Jesus' teaching?

2. From Matthew 6:9-13, what do you learn about prayer?

3. Why is it important to pray? When should you pray? What should we pray about?

4. Give an example of a time God answered your prayers.

TO TRAP A TEACHER

CHARACTERS

THOMAS
MATTHIAS
LYNAS

THOMAS: I still don't understand why we have to be here.

MATTHIAS: How many times do we have to tell you? It's part of the job.

LYNAS: Right! If you want to be a leader, then you have to accept responsibilities as well as privileges.

THOMAS: Well, I still don't see what's so important about coming up on this cold mountain first thing in the morning.

MATTHIAS: Weren't you listening at the meeting yesterday?

THOMAS: Well, of course...

LYNAS: He was probably sleeping again.

THOMAS: I was not...

MATTHIAS: Or daydreaming again.

THOMAS: I was not asleep or daydreaming! I just don't see what's so important.

LYNAS: Do you remember when the chief priest got up to speak?

MATTHIAS: Do you remember how he impressed upon us that we are the leaders of God's people?

LYNAS: Do you remember when he told us to make certain that Israel's religion remained pure?

MATTHIAS: Do you remember when he told us we had to set aside petty differences and have a common goal?

THOMAS: Please! I was at the meeting yesterday. It was long enough then. I don't need it rehashed again today.

LYNAS: Then you should remember why we are here today.

MATTHIAS: You know that it's our job to watch over this Jesus, to listen to every word He says.

THOMAS: That's the part I don't understand. Why is it so important to come all the way out to listen to some wandering teacher? Really! He's from Galilee. Nothing important has ever come from Galilee.

LYNAS: You really weren't listening, were you?

MATTHIAS: Haven't you noticed all these people out here this morning? They ARE listening to Him. They believe He's some kind of prophet. We have to be sure that He is not leading all of His listeners astray.

THOMAS: Why would people think He's a prophet? They can hear His Galilean accent. Surely they know that God wouldn't use a Galilean for a prophet.

LYNAS: Never underestimate people's ability to fall for anything. They're convinced that He's a prophet, and they listen to Him.

MATTHIAS: So we have to hear what He says if we're going to persuade people that He's telling lies.

THOMAS: But what if His teaching isn't false?

LYNAS: You not only don't listen at meetings, you don't even listen to yourself. Where does this man come from?

THOMAS: Galilee.

LYNAS: And has anything good ever come out of Galilee?

THOMAS: Well, there've been a few good jokes. You know, like how many Galileans does it take to start a fire?

MATTHIAS: Forget the jokes. Don't you understand?

LYNAS: Let me make it plain. He comes from Galilee. Therefore, He can't be a prophet or a teacher. Since He is not a prophet, He can't be telling the truth when He tries to teach about God. So, we have to catch Him in His lies and expose Him as a fraud.

MATTHIAS: Shh! He's starting to speak.

THOMAS: What's He talking about?

LYNAS: Don't tell me you not only can't remember, but you also can't hear?

MATTHIAS: Shh! Jesus is saying that people should pray.

THOMAS: If that's all He's saying, I don't think we'll catch Him in any lies.

LYNAS: Be quiet and listen. He's saying more than that.

MATTHIAS: He's saying that people shouldn't stand on street corners to pray but they should pray privately.

THOMAS: Then we've got Him! Everybody knows you're supposed to pray with a loud voice where lots of people can hear you.

LYNAS: Will you be quiet and let us listen? Everybody doesn't know that. Some may agree with Him. Give Him time to say more. The more He speaks, the more we'll hear and have a chance to prove Him false.

MATTHIAS: Did you hear that? He said that we Pharisees pray in public to impress people, and we will not have any other reward than that. This man could be dangerous if people believe Him.

THOMAS: But why would they believe Him? I can hear His accent quite plainly. Say, did you hear the one about the Galilean who was walking with his donkey—

LYNAS: Would you stop with the Galilean jokes already? We are supposed to be listening to HIM, not you. Now stop chattering and listen!

THOMAS: But I can't hear Him clearly.

MATTHIAS: Then be quiet and let us listen. We'll tell you what He says.

LYNAS: Listen to Him now. Telling people not to imitate the heathen who pray with vain repetitions. Sometimes this man makes sense.

MATTHIAS: There's no doubt how dangerous this man is. Listen to Him mixing truth and lies together. He will definitely confuse people if He's allowed to continue.

LYNAS: Now He's giving an example of how to pray. "Our Father who is in heaven..."

THOMAS: I thought we were supposed to pray to God?

MATTHIAS: We are.

THOMAS: Then we've got Him, because my father's not in heaven. He's in Jerusalem. In bed. Where I should be.

MATTHIAS: He doesn't mean pray to your father. He means God is your real Father. Your Father in heaven.

THOMAS: Oh, I get it.

LYNAS: Quiet, you two. I'm trying to listen to this guy's prayer. It's not a bad prayer, for a Galilean.

MATTHIAS: What's He been saying while I've been trying to explain things to our thickheaded friend?

LYNAS: First, He praises God for being holy.

MATTHIAS: That's a good beginning.

LYNAS: Then, He asks for God's commands to be obeyed on earth in the same way that they are in heaven.

MATTHIAS: That's a nice thought, but it sounds like wishful thinking.

LYNAS: Then He asks God to supply our needs for today.

MATTHIAS: I can't argue with that.

LYNAS: Next, He asks God to forgive us in the same manner that we forgive people who have sinned against us.

THOMAS: Say, did you hear about the Galilean who was asked if he could multiply—

LYNAS AND MATTHIAS: Cut it out!

MATTHIAS: What else did He say in His prayer?

LYNAS: He asks God not to let Him be tempted but instead to deliver Him from evil. Then, He closes with a little praise about power and glory being for God.

MATTHIAS: We had better get back to the Council to report on this Jesus. He could be a lot of trouble to us.

LYNAS: You're right. He's going to confuse people by mixing truth and lies the way He does. Let's go. *(LYNAS and MATTHIAS exit.)*

THOMAS: *(Yawns.)* Hey! Where did they go? Oh well. I think I'll go home and have a little more breakfast and maybe a little more sleep. Maybe I'll tell my wife the one about how many Galileans it takes to make a bed. If I can remember it....

Waste Nard, Want Nard

SCRIPTURE: Matthew 26:6-13; Mark 14:3-9; John 12:1-8

SUGGESTED TOPICS: Attitude in giving; stewardship

BIBLE BACKGROUND

Even being close to Jesus on a daily basis did not guarantee that the disciples instantly grasped the modeling they saw. Sometimes they must have seemed painfully slow to understand the life-changing truths unfolding before their eyes. Having lived with the very essence of selfless giving in their Master, Jesus' disciples were still blind to the message of the woman who gave the most precious thing she had to honor Him.

The apostle John is often pictured as a quiet man. After all, he was the beloved disciple. Most people tend to forget that he and his brother, James, were fishermen known as the "Sons of Thunder." This nickname suggests quick tempers and loud voices. This skit uses James and John to reflect the unthinking attitudes which occasionally trip up all Jesus' followers.

PERFORMANCE TIPS

1. Suggested props: Bible-times costumes.
2. James and John should speak in a scornful tone of voice.
3. Read Mark 14:6-9 after the skit and discuss Jesus' response.

DISCUSSION QUESTIONS

1. Compare the attitudes of James and John and the woman.
2. Who showed love for Jesus? How?
3. Read 2 Corinthians 9:7. What does the Bible say is the wrong way to give? What is the right way to give?
4. What can you give to show your love for God?

Waste Nard, Want Nard

CHARACTERS

JAMES
JOHN

JAMES: You know, following Jesus certainly does have its good points.

JOHN: You're right. Take this meal we're having, for example. Being invited to a prominent man's home. Being served the best food that money can buy. Nothing is too good when Jesus is visiting.

JAMES: Yes. It is good to have meat to eat. I was getting tired of fish.

JOHN: Say! What's that woman doing over near Jesus?

JAMES: She isn't one of the serving girls. What do you suppose she's planning to do with that box?

JOHN: I have no idea. She's holding it as if it's valuable.

JAMES: I wonder what's in it?

JOHN: Look at that! She broke the box! She's pouring the contents over Jesus!

JAMES: Well, now we know what was in the box. There's no mistaking the smell of spikenard! I wonder why she's being so wasteful. That stuff's very expensive.

JOHN: Somebody should reprimand her for this waste. In fact, I think I'll do it myself. Do you want to help?

JAMES: Gladly! I abhor waste.

JOHN: Hey! Woman! What's the matter with you?

JAMES: Yeah! That's expensive stuff you're pouring all over the floor!

JOHN: Do you know how much that stuff is worth?

JAMES: She probably does, since she bought it.

JOHN: Oh, yeah. That's right. Anyway, that would cost the average worker a whole year's wages! And you're pouring it out like it was cheap wine!

JAMES: You should have sold it and given the money to the poor. At least then somebody would have benefitted from the expense.

JOHN: Wait! Jesus is speaking. Oh, oh. We're in trouble again.

JAMES: Honest, Jesus. It wasn't my fault. *(Points to JOHN.)* It was all his idea.

GOING FISHING

SCRIPTURE: John 13:1-17; 21:3-8

SUGGESTED TOPICS: Serving others; humility

BIBLE BACKGROUND

Jesus' disciples needed to learn the importance of being a servant. To teach this, He chose the worst imaginable task: washing feet.

In biblical times, feet were always dirty. The footwear of the day was sandals, the roads were dusty, and the most common mode of travel was walking. If a man, particularly a wealthy man, invited guests to dinner, he made certain his guests had their feet washed by one of his servants. Because washing people's feet was possibly the least desirable task in the household, it usually fell upon the servant of the lowest rank.

Jesus, the King of Kings and Lord of Lords, humbled Himself to the most lowly position imaginable to demonstrate the servant's heart to His disciples. It must have been a profoundly moving experience for them, particularly after His death a few days later.

PERFORMANCE TIPS

1. Suggested props: one or more large fish nets.

2. The skit indicates the presence of seven men on the boat. However, only three men have speaking parts. The other four can be invisible or can be played by four others who help to pantomime casting out the nets, pulling in the nets, rowing the boat, etc.

3. Have Peter and Thomas look at the shore while Nathaniel pulls up the net. If your room is reasonably soundproof, Peter can yell to the man on shore. Or have Peter mimic shouting by placing his hands around his mouth.

DISCUSSION QUESTIONS

1. What are some jobs people do for you?

2. What are some things you could do to help others?

3. Read Jesus' words in Mark 10:43,44. What did Jesus say about the way to be a great person? Why do you think serving others is important?

GOING FISHING

CHARACTERS

PETER
THOMAS
NATHANIEL

PETER: Thomas! Nathaniel! I'm going fishing. Are you two coming or not?

THOMAS: Sounds good to me.

NATHANIEL: I'm in, Peter. Have you got a spot in mind?

PETER: What kind of dumb question is that, Nathaniel? I always pick good spots.

THOMAS: James! John! And you other two! C'mon! Peter says he knows a good place to go fishing.

NATHANIEL: Looks like we're all coming, Peter. But level with me. You're not planning to go back to fishing, are you?

PETER: No, I don't think so. But I need a place to think. And the sea is as good a place as any. C'mon, Thomas! Hurry up!

THOMAS: We're here, Peter. Don't be so impatient. The fish aren't going anywhere.

NATHANIEL: Don't be too hard on him, Thomas. He says he wants to think. And you know how tough THAT is for him.

PETER: Some friend you are. C'mon! Let's move the boat out towards the east.

THOMAS: OK, Peter. We're underway. While we're heading towards your fishing spot, tell us what's on your mind. Sometimes it helps to think out loud.

PETER: I was thinking about the supper we had with Jesus.

THOMAS: Give us a break. Which one? We had lots of suppers with Him.

NATHANIEL: Don't pretend to be so dense, Thomas. The last one.

PETER: That's the one, Nathaniel. And this is the best fishing spot in Galilee. Help me toss the net in, Nathaniel. *(Pauses.)* Do you remember when Jesus washed our feet?

NATHANIEL: That would be pretty hard to forget.

THOMAS: Especially for you, Peter. Your quick tongue got you in trouble again.

PETER: Maybe it did, Thomas. But I had a reason for what I said and did. At least I didn't just sit there like a bump on a log and not understand what was happening.

NATHANIEL: Would you two stop arguing with each other? What's bothering you now, Peter?

PETER: Do you remember how you felt when Jesus got out the basin and the cloth and began washing our feet?

THOMAS: Of course. I was totally dumbfounded. I didn't know what to do or say. So I just sat there and let Him wash my feet.

NATHANIEL: So what do you need to think about now, Peter? Jesus explained that He was setting an example for us to follow. He washed our feet so that we should be willing to wash each other's feet.

THOMAS: Sure. It was a simple lesson. If the Master could humble Himself before His servants, then the servants can humble themselves before each other.

PETER: But here's the problem. Do you think He meant just us twelve—or eleven? Or do you think He meant we should be servants to anyone?

THOMAS: Peter, you surely do have a habit of complicating everything. We're to be the leaders of His Church on earth. Why would we be required to be servants of everyone who comes along?

PETER: That's what I thought, at first. But...do any of you doubt that He's the Messiah?

THOMAS: Not after I saw the nail holes in His hands and the gash in His side. Why do you ask?

PETER: Well, if He's the Messiah—and He is—then that means God Himself washed our feet. If He could stoop so low, how could we feel that we don't have to serve others in the same manner?

NATHANIEL: You've got a point there.

THOMAS: I think we should have a rule that Peter isn't allowed to think anymore. Every time he does, something I've just decided goes out the window. Besides, when he thinks, he loses his memory. I thought you said this was a good place to fish?

PETER: So excuse me for living. Didn't you ever have a day when you didn't catch anything before?

THOMAS: Not when somebody told me he had the best fishing spot in Israel.

NATHANIEL: Can't you two stop bickering?

PETER: I see we're not the only people out this early in the morning.

THOMAS: What do you mean?

PETER: Look. Over there on the shore. Some guy's out for a walk.

NATHANIEL: So what's he doing?

PETER: He's just standing there. Watching us.

NATHANIEL: So who is it? Do we know him?

THOMAS: It's hard to say. The light's not very good yet and it's mostly in our eyes.

PETER: Listen. The guy on the shore shouted something. He wants to know if we caught anything.

NATHANIEL: Well, isn't anyone going to answer him? We can still be civilized, even if we did have a bad night's fishing.

THOMAS: Let Peter do it. He has the biggest mouth.

PETER: Just to show how civilized I can be, I'm going to ignore that last crack. *(Shouts.)* No! We haven't caught anything. *(Speaks normally.)* Typical landlubber. He says we should try the other side of the boat. What's he think? That fish have a fence they can't cross over?

NATHANIEL: Well? What have we got to lose? The net's ready to cast again anyway. We can troll to shore and if we catch something, we won't have wasted a night. If we don't catch anything, we can teach the landlubber how to fold a net.

PETER: If you want to waste your time, go ahead. *(THOMAS and NATHANIEL cast net.)*

THOMAS: Hey! What's happening to the boat?

NATHANIEL: Well, I'll be! It's being pulled to one side by the weight of the fish in the net!

PETER: We'll have to row to shore. We'll never pull the nets in with this many fish in them!

THOMAS: Who is that guy on the shore?

NATHANIEL: I don't know. But he sure knows his fishing.

PETER: It's the Lord! It has to be!

THOMAS: Peter! What are you doing? Look at that! He jumps in the water to swim to shore and leaves the six of us to handle all these fish by ourselves. And he has the GALL to talk about being a servant!

GOOD NEWS

SCRIPTURE: Matthew 28:16-20; Mark 6:7-13; Luke 10:1-20

SUGGESTED TOPICS: Spreading the gospel; trusting in God's guidance

BIBLE BACKGROUND

Jesus had been crucified and buried. His disciples were devastated. All their plans for a new world had been dashed. But on the third day, Jesus rose. During the next few weeks, He appeared to the disciples and hundreds of other people. Just prior to His ascension, Jesus gave the disciples specific instructions. "You will receive power when the Holy Spirit comes on you; and you will be my witnesses...to the ends of the earth" (Acts 1:8).

How would the disciples react to this final message? The Holy Spirit would come and fill them with power. What did that mean? How would they know? What exactly should they do and say? They must have had thousands of questions running through their minds while waiting to celebrate Pentecost.

PERFORMANCE TIPS

1. Suggested props: Bible-times costumes.

2. Toward the end of the skit, Philip and Andrew should show in their voices and facial expressions their increasing excitement at the prospect of telling the good news about Jesus.

DISCUSSION QUESTIONS

1. What is a witness?

2. Why did Jesus tell His disciples to wait before going out to be His witnesses?

3. How can you witness about Jesus?

GOOD NEWS

CHARACTERS

ANDREW
PHILIP

ANDREW: Hi, Philip.

PHILIP: Hi, Andrew. What are you doing?

ANDREW: Just thinking about the events of the past few weeks.

PHILIP: It really has been amazing, hasn't it? Are you thinking about anything special or just things in general?

ANDREW: Mostly, I've been thinking about the last thing Jesus said to us. You know, about going into the world, baptizing people and teaching them the things that He taught us.

PHILIP: Yeah. That's quite a responsibility He's given us. What are you planning to do?

ANDREW: I don't know. I just sometimes wonder if I'm up to the task.

PHILIP: Well, Jesus must have thought that we are capable of doing the job. If He didn't, then He wouldn't have left us with the responsibility. He would have given it to somebody else.

ANDREW: I guess that's true. Do you remember the first time He sent us out to preach and teach?

PHILIP: How could I forget? Just between you and me, I was scared witless. If I hadn't been so afraid, I probably would have told Jesus that I couldn't speak to people. But I was more afraid to say that than to go.

ANDREW: I didn't know you felt that way. I thought I was the only frightened one out of the twelve of us.

PHILIP: You sure weren't! And I bet if you spoke to the others, you'd find that all of us were scared and felt the same way.

ANDREW: Well, that helps some. Anyway, to get back to your original question, I was wondering what I was going to do about this latest assignment we've been given. Am I supposed to go out now? Do I sit and wait for further instructions? When I go, do I go alone? I guess you get the picture.

PHILIP: It really is nice to know I'm not the only one who doesn't seem to know what's happening. Maybe if we go over the first two preaching missions again, it will help us decide what to do now.

ANDREW: That sounds good to me. I remember that first mission. The twelve of us were sent out two by two.

PHILIP: Right. And when the seventy were sent out, we went two by two again.

ANDREW: I think we've maybe hit on the answer to one of our questions already.

PHILIP: Go with somebody, not alone.

ANDREW: Remember when we were first sent out? All those sick people healed. And Jesus gave us power over the unclean spirits. He told us, even before we went, that we had more authority than they did.

PHILIP: We learned that again on the second journey. All the spirits obeyed us because we spoke with the authority given to us by Jesus. It was so exciting! We were nearly bubbling over.

ANDREW: He also gave us authority over serpents and scorpions—in fact, all the power of the enemy. We didn't have to be afraid of anything.

PHILIP: I think we've just hit on something else.

ANDREW: Right. If Jesus is sending us, we have authority and we don't need to be afraid. Just knowing that helps. But what are we going to eat? How will we earn a living if we're teaching and preaching?

PHILIP: I think that concern was answered on our first two journeys, also. What did we take with us then?

ANDREW: Other than the clothes on our backs and a staff, nothing.

PHILIP: Well, it doesn't appear to me that you starved to death.

ANDREW: That's true. We always did have enough to eat.

PHILIP: So what's different now?

ANDREW: For one thing, those were just short trips. This is now a lifetime career.

PHILIP: True. But maybe those short trips were just for practice. So we would know when we were told to do something more difficult, we would be able to.

ANDREW: That's possible.

PHILIP: What sort of things do you think we should be teaching?

ANDREW: Well, if the other times were for practice, then I think we have a pretty good idea. We were always supposed to greet whoever agreed to be our host and wish peace upon his house.

PHILIP: I don't see any reason for changing that practice. We were also to call people to repentance.

ANDREW: We might as well continue doing that. I don't see that the world has improved significantly yet.

PHILIP: And if the city won't receive us, do you think we should shake off its very dust, the way we did before?

ANDREW: Well, Jesus hasn't changed that rule, so I guess it still stands. Do you think there will be those who won't want to listen to us?

PHILIP: They crucified Jesus. I would say there's a very good chance that some will not want to hear us.

ANDREW: You know, I think you've just hit on what the main thrust of our preaching should be.

PHILIP: You mean that Jesus was crucified?

ANDREW: Yes, but not to stop there. Also, that He is risen.

PHILIP: And that He is the Lord of all creation.

ANDREW: That He's the Messiah, promised since the fall of man.

PHILIP: This is getting more exciting all the time. Should we start now? We could go out together, the two of us, and tell all that we've seen and heard.

ANDREW: No. Not yet. Remember? Jesus said He would send the Holy Spirit. I'm not sure what it feels like, to be filled with the Holy Spirit, but I am sure that when I am, I will know that it has happened. I think we're supposed to wait before we go.

PHILIP: But what do we do while we're waiting? I'm too excited to do any of the ordinary things that I used to do.

ANDREW: Maybe we should find the others. We could go some place together. And wait and pray.

PHILIP: That sounds perfect. Let's go now.

ANDREW: I'm with you. Let's go.

SCRIPTURE: Matthew 26:26-29; Luke 22:14-20

SUGGESTED TOPICS: Lord's Supper; Christian heritage

BIBLE BACKGROUND

Throughout Scripture, God gave His people symbols to help them remember important events and concepts. The Passover dinner is a reminder of how God rescued Israel from slavery (see Exodus 12:26,27). The Ark of the Covenant was a tangible reminder of God's presence with His people. Joshua's altars (see Joshua 4:5,6,20) stood as reminders of God's power shown in the conquest of Canaan.

In the New Testament, the Lord's Supper is the symbolic reminder of Jesus' death, the single most important event in history (see Matthew 26:26-28). The connection between this observance and the Passover meal is more than superficial. Not only was the original Lord's Supper celebrated at Passover, it also is a reminder of deliverance brought by God. Echoing Passover, blood is shed and a body is broken. This time the Lamb is the very Son of God, offered as a sacrifice to secure our freedom.

PERFORMANCE TIPS

1. Suggested props: several photo albums.

2. Ask group members to bring special mementos or souvenirs and describe the significance of the objects. Bring something yourself to share with the group. Comment, "Objects such as these help us remember special times in our lives."

DISCUSSION QUESTIONS

1. What things do you have at home to help you remember special people or places?

2. Where do you see symbols in our church building? What are they? Of what do the symbols remind you?

3. What symbols did Jesus talk about in Luke 22:19,20? Of what were these symbols supposed to remind people?

4. Why did Jesus want people to remember Him and His death and resurrection?

REMEMBER

CHARACTERS

JOHN
JOAN
MOTHER

JOHN: What a lousy day!

JOAN: What's wrong?

JOHN: Everything! We had a game planned for today.

JOAN: So?

JOHN: So it's raining. The game's cancelled. There's nothing to do.

JOAN: Well, you can sit here and be miserable, like you're doing, or you can find something else to do.

JOHN: Yeah, like what?

JOAN: Well, on a cold, rainy day like today, we could have some hot chocolate and look at our old photographs.

JOHN: Well...I guess so.

JOAN: Good. You go get the albums while I make the hot chocolate.

JOHN: What's the matter? My hot chocolate's not good enough for you?

JOAN: OK. You make the hot chocolate and I'll get the pictures.

JOHN: *(Pause.)* No. You make the hot chocolate. I just remembered how bad mine is.

JOAN: Right. Meet you in the kitchen.

(Pause while JOAN and JOHN move to kitchen.)

JOHN: Look. Here's a baby picture of me. I sure was bald.

JOAN: Wow! That must be almost the first picture of you that Mom and Dad took.

JOHN: Couldn't tell you. I don't remember back that far.

JOAN: I do. I remember when Mom went to the hospital. I was kind of upset.

JOHN: Why?

JOAN: I guess I felt like Mom and Dad wanted another kid because maybe I wasn't good enough.

JOHN: That's silly! Girls can sure be dumb sometimes.

JOAN: But I remember when Mom was at the hospital, Dad took me into your room and told me how I was now a big sister and how important that job was. And he asked me where we should put things so the baby's room would look really nice.

JOHN: But Dad would know where to put things. He wouldn't need your advice.

JOAN: I know that, now. But back then, that was really important to me. It told me that Mom and Dad still loved me, too.

JOHN: Look! Here's a picture of you in that dress you got for the school Christmas concert.

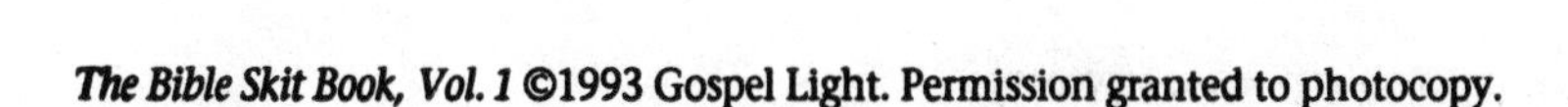

JOAN: How could you remember that? You weren't even five years old then.

JOHN: But I remember. I remember you almost fell off the stage.

JOAN: I didn't fall. Sharon pushed me.

JOHN: That's what you said. But I think you tripped. I remember.

JOAN: No you don't. I was pushed!

JOHN: Look at this old picture. Remember when we went on vacation to that Lake Minnewackamucka...I never could remember how to pronounce it.

JOAN: Winne...I don't remember either. But I remember how much fun we had.

JOHN: Me, too. Remember when I fell off the pier?

JOAN: I sure do. And I was the only one around to save you.

JOHN: I knew I was a goner. My head was sinking under water for the third time.

JOAN: So I jumped off the pier after you. With all my clothes on.

JOHN: Into about three feet of water. It was so shallow, nobody could have drowned. I sure tricked you, that time.

JOAN: And Mom and Dad laughed at us when we got back to the tent.

JOHN: I remember. Hey! Look at this old picture that fell out. Who's this old guy?

JOAN: I don't know. He can't be anybody important. I never saw him before. *(Holds up another photo.)* Look! Remember that party we had? Where we played that game where everybody tried to get as dirty as they could?

JOHN: How could I forget it? I was sure that I would win....

MOTHER: *(Enters.)* Hi, kids. Can you help me bring in the groceries, please?

JOHN: Did you get ice cream?

MOTHER: Among other things.

JOHN: I'll get the ice cream bag. *(Exits.)*

JOAN: I'll get the other things. *(Exits.)*

JOHN *(from offstage)*: Mom! Which is the bag with the ice cream in it? Mom! Mom!

JOAN: *(Enters.)* Mom. Didn't you hear John? What are you looking at?

MOTHER: This old photo of Uncle Ethan.

JOAN: Who?

JOHN: *(Enters.)* I found it...What's going on?

JOAN: Mom knows the old guy in the picture.

MOTHER: It's my Uncle Ethan. This is the only picture anybody ever took of him.

JOHN: Why? Didn't anybody like him?

MOTHER: Everybody adored him. But, way back then, most people didn't have cameras. I thought I had lost this one. Where did you find it?

JOAN: It just fell out of one of the albums.

JOHN: If he was such a great guy, how come I never heard of him?

MOTHER: Probably because when all the family gets together, the adults tell their favorite stories about Uncle Ethan while you kids are hanging out with your cousins. But almost every family has one of his carvings.

JOAN: You mean like that old wood thing in the living room?

MOTHER: Yes. That was one of Uncle Ethan's.

JOHN: It's not very good. I never knew why you had it there. I thought maybe you did it when you were a little girl.

MOTHER: It's true—he was never a great craftsman. He carved just because he enjoyed it. And everyone asked him for one of his carvings.

JOAN: But why? Why would anyone want something that wasn't very good?

MOTHER: It's a symbol. It's something to help you remember.

JOHN: Huh?

MOTHER: Look at those pictures.

JOAN: We have been. All afternoon.

MOTHER: How good are those pictures?

JOHN: They're the best pictures in the world.

MOTHER: No, they're not. Most are out of focus or overexposed. If you took them to a photo display, people would laugh at them. But they're special to you and so you see them differently than other people do. They're symbols of your lives. That's the same with Uncle Ethan's carvings. They're special because they help us to remember.

(JOHN gets up to exit.)

JOAN: Where are you going, John?

JOHN: To the living room.

JOAN: Why?

JOHN: To look at that old wood thing. The next time the family gets together, I'm going to ask about this guy.

MOTHER: Children! The grocer—never mind. Some things are more important than food. Go. Learn. And remember.

Trials, Trials, Trials

SCRIPTURE: Matthew 26:57-66; 27:11-14; Luke 22:66—23:11; John 18:12-37

SUGGESTED TOPICS: Events surrounding Jesus' death; Jesus' humility; God's love

BIBLE BACKGROUND

Jesus' earthly ministry was nearing completion. To fulfill all prophecy, He had to be betrayed and then killed. However, in order for an execution to be carried out, two trials had to be held—one under Jewish law and one under Roman law. It is interesting to note that, while both the Jewish and Roman trials of Jesus were conducted in highly irregular manners, the gospel accounts do not claim that the trial proceedings were illegal. The perspective of the writers was that of lay observers, not legal experts.

Caiaphas was a shrewd politician. With absolute cunning and disregard for the law he was sworn to uphold as high priest, he found a crime which required the death penalty and for which Jesus could be convicted: blasphemy. However, under Roman law, only a governor could sentence a man to death.

The Roman governor, Pilate, cared little for the Jews and their customs. Only the accusation that Jesus was guilty of treason against Rome held any interest for him. When he questioned Jesus, he quickly concluded that Jesus was no threat to Roman authority and sought to release Him. However, Caiaphas threatened Pilate that if he refused to sentence Jesus to death, Pilate could be found negligent in his duties by Rome. What was he to do? Simple. Pass the buck to Herod, the puppet king appointed by Rome.

Herod Antipas, one of the sons of Herod the Great. was tetrarch (ruler of one fourth of a region) of Galilee. He was in Jerusalem for Passover, even though he had no more interest in the Jews than did Pilate. He was, however, fascinated at the prospect of meeting Jesus, the miracle worker. When Jesus refused to answer Herod's questions or perform a miracle for him, Herod sent Jesus back to Pilate.

PERFORMANCE TIPS

1. Suggested props: gavel and/or black robe for Caiaphas.

2. If you have adequate space in your room, designate a separate area for each trial. March Jesus from place to place. If space is limited, march Jesus around the room each time Caiaphas, Pilate and Herod take their places.

3. Suggest that the person playing the part of Jesus act in a self-assured, calm manner. Since Jesus knew these events were part of God's plan, Jesus' attitude was not one of anger or rebellion.

4. Introduce the skit by asking the group to briefly summarize the events leading up to Jesus' arrest. Supplement their summary with information from John 18:1-12.

DISCUSSION QUESTIONS

1. What parts of Jesus' trials were illegal? Why do you think these illegal procedures were used?

2. Why did Jesus allow Himself to be arrested and tried?

3. How did Jesus' actions show God's love?

Trials, Trials, Trials

CHARACTERS

CAIAPHAS (KYE-ah-fus)
DAVID
JESUS
WITNESS ONE
WITNESS TWO
PILATE
HEROD
SERVANT

SCENE ONE

CAIAPHAS: OK. Let's begin this trial under duly appointed law...

DAVID: Excuse me, your High Priestliness.

CAIAPHAS: What is it?

DAVID: If we're operating under law, why is the trial at night?

CAIAPHAS: What are you babbling about?

DAVID: Under the law, a trial can't be held at night. Only during the day.

CAIAPHAS: Ahem. Yes. Well, sometimes one thing must bow to another. Because of Passover, we felt it was more important to resolve this matter quickly than to wait until tomorrow for the trial.

DAVID: And then, too, you wouldn't have to worry about too many of His friends showing up.

CAIAPHAS: Precisely. I mean, nonsense. Swift justice is what matters. Bring in the guilty party!

DAVID: You mean, the accused.

CAIAPHAS: Same difference. Now then, Jesus of Nazareth. You have been accused of blasphemy. How do You plead? What is it You have been teaching?

JESUS: I always spoke openly. I taught in the Temple and in the synagogues, where the Jews meet. I have said nothing in secret. Why ask what I have taught? Ask those who have heard. They know what I said.

CAIAPHAS: How dare you speak so to me? Very well, we shall assume this is a 'not guilty' plea. Bother. Bring in the first liar—I mean, witness.

WITNESS ONE: How d'you do, Your Honor.

CAIAPHAS: Now then, what did you hear this man say?

WITNESS ONE: Last Monday, I heard Him say that the Temple should be torn down.

CAIAPHAS: There you have it. Blasphemy. Is there any reason why sentence should not be passed immediately?

DAVID: Well...

CAIAPHAS: Well, what?

DAVID: Technically, He's not guilty until two witnesses agree in all aspects of their testimony.

CAIAPHAS: Very well. Call in the next li—ahem, witness.

WITNESS TWO: I'm here.

CAIAPHAS: Good. Now then, what did you hear this man say concerning tearing down the Temple on Monday?

DAVID: Isn't that leading the witness, Your High Priestliness?

CAIAPHAS: Nonsense! I'm just trying to speed up the judicial process. Answer the question.

WITNESS TWO: Oh, He said it, Your Worship. He said He could build up the walls in three days if somebody tore down the Temple. That's witchcraft, that is. And He said it.

CAIAPHAS: What about tearing down the Temple? Didn't He tell people to tear down the Temple? Think carefully.

WITNESS TWO: Uh, what is it you want me to say, Your Worship?

DAVID: Speak the truth. That's why you're here.

WITNESS TWO: Oh. Well, uh, He said He was a master builder or something like that and that He could build the Temple in three days and kind of that sort of thing.

CAIAPHAS: I'm calling a short recess. *(Calls offstage.)* Annas, check out the witnesses. See if you can find two in that crowd who can agree on a story. Now then, I think I will question the guilty party myself while we're waiting.

DAVID: You can't do that, Sir. You can't ask the accused to give evidence against Himself. It's against the law. You need two witnesses.

CAIAPHAS: Well, we'll find two witnesses if it takes all night. *(Calls offstage.)* Annas. Bring in the two witnesses that...What do you mean, you can't find two witnesses who agree in their testimony? I've had enough of this. You, Jesus! Are You the Christ?

DAVID: This is all highly irregular.

CAIAPHAS: What do I care about irregular? You heard the question. Well?

JESUS: If I tell you, you will not believe. And if I ask you, you will not answer Me nor let Me go. Hereafter, the Son of Man shall sit on the right hand of God.

CAIAPHAS: Are You, then, the Son of God?

JESUS: You say that I am.

CAIAPHAS: Hah! We have Him. What do we need witnesses for? He has accused Himself. Take Him to Pilate!

DAVID: This is all very irregular.

(Skit continues on next page.)

SCENE TWO

CAIAPHAS: This man has been perverting the nation. He has been saying that He is King. Being good, law-abiding citizens, we bring Him to you to get rid—I mean, to determine what to do about Him.

PILATE: Bring in the accused. Now then. Are you the King of the Jews?

JESUS: You say that I am. Do you say it of your own knowledge or did others tell it to you?

PILATE: I don't see that this man has done anything wrong. If He broke your Jewish laws, it's not my concern. I'm not a Jew. Try Him yourselves.

CAIAPHAS: We have done so. He is guilty. But you must pass sentence, for we cannot exact the death penalty.

PILATE: The death penalty? Surely that's a little harsh for a fellow who's only fault is maybe being a little bit crazy.

CAIAPHAS: He has been trying to incite riots for three years, beginning in Galilee and coming all the way to Jerusalem.

PILATE: Galilee? Is this man a Galilean?

CAIAPHAS: Of course. Just listening to Him, you can tell He's from Galilee.

PILATE: Wonderful! Then I don't have to make the decision. I mean, in the interests of justice, and following all the precepts of Roman law, I decide that this man should be sent to see Herod, because Galilee is part of Herod's jurisdiction.

CAIAPHAS: You're not sending Him all the way to Galilee to see Herod?

PILATE: Of course not. Herod happens to be in Jerusalem. Send Him to Herod.

(Skit continues on next page.)

SCENE THREE

HEROD: What a miserable little country. I wish I could be transferred to Rome. Nothing ever happens here.

SERVANT: Some men here to see you, my Lord. With a prisoner.

HEROD: What do I want with prisoners? Send Him to Pilate.

SERVANT: Pilate sent Him to you. Because He's a Galilean, my Lord.

HEROD: I don't care if He's a giraffe. Send Him back to Pilate.

SERVANT: Very good, my Lord. OK! Take Jesus back to Pilate.

HEROD: Wait a minute. Did you say Jesus?

SERVANT: Yes, my Lord.

HEROD: Jesus, the prophet from Galilee?

SERVANT: Yes, my Lord.

HEROD: The One who's done all the miracles? Raised people from the dead? Turned water into wine? Healed the sick? Or so I'm told.

SERVANT: That's the One, my Lord.

HEROD: Well, don't just stand there. Bring Him in! Maybe He'll perform a miracle. That would be fun.

CAIAPHAS: Here is the blasphemer, oh Herod. Sentence Him to death.

HEROD: Everything in good time. Now then. Jesus. What do You have to say for Yourself? Come on, man. Speak up. I'm the most powerful man in the country. *(JESUS is silent.)*

SERVANT: Standing mute won't help You. Speak to Herod.

HEROD: That's right. Now, it seems that the Jews accuse You of blasphemy. Well, show them they're wrong. Do a miracle. Look! Here's a glass of water. Turn it into wine.

SERVANT: It's still water, my Lord.

HEROD: I can see that. Wait a minute. *(To SERVANT.)* Does your wife still have that hideous boil on her face?

SERVANT: Yes, my Lord.

HEROD: *(To JESUS.)* You could heal her, couldn't You? I'd love to see that. Say that You'll heal her. Come on, man. Speak up!

CAIAPHAS: He has no respect for authority.

HEROD: How about walking on water? I heard You can do that. Let's go down to the river and You can walk across it. If You get to the other side, You're a free man. What do You say? Go ahead. Do it.

SERVANT: What's the matter with You? Don't You want to go free?

HEROD: I've had enough of this. Who cares if He comes from Galilee? His crimes were committed in Jerusalem. Send Him back to Pilate. Let Pilate make the decision.

THE SACRIFICE

SCRIPTURE: Matthew 27:15-66; Luke 23:18-56; John 19

SUGGESTED TOPICS: Death of the Savior; God's plan of salvation fulfilled; God's love

BIBLE BACKGROUND

The fullness of time had finally come. For centuries, Satan had challenged God's control. When the long-promised Messiah was born, Satan, through Herod, had attempted to murder Jesus while He was still a child. Finally, the Savior was about to be crucified. Satan was sure he had finally won.

Sacrifice is never easy, not even for the One who is perfect (see Matthew 26:39-44). Jesus, the perfect Son, knew the pain He must endure for His Father's plan to be completed. Willingly, He took the sin of the entire world upon Himself, giving all mankind the only hope of being reconciled to God.

PERFORMANCE TIPS

1. Suggested props: chalk and chalkboard for coach to use in sketching the trick play.

2. By the end of the skit, Josh's voice and gestures must show that he is certain of his actions. He should show his determination to do whatever is needed for his team to win. The other players on the team are still questioning the wisdom of the trick play.

DISCUSSION QUESTIONS

1. Why was it necessary for Jesus to die on the cross?

2. When Jesus died, what did most people who knew Him think about Him?

3. Instead of ending God's plan, the Bible tells us that Jesus' death was the fulfillment of God's plan. Because He followed God's plan, Jesus is able to offer us the gift of eternal life. What do you need to do to accept this gift?

The Sacrifice

CHARACTERS

COACH
PLAYERS
PETE
JIM
JOHNNY
JOSH

COACH: OK, guys. Listen up. The big game's almost here.

PLAYERS: Yeah! Let's get 'em! We're number one!

COACH: Hold it down! Hold it down!

PLAYERS *(softly)*: We're number one!

COACH: That's better. Now, you all know that this is the most important game of our lives. We've GOTTA win this game!

PLAYERS: No problem! Beat 'em! Crush 'em! We're number one!

COACH: Hold it down!

PLAYERS *(softly)*: We're number one!

COACH: OK. What we need is a trick play. Something we can count on if we need to score a last-minute touchdown. Something the opposition won't expect.

PLAYERS: Trick play! Trick play! We're number one!

COACH: Hold...

PLAYERS *(softly)*: We're number one!

COACH: Now, then. I don't have to tell you what our best play has been this season.

PETE: I seal the defensive end!

JIM: I kick out the outside linebacker!

JOHNNY: I cut the middle linebacker!

JOSH: And I run for daylight! Touchdown!

PLAYERS: Yeah, Josh! Score, score, score! We're number one!

COACH: Now, the trick play is a variation of this.

JOSH: So where do I run?

PETE, JIM AND JOHNNY: And who do we hit?

COACH: First, Pete. When you seal the end, don't block him as well as normal.

PETE: You mean, miss him?

COACH: No, but just a brush block. Not your usual crushing blow.

PETE: I don't know...

COACH: Jim. Pretend to block the outside backer, but let him get inside of you.

JIM: I don't know...

COACH: Johnny. Make a show of cutting the middle linebacker, but let him jump over you.

JOHNNY: I don't know...

COACH: In the meantime, Pete, you miss three more blocks.

PETE: Three blocks! I'd never miss three blocks. I'm too good!

JOSH: Wait a minute, Coach. If they do that, I'm going to get creamed.

COACH: Yes, Josh. You will.

JOSH: But I'm your best player! I'm your son! Don't you love me any more or what?

COACH: Of course I do. It's because I love you that I want you to win this game.

JOSH: Sure. But if I'm buried, how will the play ever work?

COACH: Simple. You won't have the ball.

PETE, JIM AND JOHNNY: But they'll kill him!

COACH: No they won't. They'll think they have. But Josh will rise to play again.

JOSH: So what happens to the ball?

COACH: Before you're hit, you hand the ball to Bart. He runs the opposite direction. You pretend you still have the ball, and while the enemy is concentrating on you, Bart gains big yardage.

JOSH: Will it work?

COACH: Guaranteed.

JOSH: If I sacrifice myself, we'll win?

COACH: Absolutely.

JOSH: Then I'll do it. Let's go through it once again so I've got everything straight. We don't want to mess this up.

He's Alive!

SCRIPTURE: Matthew 28:1-10; Luke 24:1-12; John 20:1-18

SUGGESTED TOPICS: Jesus' resurrection; God's plan of salvation fulfilled

BIBLE BACKGROUND

Jesus was dead! His disciples, in fear for their own lives, were in hiding. Because Jesus' death had occurred so close to the beginning of the Sabbath, Joseph of Arimathea and Nicodemus had not had time to properly prepare His body for burial. Now, on the first day of the week, a small group of women made their way to the tomb to pay their last respects to the dead.

The Bible leaves no ambiguity with respect to Jesus' death and resurrection. This is the most important series of events in human history and the crux of Christianity (see 1 Corinthians 15:12-19). For centuries, people have tried to prove it false; for centuries, people have failed.

PERFORMANCE TIPS

1. Suggested props: Bible-times costumes.

2. In Scene One the three women should walk slowly towards one end of the room designated as the tomb. Designate another area of the room as the house where Peter and John are staying.

3. Peter and John should sound as if they are convinced that Mary is completely out of her mind. Because they saw Jesus die, they are certain He is dead.

DISCUSSION QUESTIONS

1. Suppose you saw a friend die and were later told he or she was alive again. How would you feel? What would make you believe the report?

2. Do you agree or disagree with the statement, "Jesus' resurrection is the most important event in history"? Why or why not?

3. How does the death and resurrection of Jesus affect your life now? What difference does it make today whether or not Jesus rose from the dead?

HE'S ALIVE!

CHARACTERS

MARY MAGDALENE
MARY (MOTHER OF JESUS)
JOANNA
PETER
JOHN
ANGEL
JESUS

SCENE ONE

MARY MAGDALENE: So? How are we going to do it?

MARY: I don't know.

JOANNA: It's a very heavy stone.

MARY MAGDALENE: Maybe if we all push together?

MARY: Don't be silly.

JOANNA: Maybe the guards will help us.

MARY: Maybe, maybe, maybe. We should go and get some of the men to help us. Four of the stronger ones should be enough to roll away the stone.

MARY MAGDALENE: No way! If the guards saw so many men coming, you know what would happen. They'd attack first and ask questions later. But maybe they'll help three women.

JOANNA: Why wouldn't they? We're only going to make sure that the body is properly buried. They'll be there the whole time. It's not like we're going to steal anything.

MARY MAGDALENE: Well, maybe they'll help.

MARY: It's the only hope we have.

JOANNA: Are we almost there?

MARY MAGDALENE: Of course. You know where the tomb is.

MARY: It's right over there.

JOANNA: But where are the guards?

MARY MAGDALENE: And why is the stone over on the side and not in front of the entrance?

MARY: There's something strange going on here.

JOANNA: The body's gone!

MARY MAGDALENE: I'd better go and tell Peter and John. *(She runs off.)*

MARY: Should we go in?

JOANNA: It's awfully dark.

MARY: But we must know what happened.

JOANNA: But it's awfully dark.

MARY: No it's not. It's light. Where did the light come from?

ANGEL: Who is it that you seek?

MARY AND JOANNA: Who are you, Sir? And why do you shine?

ANGEL: I am an angel of the Lord. Why do you seek for the living among the dead? Do you not remember that He said evil men would kill Him, but on the third day, He would rise again?

MARY: Are you telling us that He's alive?

JOANNA: Just as He said in Galilee. I remember.

ANGEL: Go to the disciples and tell them the good news. He's alive.

MARY AND JOANNA: We will! We will! *(They run off.)*

SCENE TWO

PETER: Who's banging on the door?

MARY MAGDALENE *(gasping for breath)*: Mary.

PETER: Who?

JOHN: She said, "Mary."

PETER: It could be a trick. Mary who?

MARY MAGDALENE *(gasping for breath)*: Mary...*(Gasps.)* Magdalene.

JOHN: It sounds like her. Let her in.

PETER: OK. You're in. What is it?

MARY MAGDALENE *(gasping for breath)*: Jesus. Tomb. Stone. Gone. Body.

JOHN: Whoa. Whoa. Whoa.

PETER: Pull in your nets, woman. Take a deep breath and start over.

JOHN: You're not making any sense.

MARY MAGDALENE: We went to Jesus' tomb.

PETER: Why'd you do that?

MARY MAGDALENE: To anoint His body. To give it a proper burial.

JOHN: Well that was dumb. How are you women going to move that stone?

MARY MAGDALENE: We didn't have to. It was already moved.

PETER: Sure it was. With guards all around the tomb.

MARY MAGDALENE: I'm telling you. It was rolled away from the entrance.

JOHN: You must have gone to the wrong place.

MARY MAGDALENE: No we didn't. Go! See for yourselves.

PETER: We will! C'mon, John.

JOHN: Just far enough to see the guards.

PETER: Well, of course. No point in getting killed because some hysterical women can't find the right tomb.

MARY MAGDALENE: We were at the right place! Somebody's taken the body.

JOHN: Sure they did. Let's go and see, Peter. *(They run off to the tomb.)*

PETER *(puffing while jogging)*: It looks peaceful enough so far.

JOHN *(also puffing)*: Try to keep up! But be quiet. We don't want to alert the guards.

PETER: I am being quiet. Just over this hill, we'll see the tomb. Don't get so far ahead.

JOHN: I can see the tomb.

PETER: And?

JOHN: I can see the stone.

PETER: And?

JOHN: I can't see the guards.

PETER: What?

JOHN: I can't see the guards. They're not there.

PETER: What? Let me see. What's the stone doing way over there?

JOHN: I don't know.

PETER: Where are you going?

JOHN: To get a better look. C'mon.

PETER: Well, slow down. Don't go running into danger.

JOHN: What danger?

PETER: How do I know? But something strange is happening.

JOHN: C'mon. Maybe Mary was right.

PETER: Slow down. OK, you got here first and you're blocking the entrance. So what do you see?

JOHN: Nothing.

PETER: What do you mean, "nothing"? Get out of the way.

JOHN: Well, you don't have to push.

PETER: Look. Look at the burial cloths!

JOHN: What about them?

PETER: They're still completely wrapped. Just like the body floated out of them. Whoever did this was certainly neat.

JOHN: Something's wrong.

PETER: What do you mean?

JOHN: Where's the headpiece?

PETER: I don't know. Must have been taken with the body.

JOHN: But why? Why would anybody steal a body with the head piece and then rewrap the linen cloths?

PETER: They didn't.

JOHN: What?

PETER: They didn't take the head piece. It's wrapped up over here in the corner.

JOHN: What? Peter! He's alive! He must be.

PETER: What are you talking about?

JOHN: Jesus is alive! It's the only thing that makes sense!

PETER: He's dead. You saw Him crucified. You saw the spear in His side.

JOHN: But nobody would rob a grave this way. He's alive, I tell you!

PETER: Maybe. I want to study this some more. Let's go.

JOHN: But He's alive! We have to tell the others.

PETER: Just keep quiet. Dead people don't come back to life.

JOHN: What about Lazarus?

PETER: Just keep quiet and let me think. *(They leave for home.)*

SCENE THREE

MARY MAGDALENE *(sobbing softly)***:** Why? Why? Why?

ANGEL: Why do you weep?

MARY MAGDALENE: Because somebody took away my Lord. And I don't know where they put Him. *(She sinks to her knees and covers her face with her hands.)*

JESUS: Woman, why do you weep?

MARY MAGDALENE *(sobbing)***:** Sir?

JESUS: Whom do you seek?

MARY MAGDALENE: Sir, if you are the gardener and took away my Lord, please tell me where to find Him. Let me take Him to another place so that we can visit His grave.

JESUS: Mary.

MARY MAGDALENE: *(Looks up, amazed.)* Master?

JESUS: Go and tell My brothers that I am going back to My Father and your Father; to My God and your God.

MARY MAGDALENE: I will. I will. *(She gets up.)* He's alive! He's alive!

ACTS

SCRIPTURE: Acts 1; 2

SUGGESTED TOPICS: Early church; arrival of the Holy Spirit/Pentecost; witnessing

BIBLE BACKGROUND

Jesus had risen! For the next few weeks, He appeared to hundreds of people. All had the same exciting message to tell their friends. "He's alive! Jesus is risen!" But Jesus knew His earthly ministry had ended. He would not remain on earth forever. He would ascend to take His rightful place as the King of Kings and Lord of Lords. He would not, however, leave His followers defenseless. He promised to send the Holy Spirit.

Luke, writer of the Gospel which bears his name and the book of Acts, was a medical doctor. Most of Acts was written from firsthand experience as he traveled with Paul. Being a doctor, he would be trained to observe. Surely, his firsthand accounts, however incredible some of the events may seem, can be considered reliable.

As a confidant of Paul, Luke had opportunity to meet most of the apostles and many other witnesses of Jesus' life and the life of the early church. His history is a record of the period in which he lived. No other work of history refutes his. The Church of Jesus Christ did spread throughout the Roman Empire in spite of severe persecution. If his writing were false, where are the arguments which could have corrected his errors? The record says his book must be accepted as an accurate account of the time.

PERFORMANCE TIPS

1. Suggested props: table, chair, pad of paper and pen.
2. After the skit, read Acts 2:42-47 to find out ways the Holy Spirit helped the believers as they began the early church.

DISCUSSION QUESTIONS

1. Read John 18:15-18,25-27 and Acts 2:38-41. How did Peter act when Jesus was on trial? How did he act after Pentecost? Why do you think he changed so much in 50 days?
2. According to John 14:26 and Acts 1:8, why do people need the Holy Spirit?
3. What is one way the Holy Spirit can help you?

CHARACTERS

MARK
LUKE

MARK: Who are you writing to, Luke?

LUKE: To Theophilus again.

MARK: Is this one going to be as long as the first?

LUKE: Hard to say. I have a lot to tell him.

MARK: You told him all about Jesus in the first letter. Why do you need to write another?

LUKE: It's important that he hear everything that's happened since then.

MARK: C'mon. There's not enough paper and ink to tell everything that's happened since Jesus rose. You're going to have to pick and choose.

LUKE: I meant the important things. I think I should begin with Jesus' ascension into heaven. And the angels.

MARK: Like what?

MARK: Maybe you should leave the angels out.

LUKE: Why should I do that?

MARK: Most people have never seen angels. They'll think you made it up.

LUKE: I've talked personally to most of those who were there. You know what everyone says happened. Were there angels?

MARK: Well, yes.

LUKE: And was their message important?

MARK: That Jesus was taken up into heaven and would return again? Yes.

LUKE: Then I must include it. It should be written accurately.

MARK: Then you'll probably write about Peter's sermon.

LUKE: All in good time. He should know about the waiting period.

MARK: Why? Nothing exciting happened until the Feast of Pentecost.

LUKE: I'm not trying to write a thriller. I'm writing history.

MARK: What's so important about waiting?

LUKE: Have you learned so little? People need to know that God has a time for all things. It's important not to rush off and try to do things on our own. It's also important to tell that Matthias was chosen to be an apostle in Judas' place.

MARK: Why is that important?

LUKE: To show that the apostles are people of God. People who seek His will.

MARK: OK. Then, of course, the tongues of fire.

LUKE: Naturally. But I need some help. I have, of course, heard it described. But I need an eyewitness to be certain that I have all the details correctly recorded.

MARK: Well, we were all in the same place...

LUKE: About one hundred twenty of you?

MARK: Yes. Suddenly, there was a sound like a strong wind blowing. The noise filled the whole house. But there was no breeze.

LUKE: I wish I had been there. And then, the fire.

MARK: I remember looking at Peter. And above his head was what looked like a small flame. And I thought, "Wow! God chose Peter to be someone extra special." Then I looked around. And the same kind of flame was over everyone's head.

LUKE: And then?

MARK: Everybody began to speak in different languages.

LUKE: That must have been very confusing.

MARK: Yes and no. It should have been, but everyone sensed the presence of the Holy Spirit, and there was peace in the noise.

LUKE: You see why I included the angels. Many will find this hard to believe, also. But since it is the truth and it's important, it must be included.

MARK: Yes, I see what you mean. Then, Peter's sermon.

LUKE: That's right. Everything in good order. Peter's sermon on that day.

MARK: Nobody will have trouble believing that. Lots of people who heard it are still living, even those who didn't believe.

LUKE: I still have trouble believing that some people thought the apostles were drunk.

MARK: Why is that so hard to believe?

LUKE: How many people, when they are drunk, can speak another language perfectly? To call the men drunk! Why, that's crazy.

MARK: Some would rather believe anything than to believe in Jesus.

LUKE: True. And sad. But back to that day.

MARK: Peter's sermon was really something. Just think—this was the same Peter who, only a few short weeks before, had denied that he even knew Jesus. And now he was standing in front of a huge crowd, telling them that Jesus, who had been crucified, is the Messiah, the Son of God.

LUKE: God used that sermon to touch many lives. More than three thousand. Incredible!

MARK: So what else are you going to write about?

LUKE: Many things. Baptism of the Gentiles. Preaching missions.

MARK: You're not planning to mention that little homesickness episode of mine, are you?

LUKE: Now that you mention it, I think I shall.

MARK: *(Groans.)* Why?

LUKE: Everyone knows the solid friend you've become. It's good for people to know that you don't have to be perfect in order for God to use you.

MARK: Well, OK. But go a little easy on me, will you? After all, I was pretty young then.

LUKE: And now, you're a strong man of God. Don't worry. People will remember your faith more than your failings. But I'm getting a cramp in my writing hand. I wish there were a faster way to get all this down on paper. I'll write some more tomorrow.

CRIPPLED

SCRIPTURE: Acts 3:1—4:22

SUGGESTED TOPICS: Acts of the Holy Spirit; opposition to the early church; witnessing

BIBLE BACKGROUND

The Sanhedrin, the highest Jewish court of justice during the Greek and Roman periods, thought they had solved the problem of Jesus. He was dead. His body, however, had disappeared. Pulling all the political strings possible, they spread the rumor that the apostles had stolen the body. Surely now their problems were over.

However, fifty days later, during the Feast of Pentecost, new problems arose. Peter preached a sermon convincing three thousand people that Jesus is the Christ. As if that was not bad enough, while going to the Temple to pray, Peter and John had healed a lame man and credited Jesus with the healing. In order to preserve their prestige and power, the Sanhedrin had to act quickly. The Sanhedrin had a great deal of power with which to threaten the disciples. Jesus had been crucified; the disciples had to face the possibility that they would meet the same fate. Did this deter them, weaken their resolve, slow them down? No. Because they knew whom they believed and that what they believed was true.

PERFORMANCE TIPS

1. Suggested props: table and three chairs.

2. Caiaphas and Annas should show by their forceful mannerisms and voices that they are the leaders of the group. Alexander should sound as if he doesn't quite understand what is happening.

3. After the skit, read or briefly summarize Acts 4:18-20 to find how the disciples reacted to the Sanhedrin's threats.

DISCUSSION QUESTIONS

1. What did the Jewish leaders threaten to do to Peter and John if they kept preaching about Jesus? Why did the Jewish leaders think their threats would be successful?

2. How might Peter and John have felt when they first heard these threats? How would you have felt?

3. Why did Peter and John keep on preaching about Jesus? Why were the threats ineffective?

4. When have you been reluctant or afraid to tell someone about Jesus? Who helped Peter and John have courage? Who can help you?

CRIPPLED

CHARACTERS

ANNAS (ah-NAHS)
ALEXANDER
CAIAPHAS (KYE-uh-fus)

ANNAS: Gentlemen, we have a problem. The cripple who's usually outside the Temple gate isn't there.

ALEXANDER: You mean the one always begging?

CAIAPHAS: Precisely.

ALEXANDER: That's no problem. He always annoyed me when I came to the Temple to pray. If he's missing, good riddance.

ANNAS: He's not missing. He's running and jumping INSIDE the Temple courts.

ALEXANDER *(confused)***:** The cripple?

CAIAPHAS: Right.

ALEXANDER: Do all you priests and scribes know the meaning of the word "cripple"?

CAIAPHAS: Of course we do!

ALEXANDER: Then how can he be running and leaping? He's a cripple!

ANNAS: Obviously, he's been healed.

ALEXANDER: Then he's no longer a cripple?

CAIAPHAS: Right.

ALEXANDER: So he can make his own living and won't be begging anymore?

CAIAPHAS: I suppose so.

ALEXANDER: Then what's the problem? He's gone. I can come to pray in peace.

ANNAS: If you'll be quiet and listen, you'll know what the problem is. At three o'clock this afternoon the cripple was sitting at the Temple gate, as usual...

CAIAPHAS: Begging, as usual...

ANNAS: When two men came up to him and spoke to him.

CAIAPHAS: But instead of giving him money, one of them reached out...

ANNAS: Took his hand...

CAIAPHAS: And pulled him to his feet.

ANNAS: Now he's leaping all around the Temple.

ALEXANDER: I still don't see a problem.

CAIAPHAS: The man's a fool.

ALEXANDER: Just because he's leaping and running is no reason to call him a fool.

CAIAPHAS: Not him! You!

ALEXANDER: Me? Did you hear that? He called me a fool.

ANNAS: With good reason. Don't you ever think?

ALEXANDER: Well, let's see. About noon, I thought I was hungry.

CAIAPHAS: A fool. A complete fool.

ANNAS: Sit down. Try not to speak. Just listen.

CAIAPHAS: A lame man was suddenly healed this afternoon.

ANNAS: Everybody in the Temple heard about it.

CAIAPHAS: There was a great uproar.

ANNAS: Everybody wanted to see the healed man.

CAIAPHAS: AND the men who had healed him.

ANNAS: Now do you see the problem?

ALEXANDER: I sure do. Why, everybody in Jerusalem will be flocking to these two doctors. All the other doctors will go broke.

CAIAPHAS: A fool. The man's a fool.

ANNAS: Alexander. Try to understand. The two men are not doctors.

ALEXANDER: And you call me a fool. Only doctors can heal the sick.

CAIAPHAS: How long has that man been lame?

ALEXANDER: I don't know. I've been coming to the Temple for thirty years and he's always been begging at the door.

ANNAS: Precisely. And he was lame before that. He was born lame.

CAIAPHAS: Maybe forty years ago.

ANNAS: No doctor has ever been able to help him.

CAIAPHAS: Suddenly, he's healed.

ANNAS: What do you think happens?

ALEXANDER: He signs up for dancing lessons?

CAIAPHAS: NO! Everybody in the Temple runs to see what happened.

ANNAS: They want to see this miracle.

CAIAPHAS: And they want to see the men who did it.

ALEXANDER: Well, I should think so. What's the big deal?

ANNAS: Those two men are preaching right now. Here in the Temple.

CAIAPHAS: About Jesus.

ALEXANDER: So? Jesus is dead. What's the big deal?

ANNAS: Those men claim He's no longer dead...

CAIAPHAS: That it was Jesus' power that healed the lame man...

ANNAS: And that everyone must believe in Jesus as the Son of God.

ALEXANDER: Well, that's just plain crazy. Jesus is dead. We saw to that.

ANNAS: But they're saying that He rose from the dead.

ALEXANDER: Nobody believes that.

CAIAPHAS: Many do. Remember—there's no body. The tomb is empty.

ALEXANDER: Sure. But His disciples stole the body. Remember?

CAIAPHAS: A fool. An utter, complete fool.

ANNAS: Alexander, do you remember how that story was started?

ALEXANDER: Sure. We paid the guards to say they fell asleep on duty.

CAIAPHAS: So, do you really believe the disciples stole the body?

ALEXANDER: Well, sure. What else could have happened?

ANNAS: We don't know. But we don't want people going around teaching that Jesus came back to life. If people believe Jesus is the Son of God, what happens to us?

ALEXANDER: Why should anything happen to us?

ANNAS: Because He was crucified.

ALEXANDER: Sure. But the Romans did that.

CAIAPHAS: Because we demanded it.

ALEXANDER: Oh.

ANNAS: So you see what that means?

ALEXANDER: People might not like us much.

CAIAPHAS: Who cares about liking us? They might stop respecting us.

ANNAS: They might refuse to listen to us anymore.

CAIAPHAS: We'd lose much of our power over the people.

ALEXANDER: We have to stop these radicals.

ANNAS: Finally, he begins to understand.

CAIAPHAS: Now that we've agreed there is a problem, we must decide what to do.

ALEXANDER: We can pretend the miracle didn't happen.

ANNAS: How can we do that?

ALEXANDER: We can say the healed man is an imposter.

CAIAPHAS: Who's going to believe that?

ALEXANDER: They believed that the guards fell asleep.

ANNAS: True. Maybe...no. Too many people know this man. That lie wouldn't work.

CAIAPHAS: I have it! We simply have to stop the story from spreading.

ALEXANDER: How can we do that?

CAIAPHAS: We order those two to stop talking about Jesus.

ALEXANDER: How much are we going to have to pay them? Bribing those guards cost our treasury most of its ready cash.

ANNAS: He has a point, Caiaphas. Even if we had cash, I doubt we could bribe them.

CAIAPHAS: Of course not. Money wouldn't silence them. But threats...

ANNAS: Ah...

CAIAPHAS: Beatings.

ANNAS: Long-term imprisonment.

CAIAPHAS: That's the trick. Nobody will keep telling lies if they have to suffer for it. If we can just make them suffer, they'll be silent.

ANNAS: I like it. OK, bring the Temple guards along and we'll lock these men up for the night. That should put a stop to all this nonsense.

Encourage One Another

Jr. High
2-1-95

SCRIPTURE: Acts 2:42-47; 4:32-37

SUGGESTED TOPICS: Encouragement; conflict; Christian life; responsibility to body of believers

BIBLE BACKGROUND

The Church had been growing at a tremendous rate as the apostles continued preaching with courage and conviction. As it grew, many problems should have driven wedges between various believers. Although this threatened to happen, the love and encouragement of the believers to one another overcame the danger of separation.

This skit explores the challenge of encouraging others to use their abilities for the good of the group. The skit takes a look at the biggest problem facing every coach of a sports team: getting the team to play together as a team rather than a group of individuals. Nothing breaks down a team more quickly than bickering among the players. And nothing hinders the work of the gospel more than lack of cooperation and mutual support.

PERFORMANCE TIPS

1. Suggested props: hat, whistle and clipboard for coach; soccer shirts and ball for players.
2. If you are not familiar with coaching techniques, invite a coach to come to your group. Ask the coach to describe ways of encouraging a team to work together.
3. Soccer players in your group will be familiar with the terms used in the skit. Ask them to play the parts of the players. They may also explain terms to group members who are unfamiliar with the game of soccer.

DISCUSSION QUESTIONS

1. What was the coach trying to accomplish in his half-time pep talk?
2. What might have happened if the players had kept arguing with each other? Why?
3. What does it mean to encourage someone? How did the team members encourage each other? What are some benefits of encouraging others?
4. Who are some people you spend time with? What are specific ways you may encourage them?
5. Read Hebrews 10:24,25. How do these verses say Christians should encourage each other? How do the people in your church encourage each other? What can you do to encourage another Christian?

Encourage One Another

CHARACTERS

COACH
PETE
JIM
TOM
JOHN

COACH: OK, guys! Off the field! C'mon over here. We need a half-time chat.

PETE: I'll say! These turkeys can't do anything right!

JIM: Oh yeah? Well, if you'd pass the ball...

PETE: I would, if anyone could shoot.

COACH: Enough! Settle down and listen.

PETE and JIM: OK.

COACH: Good. Now, we're not out of the game. We're only down two goals and we have a full half to play. We can come back, if we play as a team.

JIM: What good would it do? Didn't you see those two soft goals Tom let in?

TOM: What do you mean, soft? If I had any kind of defensive help...

JOHN: What do you think we've been doing out there? Playing checkers? We've been working a lot harder than you.

COACH: Enough! I mean it.

TOM and JOHN: OK.

COACH: Listen, guys. Soccer is a team sport. It's played by a team of eleven people. No one person wins a game and no one person loses a game. It's won or lost by a team.

PETE: Yeah, but some of these guys...

COACH: Let's try something. Everyone who has played a perfect game, step over here.

JIM: Well, maybe not perfect but better than...

COACH: I didn't say better than. I said perfect. Has anybody here played a perfect game today?

PETE, JIM, TOM and JOHN: No.

COACH: Alright. The only person who is in a position to criticize is the person who played a perfect game. If you haven't been perfect, the only person you should criticize is yourself.

PETE, JIM, TOM and JOHN: OK.

COACH: Now, we have the kickoff in the second half. I think we can catch these guys napping, if we play as a team. On the kickoff, tap the ball back to Bart.

PETE: Why?

COACH: Who's the best passer on the team?

PETE: Bart is.

COACH: That's why the ball goes to him, first. Bart, lead Andy with a pass down the right sideline.

JIM: Why Andy? I score more goals than he does.

COACH: Who's the fastest man on the team?

JIM: Well, Andy. But...

COACH: That's why the pass goes to Andy. We can beat their left side with speed. Andy, once you've passed the left fullback, break for the goal. When you get to the penalty area, shoot. Any shot not directly at the goaltender should score.

JOHN: But even if it does work, it'll only work once.

COACH: True. But if it works once, they may overcorrect for fear it'll work again. That will open up other areas of the field.

PETE: But what if they score again?

COACH: They shouldn't. We have a good goaltender and a good defense. We're just not playing together as well as we can. Tom, remember—you can see the whole field from the goal. Talk to your fullbacks. If you want them to move, tell them. They can't read your mind.

TOM: OK. Hey, John. You see that number eleven? If you and Matt double team him every time he gets the ball, we should be able to rattle him.

JOHN: You got it. Nobody gets a decent shot against us this half.

COACH: OK, the half's about to begin. Remember the plan. There's the whistle! Let's go!

PETE: It's all yours, Bart.

JOHN: Beautiful pass, Bart! Nobody's gonna beat Andy to it!

TOM: C'mon Andy! Run. Use your speed. That's the way! You've got him beat!

JIM: You're clear, Andy! Hit it! Hit it!

PETE: Yes! Goal! Good shot, Andy! Way to go!

COACH: Great play, team! We're only down one, now!

JOHN: No problem. We'll get it back.

JIM: And they won't beat our defense again.

COACH: Let's go, guys. Lots of time to win this one.

OPEN DOORS

SCRIPTURE: Acts 5:12-26

SUGGESTED TOPICS: Acts of the Holy Spirit; early church; witnessing; response to injustice; courage under persecution

BIBLE BACKGROUND

The disciples, having been filled with the Holy Spirit, were actively preaching the gospel throughout Jerusalem. Many people accepted the apostles' teaching and were converted to "The Way." The Jewish council, comprised of Pharisees and Sadducees, finally agreed that teaching about Jesus had to be stopped. In the past, they had called in Peter and John and ordered them to cease their preaching. But no punishment had yet been meted out, for they could find no law which had been broken and were wary of the general population which was excited about the miracles that they had seen performed. However, warnings alone could not stop the apostles and the Council decided that more drastic action must be taken.

What were the motives of these religious leaders in trying to stop the preaching of the disciples? Were they jealous of the attention that this new teaching was bringing to the apostles? Were they afraid that this new teaching would lead Israel astray and that God's displeasure would erupt into the destruction of the nation? Were they afraid of a potential uprising against the Roman government and the resulting martial law that would be imposed? Were they afraid if Rome had to intervene directly that they could lose their political power?

Any of the above could be true. But whatever their motives, their actions were wrong. God called them to account for their behavior because, as religious leaders, they should have been the most receptive to Jesus the Messiah. They should have been ready to lead Israel to God, when in fact they did the opposite.

PERFORMANCE TIPS

1 Suggested props: Bible-times costumes.

2. Before the skit, explain to the group that we tend to think of prisons as modern facilities where prisoners are treated well. However, in Roman times, prisoners often died from neglect and mistreatment. The threat of imprisonment was powerful.

3. After the skit, read or summarize the conclusion of the story as found in Acts 5:27-42.

DISCUSSION QUESTIONS

1. What words would you use to describe Peter's actions?
2. Do you think Peter and the other believers were afraid? Why or why not?
3. What does God promise His followers in Hebrews 13:5,6?
4. When is a time you need to remember these promises?

Open Doors

CHARACTERS

CAPTAIN
ANNAS (ah-NAHS)
CAIAPHAS (KYE-uh-fus)
ALEXANDER
JOHN
OTHERS
PHARISEES
MESSENGER

SCENE ONE

CAPTAIN: O Your Holinesses, we have a problem.
ANNAS: What kind of problem, Captain?
CAPTAIN: Well, you remember those apostle characters?
CAIAPHAS: You mean those blasphemers who tried to make people believe that Jesus of Nazareth is the Messiah?
CAPTAIN: The very same, Your High Priestliness.
ANNAS: What about them?
CAPTAIN: They're doing it again, Your Most Worthiness.
CAIAPHAS: Cut the fancy titles! What are they doing?
CAPTAIN: All kinds of terrible things.
ANNAS: Such as?
CAPTAIN: They're healing the sick.
CAIAPHAS: Didn't we tell them to stop doing that?
ANNAS: We certainly did! We have doctors to heal the sick. What else?
CAPTAIN: They're casting out demons again.
CAIAPHAS: Oh, infamy!
ANNAS: Disgraceful!
CAPTAIN: And...
CAIAPHAS and ANNAS: AND?
CAPTAIN: And they're saying that Jesus gives them the power to do these things.
CAIAPHAS: Blasphemy!
ANNAS: Double blasphemy!
CAIAPHAS: Call the council!
CAPTAIN: Council!

ANNAS: Not you. Me. Council! Convene immediately.

ALEXANDER: What is it, Annas? I was just settling down to a refreshing study of the law.

JOHN: And I was trying to decide if we've been too lax about the Sabbath. Maybe we should add some more regulations.

CAIAPHAS: That can wait. This can't.

ALEXANDER: Then it must be important.

ANNAS: More than important.

JOHN: Then we're all ears. What happened?

CAIAPHAS: You remember those blasphemers.

JOHN: Which ones? So many fail to keep the Sabbath anymore.

ANNAS: Not mild offenders. Blasphemers!

ALEXANDER: Well, I don't think that those who fail to keep each minor regulation can be described only as minor offenders. After all, our tradition...

ANNAS and CAIAPHAS: Be quiet and listen!

JOHN: You don't need to yell.

ALEXANDER: We're listening.

ANNAS: We're talking about the blasphemers.

CAIAPHAS: The ones who claim to have seen the Messiah.

JOHN: Oh, those blasphemers.

ALEXANDER: What's the big deal about them?

CAIAPHAS: They're out healing.

ANNAS: And casting out demons.

CAIAPHAS and ANNAS: And preaching!

ALEXANDER: Oh, infamy!

JOHN: Disgraceful!

ALEXANDER: Blasphemy!

JOHN: Double blasphemy!

ANNAS: Our feelings precisely.

CAIAPHAS: So what do we do?

ALEXANDER: This requires thought.

JOHN: We need time.

ANNAS: They must be stopped.

CAIAPHAS: Aha!

ALEXANDER, JOHN and ANNAS: What?

CAIAPHAS: An idea. Captain!

CAPTAIN: Present and accounted for, Your High Priestliness.

CAIAPHAS: Go and arrest those men.

CAPTAIN: Which men?

ANNAS: The blasphemers!

CAPTAIN: Which ones? There are so many these days.
CAIAPHAS: The ones who call themselves apostles.
CAPTAIN: Oh, them. Where should I take them?
CAIAPHAS: To prison!
ANNAS: Throw them into a cell.
ALEXANDER: A small cell.
CAPTAIN: But there are twelve of them. Shouldn't I use a large cell?
ALEXANDER: A small, dark cell.
CAIAPHAS: While they're cooling their heels, we'll have a good night's sleep.
ANNAS: And awake to consider the matter with cool heads.
CAPTAIN: That's a good one. Cool heels and cool heads.
ALEXANDER: Are you still here?
JOHN: Go and arrest those men.
CAIAPHAS: Good night, gentlemen. We'll meet here tomorrow morning.
ANNAS: And throw the book at those blasphemers.
JOHN: After giving them a fair trial, of course.
CAIAPHAS, ANNAS and ALEXANDER: Of course.

(Skit continues on next page.)

SCENE TWO

CAIAPHAS: Good morning, gentlemen.

OTHERS: Good morning.

CAIAPHAS: I see some of you who were not here yesterday. Guard, go get the prisoners.

CAPTAIN: At once, Your High Priestliness.

ANNAS: You? I thought you were a captain. Why isn't one of your men doing this job?

CAPTAIN: I wanted to see this trial.

ALEXANDER: Well, go and get the prisoners.

JOHN: We can't start the trial until they arrive.

CAPTAIN: At once, with the greatest of haste, I obey your every command...

PHARISEES: Go already!

CAIAPHAS: While he's bringing the prisoners, I'll explain the situation to those who were not here yesterday. Those blasphemers have started up, again.

OTHERS: Hmm.

ANNAS: And you'll remember how we specifically warned them to stop.

ALEXANDER: With words of unmistakable meaning.

JOHN: And yet with kindness.

CAIAPHAS: And how has our consideration been repaid?

ANNAS: With treachery.

ALEXANDER: Yesterday, they were healing.

JOHN: And casting out demons.

CAIAPHAS: And preaching that Jesus is the Messiah.

OTHERS: Oh, infamy! Disgraceful! Blasphemy! Double blasphemy!

CAIAPHAS: Our feelings precisely.

CAPTAIN: Excuse me, Your High Priestliness.

CAIAPHAS: Oh, you. Well, speak up. What is it?

CAPTAIN: If we could have a word in private...

CAIAPHAS: Nonsense! We're ready to start the trial. Bring the prisoners.

CAPTAIN: There may be a slight delay.

ANNAS: What do you mean, a slight delay?

ALEXANDER: We're busy men. We have important things to do.

JOHN: Bring the prisoners. Let the trial begin.

CAPTAIN: That's the reason for the delay.

CAIAPHAS: What reason?

CAPTAIN: The prisoners.

CAIAPHAS: What about the prisoners?

CAPTAIN: We, uh, well, uh...it's kind of, uh...

ANNAS: Stop humming and hawing. Where are the prisoners?

CAPTAIN: Well, we're not sure.

PHARISEES: What?

ALEXANDER: You put them in prison last night, didn't you?

CAPTAIN: I sure did.

JOHN: And you let them escape.

CAPTAIN: Not exactly.

ANNAS: Then you have them in custody.

CAPTAIN: Not exactly.

ALEXANDER: Then where, exactly, are they?

CAPTAIN: We're not sure.

CAIAPHAS: Explain yourself, Captain, or you will soon be a former captain!

CAPTAIN: Well, I went to the Temple with my men yesterday and did just what you told me to do. I found those men healing and casting out demons and preaching...

PHARISEES: Infamy! Disgraceful! Blasphemy! Double blasphemy!

CAPTAIN: And I arrested them. I said, "In the name of the Most Holy Council and by the authority of His Great High Priestliness..."

CAIAPHAS: Get on with it!

CAPTAIN: Yes, Sir. So I took them to jail.

ALEXANDER: And...

CAPTAIN: And I found a cell just like you described.

JOHN: To the letter?

CAPTAIN: Exactly. And I threw all twelve of them in.

ALEXANDER: And...

CAPTAIN: I got to thinking—that many in one cell, maybe they'll break down the door.

ANNAS: And so you took precautions.

CAPTAIN: No, Sir! If any precautions are missing, I didn't take them.

CAIAPHAS: Please, just finish your story.

CAPTAIN: Yes, Sir. Well, I put extra guards at the door all night.

CAIAPHAS: Excellent. So what is the problem?

CAPTAIN: I went down this morning, unlocked the door and ordered the prisoners out of the cell. When they didn't come out, I went in after them. But they weren't there. The bars were all firmly in place, the door was securely locked, the guards were all on duty, but the jail cell was empty. The prisoners were gone.

ANNAS: You expect us to believe this fairy tale?

MESSENGER: Pardon me, gentlemen. But those men you arrested yesterday are back in the Temple. They're teaching the people again.

CAIAPHAS: What?

ANNAS: You! Go and arrest them and bring them here.

CAPTAIN: I will! I'll take my men and we'll beat them and whip them and...

CAIAPHAS: No! Who can tell what that might do to a crowd. We don't want a riot. Go and bring them quietly. We can deal with them here. Oh, my head. How it aches!

SAMARIA TODAY

SCRIPTURE: Acts 8:1-25

SUGGESTED TOPICS: Witness of the early church; acts of the Holy Spirit; free gift of eternal life

BIBLE BACKGROUND

Having been filled with the Holy Spirit, the disciples preached in Jerusalem and thousands embraced the new faith. However, Jesus' command to the disciples had been to preach the good news in Jerusalem, in Judea, in Samaria and to the farthest parts of the world.

The religious leaders in Jerusalem were angered by the preaching of the apostles. To quell the preaching, these leaders began to persecute the believers. They tried everything from arresting entire families to the murder of Stephen (only a Roman governor was permitted to sentence anyone to death under Roman law).

In response to the persecution, many believers fled Jerusalem. They went to Judea, to Samaria and to faraway parts of the world. Wherever they went, they shared the gospel, fulfilling the Great Commission.

The Samaritans were a mixture of Jews and Gentiles. During and after the years of the captivity, Samaria had perverted the true faith, Judaism. As a result, Jews looked down upon Samaritans perhaps even more than they did on any other group. Centuries of animosity existed between these closely related ethnic and religious groups.

All cultures have some form of ethnic joke. Most of these "jokes" are not worth the breath expended to tell them. However, they persist because some people find them humorous. The Samaritans and the Jews were bitter enemies and it is reasonable to assume there would be Samaritan jokes told in Israel and vice versa. Although the "Jewish jokes" told in Perez' monologue are not funny, they might be to a certain mentality of Samaritan, simply because they are "Jewish."

PERFORMANCE TIPS

1. Suggested props: table and chairs set up as for a TV talk show; large APPLAUSE, LAUGH and CHEER signs to direct audience response at the appropriate times.

2. Introduce the skit by discussing the hatred between the Jews and Samaritans. (The Jews looked down on the Samaritans because the Jews believed the Samaritans had distorted their religion. It was not likely that a Samaritan would even want to hear about a new Jewish religion, much less believe in it.)

DISCUSSION QUESTIONS

1. This skit uses several ethnic jokes which make fun of Jews. Read Matthew 5:43,44. How does Jesus tell us to treat others?

2. Why must it have been hard for Simon to become a Christian?

3. What changes did Simon make in his life after he believed in Jesus?

4. What changes might a person today make in his or her life after becoming a Christian? Would these changes be hard or easy?

SAMARIA TODAY

CHARACTERS

AZARIAH (aa-zuh-RYE-uh)
AUDIENCE
PEREZ (peh-REZ)
SIMON

AZARIAH: Welcome to Samaria Today! Tonight, an all-star magic show, featuring none other than Samaria's own—Simon, the Sorcerer! And now, a big Samaritan welcome to the star of the show, the man who makes all others fear to show their faces, Perez!

(AUDIENCE cheers loudly.)

PEREZ: Thank you, thank you, thank you. Well, let's see what's happening in the news. There's been lots brewing in Jerusalem, and it's not just coffee.

(AZARIAH chuckles.)

PEREZ: The followers of that Galilean upstart, Jesus, are trying to turn the city upside down. I guess that's an extension of Jesus' claim that He could rebuild the Temple in three days.

(AUDIENCE sits silently. AZARIAH laughs.)

PEREZ: See, it's an even bigger miracle—the streets up in the air, the houses pointing down...OK, so there are no miracle lovers here today. Well, how 'bout those Israelites. There are SO MANY Israelites spread throughout the Empire...

AUDIENCE *(shouting)*: How many are there?

PEREZ: There are so many Israelites spread throughout the Empire that every other woman's name is JEW-dy.

(AUDIENCE laughs.)

PEREZ: And she sells JEW-elery.

(AUDIENCE laughs louder.)

PEREZ: And her birthday is in JEW-ly.

(AUDIENCE laughs louder.)

PEREZ: And last but not least, how 'bout Saul?

AUDIENCE *(shouting)*: How 'BOUT Saul?

PEREZ: He's out arresting all those Christians. I guess he's discovered an eleventh commandment—Thou shalt not think.

(AUDIENCE laughs loudly.)

PEREZ: Thank you. We'll be right back with the rest of the show, including the truly amazing magical wizardry of Simon, the Sorcerer! Stay tuned.

AZARIAH: And now, a special word from our new sponsor, Sylvan's Water. Are you tired of having to travel every day to Jacob's Well to draw fresh water? Well, you're about to receive the best news you've heard since Babylon took Israel into captivity. Sylvan's special caravan will travel to the well, draw the water and deliver it right to your door. Don't wait! Call Sylvan today! And now, back to the show.

(AUDIENCE cheers.)

PEREZ: Thank you. Thank you. We've got a great show today, so let's get right to it. Here's a man we've all seen before. He's wowed you in the streets! He's dazzled you in the high places! The man known far and wide as "The Great Power of God!"—Simon, the Sorcerer!

(AUDIENCE cheers as SIMON enters.)

PEREZ: Welcome to the show.

SIMON: Thank you. It's a pleasure to be here.

PEREZ: I know you've got lots of magic to show us, but first, let's talk a bit.

SIMON: Actually, I don't have any magic to show.

PEREZ: Always the kidder. So, what's happening in the life of the sorcerer?

SIMON: I don't call myself a sorcerer any more.

PEREZ: OK, then. What's happening in the life of "The Great Power of God?"

SIMON: I don't use that title any more, either.

PEREZ: OK, then. What do you call yourself?

SIMON: A believer.

AZARIAH: Not very catchy. "Simon, the Believer!" If I were you, I'd change back.

SIMON: But I don't want to change back. I prefer being a believer.

PEREZ: Tell us about this believer bit. What kind of believer?

SIMON: A believer in the Lord Jesus Christ.

PEREZ: That Israelite heresy?

SIMON: It's not Israelite and it's not heresy. It's truth for all people.

PEREZ: How does an intelligent magician like yourself allow himself to be fooled by something that comes out of Judea? Or Galilee, of all places.

SIMON: Because this isn't something foolish.

PEREZ: How can you say that? If you're a believer living in Jerusalem, you could be killed. It sounds foolish to believe something that could get you killed.

SIMON: It is foolish to believe lies. Intelligence believes the truth.

PEREZ: But you're a magician. A great man.

SIMON: I WAS a fraud. A fake. All of my magic was nothing more than tricks. But I heard about a man named Philip, one who performed miracles. So I went to see what the competition was doing.

PEREZ: And what was this Philip doing?

SIMON: Real miracles. Healing the sick. Casting out unclean spirits.

PEREZ: If he's doing all that, why haven't I heard about him?

AZARIAH: We tried to get him on the show, but he wouldn't come and perform his magic for us.

SIMON: He doesn't perform magic. He works miracles by the power of the Lord Jesus Christ. Not for applause. Not for fame. But for the glory and honor of God.

PEREZ: Why would someone waste great talents like that?

SIMON: That's what I wanted to know. So I went to see what he did and how he did it. That's when I discovered he doesn't do tricks. He uses the power of the true God to perform miracles. That made me a believer and I was baptized.

PEREZ: This is great! I thought we were going to see some of your magic tricks. But, if you've been baptized and believe, then you can actually do miracles here for us! What do you say, audience? Do you want to see a miracle?

AUDIENCE *(cheering loudly)*: Yes! Yes!

SIMON: We don't do miracles so that people will be entertained. Only so that God will be glorified.

PEREZ: C'mon. Show us a miracle. We'll double your fee.

SIMON *(shaking his head)*: You're just the same as I used to be. I thought that money could buy everything. But I was wrong.

AZARIAH: For a real miracle, we'll triple your fee.

SIMON: You don't understand. God's power is not for sale. I thought it was. But I was wrong.

PEREZ: We'll quadruple your fee. But that's our last offer.

SIMON: But you can't buy God's power. I learned that from Peter.

PEREZ: Who's Peter?

AZARIAH: A rabbit, isn't he?

SIMON: No, the apostle Peter.

PEREZ: I've never heard of him.

SIMON: He was one of the twelve who followed Jesus. When he heard that people in Samaria were being baptized and believing in Jesus, he and John came to help. I saw them pray that the new believers would be filled with the Holy Spirit.

PEREZ: What's so special about that?

SIMON: It's more proof that this is real. Magicians never tell anybody how they do a trick. They guard their secrets. But the apostles want all believers to have the power of the Holy Spirit to help them in their faith. I watched as Peter and John prayed for the new believers, and I saw them filled with the Holy Spirit!

PEREZ: Wait a minute. These apostles are Jews. The Jews hate Samaritans. Why would they want Samaritans to have anything good? Maybe it's some kind of a trick.

SIMON: It's no trick. I lived with tricks all my life. This is real. This is the gospel, the good news for all people. I saw the power that Peter and John had, and I knew it was far more than my own. So I asked them, how much? How much to give people the Holy Spirit?

PEREZ: And how much was it?

SIMON: That's when I learned that God is not for sale. Peter told me, "You can't purchase God's gift! You're still in sin and can't be a part of the believers because you treasure money more than God."

PEREZ: Then how can you call yourself a believer?

SIMON: Because Peter told me to pray, to ask God to forgive my greed. And he helped me. He prayed with me. And God forgave my sin. That's the good news of Jesus Christ—that God loves us and wants to forgive our sins. Not just the Jews' sins, but everybody's.

PEREZ: Interesting story. But we're almost out of time. We do have enough left for one bit of magic. How about it, Simon? Show us one of your old tricks—a bit of the old Simon, "The Great Power of God."

SIMON: You haven't heard a word I said. I am not the great power of God. I never was. The great power of God is His love for us, a love that would surrender His only Son, Jesus Christ, to die for us on the cross...

PEREZ: Well, that's the show for tonight, folks. Sorry that there wasn't any magic, but tomorrow's show will more than make up for it: singers, dancers and jugglers. See you tomorrow, same time, same place.

The Bully

SCRIPTURE: Acts 9:1-31

SUGGESTED TOPICS: Trust; Christian life; prejudice; courage under persecution

BIBLE BACKGROUND

Everyone has met a bully. Everyone has known an enemy, someone who was tougher and meaner than everybody else. How would you react to meeting that person years later? If that person claimed to have changed, would you believe it?

That was the dilemma that faced the followers of Jesus in Damascus and then in Jerusalem. Saul was a notorious enemy of the believers. He had been instrumental in the murder of Stephen and was threatening a similar fate for any other followers of the Lord. Who could believe that such a man could change? Who could believe that this specific man had changed?

PERFORMANCE TIPS

1. Suggested props: baseball hats and gloves, baseball, chewing gum.
2. Doug and Joe chew gum and play catch during the skit.

DISCUSSION QUESTIONS

1. If you were Doug or Joe, would you believe Tough Tony had changed? Why or why not?
2. When Saul became a Christian, the believers in Jerusalem were afraid of him because of his past hatred of Jesus' followers. What does Acts 9:26-28 say about the way Barnabas helped Saul?
3. What does Galatians 6:10 say about the way we should treat others?

THE BULLY

CHARACTERS

DOUG
JOE
BARNEY
TONY

DOUG: Did you hear the news?
JOE: What news?
DOUG: Tough Tony.
JOE: What about him? He moved away. We don't have to worry about him.
DOUG: Oh, yeah? He's back.
JOE: He CAN'T be back!
DOUG: Well, he is.
JOE: And just when things were starting to settle down.
DOUG: I heard that he changed. He's not a bully anymore.
JOE: Sure. Like cows fly.
DOUG: Maybe he did change.
JOE: No way. People like Tony don't change.
DOUG: You're right. Now his gang has a leader again.
JOE: And I was just getting used to not looking over my shoulder all the time.
DOUG: They'll be stealing everything we have.
JOE: Maybe we can avoid him.
DOUG: Yeah, right.

(BARNEY enters with TOUGH TONY.)

BARNEY: Hi, guys.
JOE: Hi, Barn—
DOUG: Barney! What are you doing with him?
BARNEY: Guys, meet my friend, Tony.
TONY: Hi, guys.
JOE: Barney! Are you crazy? Why'd you bring Tough Tony here?
BARNEY: His name's not Tough Tony.
TONY: It's just Tony, now.
DOUG: Right. Well, we don't want him here. You know what he did to us before.
BARNEY: But that was before. He's different now.
JOE: Oh, yeah! How? Is he only going to beat us up every other day instead of every day?
TONY. Honest, guys—I've changed. I'm not the same as I was before.

BARNEY: Listen, guys. Tony has changed. And he wants to be friends with us.

DOUG: Well, we don't want to be friends with him.

JOE: Yeah. How do we know he's changed?

TONY: I really have changed.

JOE: No way. Once a bully, always a bully.

BARNEY: But he has changed. When he moved to the other side of town, he met some new friends. And they invited him to Sunday School with them. Now, he's different.

DOUG: Come off it, Barney! Sunday School doesn't change people.

BARNEY: Sure it does.

TONY: No, he's right, Barney. Sunday School doesn't change people.

BARNEY: What?

JOE: See, I told you. He's just pretending.

TONY: Sunday School doesn't change people. But Jesus does.

DOUG: What are you talking about?

TONY: I met Jesus.

JOE: Right! Jesus died a long time ago. He's history.

BARNEY: Joe, I thought you were a Christian.

DOUG: Sure he is. We both are.

BARNEY: Well, you don't talk like you are.

JOE: What do you mean?

BARNEY: Jesus is alive.

DOUG: Well, yeah. But you don't meet Him.

BARNEY: Maybe you don't. But you can—you can pray.

DOUG: Maybe. But Jesus doesn't talk to people today.

TONY: You're wrong, Doug. Jesus spoke to me.

JOE: Prove it. How did Jesus speak to you?

TONY: He used a Sunday School teacher—a man who used to be a gang leader.

BARNEY: And now, Tony knows Jesus. And he's changed.

TONY: Please, guys. I'm sorry for all the stuff I did before. Please forgive me and let me be your friend.

JOE: We'll think about it.

DOUG: But don't hold your breath.

JOE: Yeah! We're not sure about you. *(JOE and DOUG exit.)*

TONY: How can I make them believe me?

BARNEY: It may take awhile, but together, we'll convince them. I'll tell them what you've done. You'll have to show them by the way you live. Hey! I'll ask Mom if you can come for supper tonight.

TONY: Great!

WITHOUT A PREACHER

SCRIPTURE: Acts 8:26-40

SUGGESTED TOPICS: Witnessing; prejudice; salvation is for all people

BIBLE BACKGROUND

Fleeing persecution in Jerusalem and Judea, the Christians moved into Samaria and began preaching Jesus to the Samaritans. In the midst of this exciting time, Philip was called by God to leave the city and go out into the desert. There, in the middle of nowhere, Philip encountered a black man who was traveling home to Ethiopia. Using the words of the prophet, Isaiah, Philip introduced the man to Jesus. Now the Word was spread into Africa, for the black man was none other than the treasurer of the court of Candace, queen of Ethiopia. Acts 8 shows us that God intends to be God of all people—not only the Jews, not only the Samaritans, but all people.

PERFORMANCE TIPS

1. Suggested props: several books, a Bible and bookmark.
2. Either before or during the skit when the Bible passage is mentioned, read Isaiah 53:7,8.
3. The nationality of the people playing the parts of Malcolm and Phil is unimportant. If you have a mixed ethnic group, you might ask a Caucasian to play the part of Malcolm and someone of another race to play the part of Phil.

DISCUSSION QUESTIONS

1. In the skit, Malcolm is unsure about the beliefs of his religion. Why is it important to know what you believe?
2. What does 1 Peter 3:15 say you should be ready to do? How can you better prepare yourself to explain your beliefs to others?
3. Do you agree or disagree with the statement, "It's not important what you believe. It's only important that you believe something." Why or why not?
4. If you are a Christian, should you be friends with someone who isn't? Why or why not?

WITHOUT A PREACHER

CHARACTERS

PHIL
MALCOLM

SCENE ONE

PHIL: Hey, Malcolm!

MALCOLM: What? Oh. Hi, Phil.

PHIL: Where are you going?

MALCOLM: Just to the store. Errand for Mom. What about you?

PHIL: I'm off to the library. Have to return these books before the holiday. By the way, Happy Easter.

MALCOLM: What?

PHIL: Happy Easter. This Sunday. Easter. Remember?

MALCOLM: Easter! *(Sneers.)* White man's religion.

PHIL: What do you mean?

MALCOLM: Christianity! It only works for whites.

PHIL: You don't really mean that.

MALCOLM: I sure do.

PHIL: Then what do you believe?

MALCOLM: Islam. That's the belief of my people.

PHIL: We have got to talk. But I have to get these books returned and you have to get your Mom's groceries. Could I come over to your place tonight so we can talk?

MALCOLM: You mean so you can shove the Bible down my throat. No thanks. Besides, I have to baby-sit my kid sister tonight.

PHIL: I like kids. How about if I help? And we can talk, not argue.

MALCOLM: Well, I guess so. But I won't change my mind.

(Skit continues on next page.)

SCENE TWO

MALCOLM: I figured you'd bring your Bible.

PHIL: Of course. How else can I show you what I believe? And why.

MALCOLM: I suppose. But you won't get me believing white man's religion.

PHIL: Why do you call Christianity "white man's religion"?

MALCOLM: Because it is. Islam is the religion for blacks.

PHIL: But they both started in the same part of the world.

MALCOLM: What are you talking about?

PHIL: Who started Islam?

MALCOLM: Mohammed. The great prophet.

PHIL: And he was an Arab. From the Middle East. Christianity grew out of Judaism, also from the Middle East. So they're both Middle Eastern religions if that's how you judge.

MALCOLM: Well, Islam is for blacks and Christianity for whites.

PHIL: Can I show you something from this book?

MALCOLM: Why should I believe anything from it?

PHIL: Because it's from the prophet, Isaiah.

MALCOLM: So?

PHIL: Islam recognizes Isaiah as a prophet.

MALCOLM: It does?

PHIL: Yes. I thought you knew about Islam?

MALCOLM: Well, I'm kind of new. I don't know everything yet.

PHIL: Look at chapter fifty-three. What do you think it means?

MALCOLM: *(Reads chapter silently.)* I don't know. Sounds like somebody's being oppressed. Who? The prophet or somebody else?

PHIL: Somebody else asked the same question. A black man.

MALCOLM: What black man?

PHIL: Let's look at the book of Acts.

MALCOLM: White man's book.

PHIL: No, it's a book for everybody. And it shows who asked the question. Look in chapter eight, verse thirty-four.

MALCOLM: So. He asked the same question. Why do you say he was black?

PHIL: Look back a few verses. Who was he?

MALCOLM: An Ethiopian.

PHIL: Right. So let's look back at the prophet.

MALCOLM: OK. So who is the prophet talking about?

PHIL: He's talking about Jesus.

MALCOLM: No way. I may not know a lot, but I know Jesus wasn't even born then.

PHIL: But the prophet was talking about the future. Prophets do that, if they're true prophets.

MALCOLM: You expect me to believe that?

PHIL: Islam believes it.

MALCOLM: OK, then. How do you know it means Jesus?

PHIL: Because He fits the description perfectly.

MALCOLM *(scornfully)*: Yeah? Prove it.

PHIL: You see the first part of the chapter? A man despised, rejected, someone not held in esteem.

MALCOLM: Sounds like a black man gettin' dumped on.

PHIL: Or a Galilean.

MALCOLM: Huh?

PHIL: Jesus came from Galilee. And He knew about prejudice.

MALCOLM: How? He was a Jew living in Israel.

PHIL: But Galileans were looked down on by the rest of Israel. Other Jews thought that they were second-class citizens, not very bright. See, prejudice isn't new. It's existed for centuries.

MALCOLM: So, people were prejudiced against Him. So what?

PHIL: So, when He was crucified, all His friends ran away. Left Him to face punishment alone.

MALCOLM: His friends deserted Him?

PHIL: They sure did. But read on.

MALCOLM: It says we thought He was being punished by God.

PHIL: Which is exactly why Jesus was found guilty by the Jewish court. They believed that He was a blasphemer.

MALCOLM: What's that?

PHIL: In Jesus' case, someone who claims to be God. And under Jewish law, God says that blasphemers are to be put to death.

MALCOLM: That sounds rough.

PHIL: But look at the rest of the chapter. Why was He bruised, wounded and oppressed?

MALCOLM: It says He was killed because of us?

PHIL: That's right. He was killed because people—all people—had sinned. Not just white people or black people. Not just one nation. But all people.

MALCOLM: But that's not fair.

PHIL: True. But it IS loving. Look closely at verse seven. He didn't try to defend Himself. He accepted our punishment. Not because He was guilty, but because He knew the only way to save us was to pay the price for our guilt Himself.

MALCOLM: Why would He do that?

PHIL: Because God loves ALL His people. Regardless of race or skin color or nationality. God wants people to have the best life they can. But sin blocks people from God's love. So God took the punishment Himself.

MALCOLM: Wait a minute. You're trying to trick me. Why should I believe that Jesus is God? Only Christians believe that.

PHIL: You should believe Jesus' words, because Islam recognizes Jesus as a prophet.

MALCOLM: It does?

PHIL: Yes. Are you sure you believe in Islam? You don't seem to know a lot about it.

MALCOLM: I told you I'm new at it.

PHIL: True. Tell you what. You read what Jesus said about Himself and we can talk again.

MALCOLM: You leaving?

PHIL: Yeah, you can use some time to think abut Jesus' words. We'll talk about it again. I'll leave my Bible for you to read. In the meantime, Happy Easter.

MALCOLM: Yeah. You, too. Bye.

THE GENTILES, TOO?

SCRIPTURE: Acts 10

SUGGESTED TOPICS: Salvation for all people; prejudice; witnessing; obedience in trust

BIBLE BACKGROUND

Jesus' last command to His disciples, the Great Commission, was to go into all the world and preach the good news. How could the disciples truly understand the commission? All their lives they had been taught how God loved His chosen people, Israel, and hated all others.

Between Philip (see Acts 8) and Peter, the process had begun. Philip needed a message from an angel and the prompting of the Spirit to nudge him to approach the Ethiopian. Still, Philip saw that the man was heading south from Jerusalem and was reading from the prophet, Isaiah. Likely, the man was a proselyte, one whose nationality was not Hebrew but who had converted to the Jewish faith.

Peter also needed encouragement from God to go to Cornelius. Here was a man who was not only a Gentile but a Roman centurion. Although he was a devout and generous man, there were massive cultural barriers which would keep Peter from entering this man's house. To prepare Peter for the invitation from Cornelius, God had to tell Peter three times not to call unclean that which God has cleansed. Lest we judge Peter too harshly for needing to hear this message three times, we should recognize that he had already shown acceptance of Gentiles. A tanner treated the skins of dead animals and was thus rendered "unclean" according to Jewish law. By staying with Simon the tanner, Peter stretched the narrow limits of traditional Jewish practice.

PERFORMANCE TIPS

1. Suggested props: Bible-times costumes.

2. Before the skit, be certain the group understands how much the Jews hated the Gentiles. Ask your group to think of contemporary examples of prejudice toward others.

3. Introduce the skit by saying, "This skit refers to Jewish food laws given in Leviticus 11. Certain foods, such as meat from pigs, were considered unclean. The Jews were not to eat these foods. Other foods, such as meat from cows, were considered clean. The Jews were allowed to eat these foods. Many of these regulations made good sense for maintaining health. But, mainly, they taught God's people obedience and reminded them that they belonged to God. Listen to the skit to find how God used the examples of clean and unclean foods to teach Peter about God's love for all people."

4. Members of your group may enjoy writing and acting out an additional scene for this skit. Read the story of Peter's defense of his actions in Acts 11:1-18. Several members in the group may play the part of prosecutors, questioning Peter about his actions.

DISCUSSION QUESTIONS

1. Why do you think God gave food laws in the Old Testament?

2. What should our attitudes be toward people who are different from us?

3. In what ways can you show God's love to people who are not like you?

THE GENTILES, TOO?

CHARACTERS

PETER
SIMON
CORNELIUS

SCENE ONE

PETER: Simon, I thank you for your hospitality. But I must leave now. I have to go to Caesarea to the house of a Gentile.

SIMON: Is that wise, Peter?

PETER: Of course. Do I look like the type who would do something foolish?

SIMON: Sorry, Peter. But you know that some people do not understand how you have stayed at my house.

PETER: How so?

SIMON: I'm a tanner. I make my living tanning and preserving the hides of animals. That makes me ceremonially unclean and many people will have nothing to do with me except when they have to.

PETER: I realize that.

SIMON: Still, you accepted my invitation to stay at my home and have been with me for many days.

PETER: Why not? You are a follower of Jesus, just as I am. And I believe the Gentile I am going to visit also wants to learn of Jesus.

SIMON: But, Peter! To enter a Gentile's house is forbidden by law.

PETER: Whose law forbids it?

SIMON: You know very well, Peter. Our law.

PETER: An hour ago, I would have agreed with you. But something strange happened upstairs.

SIMON: Tell me.

PETER: It was just about noon. I was feeling a bit hungry and thinking about coming down for a bite to eat when, suddenly, I saw a vision.

SIMON: You're sure it was a vision. Not a hallucination from hunger?

PETER: It was definitely a vision. I saw a sheet, coming down from heaven, filled with all kinds of unclean animals, reptiles and birds.

SIMON: You're sure this is a vision?

PETER: Yes. And I heard a voice saying, "Rise, Peter, kill and eat."

SIMON: What did you make of it?

PETER: I knew that God was testing my faithfulness. I knew the answer and I gave it. I replied, "No, Lord. For I have never eaten any unclean thing."

SIMON: Good answer. I knew you knew the law.

PETER: But the voice answered me. It said, "Do not call anything unclean that God has cleaned." This happened a second time, and I protested again that the animals were unclean. And again the voice said, "Do not call anything unclean that God has cleaned." And it happened a third time. After the third time, the sheet was pulled up into heaven again.

SIMON: What can be the meaning of this vision?

PETER: That's what I wondered. I sat, thinking about the vision, when the Holy Spirit told me three men were looking for me and I was to go with them. The Holy Spirit said He had sent them to me.

SIMON: The Holy Spirit told you about three men? The three men who came to the house? The Roman soldier and two servants.

PETER: Right.

SIMON: They are servants of a Gentile.

PETER: Right.

SIMON: Not only a Gentile, but a Roman centurion. The enemy.

PETER: Right.

SIMON: But he is a Gentile. He is unclean.

PETER: Simon, do not call unclean that which God has cleaned.

SIMON: I see. The vision was talking about people, not animals.

PETER: Now you understand, also. That is what God was telling me with the sheet from heaven. So I must leave you now and go to see what this man, Cornelius, wants.

SIMON: But suppose some of the others come to ask for you. What shall I tell them?

PETER: The truth. Tell them I have gone to visit a Gentile.

SIMON: But, Peter! They won't understand.

PETER: Perhaps not. But I must obey God, not men. Farewell, my friend. I'll see you on my return. Thank you again for all your hospitality.

(Skit continues on next page.)

SCENE TWO

PETER: So this is the house of Cornelius. I wonder what he wants.

CORNELIUS: *(Falls on his knees.)* My Lord and Master.

PETER: Please get up. I am only a man.

CORNELIUS: Thank you for coming.

PETER: You're welcome. But why did you send for me?

CORNELIUS: I'm not sure.

PETER: What? You, a centurion, a leader of men—you don't know your own actions and thoughts?

CORNELIUS: Let me explain.

PETER: Please do.

CORNELIUS: I was praying...

PETER: To which of the Roman gods?

CORNELIUS: To the God of Israel. I have been here many years and I know that He is the only true God.

PETER: You speak wisely. What happened while you were praying?

CORNELIUS: I had a vision!

PETER: You, too?

CORNELIUS: What?

PETER: Nothing. Please continue.

CORNELIUS: In the vision, I saw an angel of God. The angel told me God had heard my prayers and had seen my charitable works. Then, he told me to send men to Joppa to find a man named Peter. He told me this man would be at the house of Simon, the tanner. You are this man? Peter?

PETER: I am he.

CORNELIUS: Then tell me what to do. The angel said you would.

PETER: For years, I believed God only loved the Israelites. Now I see how wrong I was. I see that God accepts people of all nations who believe in Him. You truly believe?

CORNELIUS: You know I do.

PETER: Yes. I have eyes. You know a little of the love and power of God. God has sent me here to tell you the rest.

CORNELIUS: Please, tell us more. We must hear the rest.

PETER: God anointed Jesus of Nazareth with the Holy Spirit to do good and to heal those who were oppressed by the devil. I am a witness of all that He did and said.

CORNELIUS: I have heard of this man. He was executed.

PETER: He was wrongly judged and executed. He died the death of a criminal. But He is no longer dead. God has raised Him to life. He appeared openly to myself and many others.

CORNELIUS: How can this be? Surely, when a man is dead, he is dead?

PETER: Jesus is no ordinary man. He is God in human flesh. He is the One of whom all the prophets spoke, the One who forgives all sins of those who believe in Him.

CORNELIUS: I believe. And all my household. We all believe.

PETER: Can this be? The Holy Spirit has descended upon this household in the same way He came to us in the Upper Room at Pentecost. You who have come with me, you see these Gentiles have received the Holy Spirit. Can we refuse to baptize with water those whom God has baptized with the Holy Spirit? Come, Cornelius, be baptized in the name of the Lord.

CORNELIUS: We shall. And you must stay. Tell us more about Jesus.

PETER: I will. But what will I tell those in Jerusalem when they ask about this thing? The truth. I shall tell them what has happened. If they don't believe me, God will have to give them a vision, also.

FREE!

SCRIPTURE: Acts 12:1-17

SUGGESTED TOPICS: God answers prayer; early church

BIBLE BACKGROUND

The Church continued to grow, much to the annoyance of the Jewish leaders. Fortunately for them, they had an ally in the latest Herod. Herod Agrippa I, grandson of Herod the Great, seemed to believe the best way to rule was to appease the Jewish leaders. Many believers were arrested on his orders and he even had James, the brother of John, executed by the sword. His next step was to have Peter imprisoned, intending to have Peter brought to a public trial in the near future.

Peter would have been not long for this world, if Herod had his way. Long-term imprisonment was not a normal practice under Roman law. There were better forms of punishment: execution, scourging, sentencing to the galleys. In Peter's case, judging from Herod's actions in dealing with James, execution was the most likely outcome.

Not only Peter, but all the other believers, must have realized this. Hence, prayer was made for Peter without ceasing (see Acts 12:5). On the very eve of Peter's intended trial, God intervened. Somewhat humorously, we find that those who faithfully gathered to pray were unprepared to accept the answer to those prayers.

PERFORMANCE TIPS

1. Before the skit, read or summarize Acts 12:1-11 which tells the story of Peter's arrest and miraculous escape from prison. Also read Acts 12:19 to find out what happened in Roman times to soldiers who allowed a prisoner to escape.

2. Arrange the skit performers so that a door is nearby. The skit should begin with the sound of Peter knocking on the closed door.

DISCUSSION QUESTIONS

1. Why is it important for Christians to pray?

2. When have you felt that God didn't hear your prayers? What could you do if you become discouraged in praying?

3. We are told in 1 Thessalonians 5:17 to "pray continually." What does it mean to pray continually? How would you say this verse in your own words?

4. What are some things you can talk to God about?

FREE!

CHARACTERS

MARY
RHODA
PETER

MARY: Who's knocking at the door? We're trying to pray. Rhoda, go and see who it is. But be careful. If it's Roman soldiers, don't let them in. We don't want to be arrested.

RHODA: Yes, ma'am.

MARY: Now then, let's continue. Oh Lord, grant our request to keep Peter safe. Preserve him from Herod and from the evil...

RHODA: Mary, Mary, Mary...

MARY: What is the matter with you, girl? Can't you see we're praying? Be quiet.

RHODA: But, but, but...

MARY: Stop stuttering and either join us in praying for Peter or go about your chores.

RHODA: But it's Peter.

MARY: Yes. We're all sad about Peter. But we'll continue to pray...

RHODA: No! At the door! It's Peter!

MARY: What are you talking about? Peter's in prison. We've been praying for his safety all evening.

RHODA: No! He's at the door. He spoke to me. I recognized his voice.

MARY: Nonsense! You're a silly girl. If he were here, he would come in. And why is someone still knocking at the door?

RHODA: Oh! I forgot to open the door. *(Runs out.)*

MARY: I don't know why I put up with the girl. She's always imagining things...

PETER: Friends!

MARY: Peter! You're here! But you're in prison! I mean, you're supposed to be in prison. No, no. I don't mean you're supposed to be there. I mean, you are there. Herod arrested you.

PETER: I was in jail. God heard your prayers and sent an angel who brought me out. I'll tell you what happened, but then, I'll have to leave. It wouldn't be safe for you if I stayed here. After I've gone, send someone to tell James and the other believers.

Paphos by Night

SCRIPTURE: Acts 13:1-12

SUGGESTED TOPICS: Respect; acts of the early church; spreading the gospel

BIBLE BACKGROUND

Much had happened since the ascension of the Lord. The believers began preaching in Jerusalem, converting thousands to faith in Jesus Christ as the Jewish Messiah and Savior of all. Vexed by the success of this preaching, the religious leaders began persecuting the new church, culminating in the death of Stephen. This persecution drove many believers from Jerusalem to the surrounding countryside of Judea and into Samaria. From Samaria, Philip was led by the Lord into the desert where he met an influential Ethiopian on his way home. Philip proclaimed the gospel to the Ethiopian, helping to spread the good news into Africa.

Completely angered by the spread of this message, Saul, a devout Pharisee from Tarsus, received permission from the high priest to pursue his persecution of the Church to Damascus. On the way, however, Saul met the Lord and was converted. Although the message of Christ had spread widely, it was still being preached only to Jews and Samaritans, who were half-Jewish. Peter changed that when he journeyed to Caesarea to present the good news to Cornelius, a Roman centurion.

Herod Agrippa, Herod the Great's grandson, seeking the favor of the Jews, began persecuting the Church with renewed vigor in Jerusalem. In response, the Church began to expand its missionary vision through Barnabas and Saul who were sent from the church in Antioch to Cyprus, Barnabas' original home.

A crucial encounter occurred on the island of Cyprus. Saul confronted a sorcerer in the presence of the Roman governor, Sergius Paulus. This dramatic moment was Saul's first declaration of the good news before a Gentile. As a result, the governor believed, and from this point on, Saul is referred to by his Roman, Hellenistic name, Paul, indicating the beginning of Paul's great ministry beyond the confines of Judaism.

As a Roman governor, Sergius Paulus' job was not filled with security. Should a rumor of his infidelity to the emperor (Claudius) reach the ears of Rome and be believed, the governor would be recalled immediately, possibly at the cost of his life. How would Rome respond to the news that one of its proconsuls had embraced the Christian faith? Certainly, he would now refuse to join in the worship of the emperor as a god. That could be considered disloyalty and ultimately treason.

PERFORMANCE TIPS

1. Suggested props: table and chairs arranged for a talk show.

2. Marcus Hamus is an intelligent individual who sees the danger of Sergius Paulus' words about his conversion to Christianity. As the skit progresses, Marcus should show increasing concern for Sergius Paulus by his facial expression and gestures.

3. Flavius should be portrayed as dense, but eager to hear about new ideas.

4. Paul and Barnabas do not insult anyone. Rather, they show respect to all persons when they speak.

5. Introduce the skit by reading Acts 13:1,2 aloud. After the skit, briefly summarize Acts 13:13-52 telling of Paul and Barnabas' journey into Pisidian Antioch and the results of their preaching to the Jews in that city.

DISCUSSION QUESTIONS

1. Why do you think Elymas didn't appear on the talk show? Read Acts 13:6-12 to find the answer.

2. How would you describe the attitudes of Paul and Barnabas towards Sergius Paulus and the talk show hosts? Why did they act respectfully?

3. Would Sergius Paulus have listened to Paul and Barnabas if they began their conversation with him by saying, "Proconsul, the religion of Rome is false and you are stupid to believe it?" Why or why not?

4. Read Acts 13:14,15. What did Paul and Barnabas do when they first went into the Jewish synagogue? What might have happened if they had interrupted the worship service without being invited to speak?

5. Throughout their journey, Paul and Barnabas showed respect to the people they met. How can you show respect to the people you meet?

Paphos by Night

CHARACTERS

FLAVIUS (FLAY-vee-us)
MARCUS
SERGIUS (SER-jee-us)
PAUL
BARNABAS
AUDIENCE

PRONUNCIATION GUIDE

Antioch (AN-tee-ahk)
Elymas (EEL-ih-mus)
Iliad (IH-lee-ad)
Paphos (PAY-fos)
synagogue (SIN-a-gog)

FLAVIUS: Welcome to "Paphos by Night," the nighttime talk show that brings you interesting people from all over the world. Tonight's guest host is the well-known actor who has just finished a worldwide tour performing *The Iliad* to sellout crowds, Marcus Hamus! Marcus' guests tonight include sorcerer and prophet, Elymas; governor of the island of Cyprus, Sergius Paulus. Also two traveling preachers who caused quite a stir today: Paul and Barnabas! And now, here's Marcus! *(AUDIENCE applauds.)*

MARCUS: Thank you. What a terrific audience. It's great to be here in Paphos. Even though the audience response has been terrific wherever we've been, the best audience in the world is always right here in Paphos. *(AUDIENCE applauds.)* But we have a really packed show tonight, so let's get right to our first guest. I think it's safe to say that everyone here has heard of this man. He's the governor of Cyprus. Well known as a man of courage and great intelligence, here's Sergius Paulus! Welcome to the show. *(AUDIENCE applauds.)*

SERGIUS: Thank you, Marcus. It's good to be here. By the way, I caught your play when you were in Antioch, and I must say, you were brilliant.

MARCUS: Thank you, Sergius, that is indeed a compliment.

SERGIUS: It's not flattery, Marcus. I really mean it.

MARCUS: OK, any more of this and I'll think you're trying to borrow money from me. Anyway, I want to ask a few questions that I think will be interesting to everybody.

SERGIUS: Fire away, Marcus.

MARCUS: Sergius, how have you managed to gain such a reputation as an intelligent man?

SERGIUS: I'm not sure what you mean, Marcus. By being intelligent, perhaps?

MARCUS: Well, we all know that many people are given political appointments because of their family connections or to repay favors. You actually seem to be qualified to be a governor.

SERGIUS: I hope so. All I can say is I just try to do the best job I can each day.

MARCUS: C'mon! Level with us. Have you done something special to please the gods so they keep you looking smart?

SERGIUS: No, nothing at all. Particularly now.

MARCUS: What do you mean by that?

SERGIUS: By what?

MARCUS: You said, "Particularly now." Why particularly now?

SERGIUS: Well, until yesterday, I thought much the same as you. I believed there were many gods and you had to be sure not to get the wrong god upset on the wrong day or you were in big trouble. But I don't believe that anymore.

MARCUS: What? You don't believe—I haven't heard...I mean, I'm no theologian. I don't have any divinity degrees. But I would think that those who do would have made some kind of an announcement about such a major change, and I haven't heard anything. Have you, Flavius?

FLAVIUS: No, I sure haven't! Of course, I WAS out of town for a few days.

MARCUS: When did this big change come about, Sergius? And why didn't anyone tell me about it?

SERGIUS: I didn't say there was an official change in Roman religious policy, Marcus. I said that I no longer believe there are many gods. I no longer believe that I must appease many gods in order to have a good day and a prosperous life.

FLAVIUS: Excuse me for interrupting, Marcus. I know you're the host but I just want to be sure I understand what Sergius is saying. Are you speaking against official Roman religious policy?

SERGIUS: Well, I guess I am, Flavius.

MARCUS: Wow! This is something! I've never heard an important official disagree with official Roman policy before.

SERGIUS: Religious freedom is allowed in the Roman Empire, Marcus. I thought you traveled throughout the world. Surely you've seen various religious practices in your travels.

MARCUS: Sure I have. But never by a governor or a deputy or any other important official before. Maybe we'd better stop right now before we get you removed from office. This would be a good time to bring out Elymas to show us some of his astounding magic.

SERGIUS: Thank you for your consideration, Marcus, but I don't think that Elymas is going to be able to make it tonight.

FLAVIUS: I think he's right, Marcus. I just checked with the director, and Elymas isn't here yet.

MARCUS: You are truly amazing, Sergius. Have you gone into the prophecy business, too?

SERGIUS: No. But Elymas was partly responsible for my change of heart regarding my religious practices.

MARCUS: Enough said, Sergius. We're trying to save your job, remember? Well, we still have the two wandering preachers waiting to come out. They're still here, aren't they, Flavius?

FLAVIUS: Oh, yes, they're here.

MARCUS: Good. OK, let's welcome these preachers, Paul and Barnabas!

PAUL: Hello, Marcus.

BARNABAS: And thanks for inviting us.

MARCUS: Paul and Barnabas? Those are unusual names to be linked together. Roman and Jewish, aren't they? I thought Roman and Jewish religion were miles apart in their doctrine.

PAUL: Absolutely. As far as the heavens are from the ocean depths.

BARNABAS: As far as the East is from the West.

MARCUS: Then how is it that you, Paul, are traveling with a Jew?

PAUL: There's really nothing unusual about it. You see, I'm Jewish. I just go by my Roman name.

MARCUS: Then you and Barnabas are actually two Jews, going around preaching together. You ARE Jewish I hope, Barnabas? You're not an Egyptian going by his Jewish name?

BARNABAS: No, I'm Jewish. Although I was born here in Cyprus.

MARCUS: Good! Then we've got that straight. Oh, I'm sorry. I don't know what has happened to my manners. I forgot to introduce you to Sergius Paulus.

PAUL: That's perfectly alright. We've met before.

BARNABAS: We sure have. How are you doing, sir?

SERGIUS: Very well, thank you.

MARCUS: Now this is perplexing. How is it that two Jewish preachers know a Roman governor?

SERGIUS: They were preaching in Paphos. They're the reason I no longer believe in many Roman gods.

MARCUS: Everything I hear confuses me more and more. What were you doing in a Jewish synagogue, Sergius? How could that possibly relate to your job as governor of Cyprus?

SERGIUS: I didn't hear them in a synagogue.

MARCUS: But I thought Jewish preachers spoke in synagogues. Isn't that right?

BARNABAS: We did speak in the synagogue. We always speak in the synagogue.

PAUL: But Sergius Paulus wanted to hear us and asked us to visit him.

MARCUS: I don't understand this. Sergius, why would you want to hear these itinerant preachers?

SERGIUS: Part of my job as governor is to keep the peace. If there is any new idea being spoken in my country, I should know what it is.

FLAVIUS: I hate to keep butting in, but since Marcus has his head in his hands and looks like he has a splitting headache, maybe I could ask the obvious question. Why did you have to ask Jewish preachers to come to see you? Jews haven't changed their teachings in all of recorded history. Didn't you already know what Jews believe?

SERGIUS: Certainly. I studied Jewish history and religion at Rome when I was learning how to be a governor. But these men were preaching something new.

PAUL: Actually, it's nothing new at all.

BARNABAS: In fact, it's the very foundation of Jewish faith.

PAUL: It's actually the fulfillment of all that was spoken by the prophets and written in the Scriptures.

BARNABAS: A fact that we try to point out to the worshipers in the synagogue when we speak to them.

SERGIUS: I was so impressed with what they said and did that I now believe in their God as the one and only true God, and in His Son, Jesus Christ. The One who is responsible for all prophecy and its fulfillment.

MARCUS: Oh, yes, I really do wish that Elymas could have been with us tonight. His act is truly worth seeing, but we're out of time. I want to thank my guests tonight—Sergius Paulus, Paul and Barnabas—for taking time out of their busy schedules to come and speak with us. Tune in tomorrow for another...uh, interesting show. Good night.

TROUBLEMAKERS

SCRIPTURE: Acts 17

SUGGESTED TOPICS: Respect; acts of the early church; spreading the gospel

BIBLE BACKGROUND

On his first missionary journey, Paul was accompanied by Barnabas and, for a short time, Barnabas' nephew, John Mark. Paul and Barnabas prepared to set out on a second journey, but they had a disagreement over whether or not to have John Mark accompany them a second time. So great was the disagreement that Paul and Barnabas went their separate ways; Barnabas took John Mark with him and set sail for Cyprus. Paul chose Silas and headed north through Cilicia. Apparently, they were also accompanied by Luke and Timothy.

The second missionary journey was filled with ups and downs. In Macedonia Paul and Silas were beaten and imprisoned for casting a demon out of a young girl (see Acts 16:16-24). Through a miracle of God, they were released from prison but were told to leave the city. The journey continued on to Thessalonica.

This skit assumes that, even though they were not alone, Paul and Silas were the two who created most of the uproar in Thessalonica. Timothy was still a young man and Luke seems to be more of a chronicler than a preacher.

PERFORMANCE TIPS

1. Suggested props: microphones, video camera.
2. Bring a map showing Paul's missionary journeys. Ask group members to locate the cities of Thessalonica, Berea and Athens and check the distances between these cities. Compare the distances to cities with which your group is familiar. Emphasize the great distances Paul walked in order to preach the gospel.
3. Carpus and Fortunatus have slightly longer passages than the other characters. If you are using these skits with children, ask two better readers to play these parts.

DISCUSSION QUESTIONS

1. Why might some of the Jews in Thessalonica have hated Paul and Silas? Read Acts 17:5 to check your answer. Why did Paul and Silas keep preaching in spite of the trouble they encountered?
2. Acts 17:16 says Paul was greatly upset when he saw Athens was full of idols. How does Paul begin his speech to the people of Athens? (Refer to Acts 17:22,23.) Why did Paul choose to preach that way?
3. What do you learn about witnessing to others from Paul's actions?

TROUBLEMAKERS

CHARACTERS

FORTUNATUS (for-choon-AH-tus)
CARPUS (KAR-pus)
TEMAN (TAY-mun)
OMAR
SOPETER
DIONYSIUS (dye-uh-NIH-see-us)

PRONUNCIATION GUIDE

Babylon (BAB-ih-lon)
Berea (buh-REE-uh)
blasphemers (BLAS-fee-murs)
blasphemy (BLAS-fuh-mee)
synagogue (SIN-uh-gog)
Thessalonica (THESS-uh-low-NYE-kuh)

FORTUNATUS: Good evening. I'm Fortunatus and this is Athens Radio News. Today's top story: "Have We Learned the Identity of the Unknown God?" With more from Mars' Hill, here's our roving reporter, Carpus.

CARPUS: Thank you, Fortunatus. Mars' Hill has been in an uproar today. A Roman citizen by the name of Paul claims to know the identity of "The Unknown God." As you all know, Athens contains magnificent temples to many gods. Just in case we might miss one, and, not wanting his wrath poured out on us, we've also erected a monument to an unknown god.

FORTUNATUS: A fact known by all our listeners, Carpus. But you say that a Roman claims to know the identity of the unknown god?

CARPUS: That's right. This man, Paul, spoke with the wise men of Athens today. I'm gathering firsthand reports from those who were there and I'll update you later in the broadcast.

FORTUNATUS: Thank you, Carpus. We'll be looking forward to that update. In other news, all is not well in Athens. We have information that a group of troublemakers may be on their way here. For more on this story, we go via satellite feed to Thessalonica. Teman and Omar, are you there?

TEMAN: We sure are.

OMAR: Ready and waiting.

FORTUNATUS: Gentlemen, I understand there has been some trouble for the Jewish community in Thessalonica.

TEMAN: Trouble? Four hundred years of slavery in Egypt was trouble.

OMAR: Being dragged off into captivity by Babylon was trouble.

TEMAN: The attempted wipeout of the Jews by Haman was trouble.

TEMAN and OMAR: This is SERIOUS.

FORTUNATUS: Please, tell us about it.

OMAR: It all started with these two blasphemers, Silas and Paul.

TEMAN: Paul is really the one to blame.

OMAR: He was just more vocal. Silas backed him up at every turn.

FORTUNATUS: Gentlemen...

TEMAN *(ignoring Fortunatus)***:** And let's not forget Jason.

OMAR: True! He should have known better.

FORTUNATUS: Gentlemen...

TEMAN *(ignoring Fortunatus)***:** But we sure showed him.

OMAR: We sure did. He won't help troublemakers again.

FORTUNATUS: GENTLEMEN!

TEMAN and OMAR: Yes?

FORTUNATUS: We seem to have lost track of the story. Perhaps if I ask a few questions, we can get this straightened out.

TEMAN: Ask away.

OMAR: Anything you want to know.

TEMAN: We've got nothing to hide.

OMAR: Always ready to help the press. That's us.

FORTUNATUS: Good. Now then, you mentioned two men by name. Troublemakers.

OMAR: Silas!

TEMAN: Paul!

FORTUNATUS: Those are the two. Just who are they?

OMAR: They claim to be Jews.

TEMAN: But they can't be.

OMAR: They've got no respect for our tradition.

TEMAN: Or the Torah.

FORTUNATUS: What exactly did they do?

OMAR: Oh, they were clever.

TEMAN: They came slinking into town.

OMAR: No they didn't.

TEMAN: Of course they did.

OMAR: No. They just walked straight in. They didn't slide down any stairs.

TEMAN: Not slinky. Slink-ING. Sneaking in.

OMAR: Oh. Right. Slinking in. That's how they came, alright.

FORTUNATUS: But what did they do?

TEMAN: What did they do? They nearly burned the city to the ground.

OMAR: They nearly turned our streets into piles of rubble.

FORTUNATUS: And how did two men do all this?

TEMAN: First, they came sneaking into the synagogue.

OMAR: And they pretended to know the Scriptures.

TEMAN: But they didn't.

OMAR: They just misquoted everything they could.

FORTUNATUS: I'm afraid I don't understand. How can talking in a synagogue create all this trouble?

TEMAN: It's all Paul's fault.

OMAR: And Silas, too.

TEMAN and OMAR: And Jason!

TEMAN: They said that Jesus is the Christ.

OMAR: They said the Christ had to suffer.

TEMAN: They said the Christ was killed.

OMAR: And that He was raised from the dead.

TEMAN and OMAR: Blasphemy!

FORTUNATUS: And how did this blasphemy nearly burn the city to the ground and turn the streets into piles of rubble?

TEMAN: Some of the Jews in the synagogue believed these blasphemers.

OMAR: This sort of thing cannot be tolerated.

TEMAN: So we got a mob—I mean, a group of concerned citizens together.

OMAR: And we stormed—I mean, we went to Jason's house.

TEMAN: And we kicked—I mean, we knocked on the door.

OMAR: And we dragged—I mean, we escorted Jason to the city officials.

TEMAN: And we yelled—I mean, we explained to the officials how Jason had harbored these criminal types in his house.

OMAR: And we screamed—I mean, we calmly showed the officials how these men were breaking the laws of Rome by claiming there was another king other than Caesar.

FORTUNATUS: So these men nearly caused a riot.

TEMAN: Nearly?

OMAR: Why, they would have destroyed the city had we not stopped them.

TEMAN: In fact, we chased them right out of the city.

OMAR: And made sure that Jason had to pay a large fine for his part in this sordid affair.

FORTUNATUS: But they're gone now. So all's well that ends well.

TEMAN: It's not all over.

OMAR: They went to Berea and tried to destroy that city, too.

TEMAN: But we heard about it.

OMAR: And marched in and stirred up trouble—I mean, we showed those ignorant Bereans the error of Paul and Silas' preaching.

TEMAN: But what can you expect from Bereans? You wouldn't believe how many of them believed these upstarts.

FORTUNATUS: Thank you for taking time out of your busy schedules to talk with us. Our satellite feed now takes us to Berea, where Sopeter can give us a firsthand account of the happenings in that city. Sopeter, welcome to Athens Radio News.

SOPETER: Thank you, Fortunatus.

FORTUNATUS: We've received reports about some troublemakers invading your city.

SOPETER: They sure have, and for no reason at all.

FORTUNATUS: Can you tell us what happened?

SOPETER: Certainly. Paul and Silas came to town...

FORTUNATUS: And tried to burn it to the ground?

SOPETER: No. Of course not. They came to visit, to come to the synagogue and speak with us. Together, we searched the Scriptures with them and learned many marvelous things about the law and the prophets and how they relate to Jesus the Christ.

FORTUNATUS: But you said they were troublemakers.

SOPETER: Not them. Some hotheads from Thessalonica were the troublemakers.

FORTUNATUS: I'm afraid I don't understand.

SOPETER: There was no trouble in Berea until some men from Thessalonica came into town and tried to convince us to lynch Paul and Silas. They caused so much trouble, we thought it best to send Paul away for his own safety.

FORTUNATUS: And where is Paul now?

SOPETER: Last I heard, he was headed your way.

FORTUNATUS: There you have it listeners, the probability that some Jewish troublemaker might be headed our way. I understand that Carpus has his update from Mars' Hill ready. Carpus?

CARPUS: Fortunatus, I'm here with Dionysius, the well-known philosopher. He was one of the men on Mars' Hill when this Roman, Paul, spoke about the unknown god.

DIONYSIUS: Actually, Paul is Jewish.

CARPUS: He is? Then why does he have a Roman name?

DIONYSIUS: Because he's a Roman citizen. But he's Jewish.

CARPUS: Can you tell us what Paul said on Mars' Hill today?

DIONYSIUS: Certainly. He spoke to us by saying that he noticed we were very devout men because we had so many monuments to the gods.

CARPUS: Perceptive enough.

DIONYSIUS: Yes. Then, he spoke to us about the unknown god. He told us that this was the God who made all things, the God who does not live in temples made with human hands.

CARPUS: Then this god would live on Mount Olympus.

DIONYSIUS: No. This God is not like other gods.

CARPUS: All gods are the same. Mostly.

DIONYSIUS: Not this one. His likeness cannot be made from gold or silver.

CARPUS: So this is a god of stone?

DIONYSIUS: No. This God's image cannot be fashioned from anything. This God creates; He cannot be created from men's work. He is the giver of all life and wants people to worship Him, not the idols we vainly set up.

CARPUS: This is all very strange. I don't understand any of it.

DIONYSIUS: The best is yet to come. He sent His Son to call people back to Him, but some people would not listen and put His Son to death.

CARPUS: And now He seeks revenge and will destroy us?

DIONYSIUS: No. This God is a loving God. He raised His Son from the dead.

CARPUS *(laughing)*: Wait! He raised Him from the dead?

DIONYSIUS: Many believe Paul. Others are interested. Others mock, as you do.

CARPUS: There you have it, Fortunatus. Some crazy Jew was on Mars' Hill trying to convince the wise men of Athens that there is a god who cares about people. And that the dead can come back to life. From Mars' Hill, this is Carpus.

FORTUNATUS: Sounds like some of those wise men have been out in the sun too long. That's the news for tonight. Next news, tomorrow at sunrise. For Athens Radio News, this is Fortunatus, saying good-night.

RIOT

SCRIPTURE: Acts 19:23-41

SUGGESTED TOPICS: Peer pressure; injustice; respect; gossip

BIBLE BACKGROUND

As Paul's preaching convinced more and more to follow the Way, jealousies were kindled in various people. Certain Jewish leaders saw their importance being diminished in the eyes of the Jews who believed. But some of Paul's fiercest enemies were those who saw their livelihoods slipping away before their eyes. The owners of the slave girl in Acts 16 accused Paul of breaking Roman law. The silversmith, Demetrius, in chapter 19, was more honest about his motives in wanting Paul stopped, and he started a riot in an attempt to achieve his ends. The mob scene which resulted is a typical display of mass hysteria in which people become incapable of rational, individual thought and become absorbed in the emotion of the crowd.

PERFORMANCE TIPS

1. Suggested props: video game cartridges or packages.
2. The entire group may participate in this skit as part of the mob. Point out the appropriate time in the script when the mob quiets down.
3. When the script calls for the mob to mutter, several lines are suggested. However, the mob may use other appropriate dialogue.

DISCUSSION QUESTIONS

1. Danny decided to use a mob to stop his business from failing. If you were Danny, would you have done the same thing? How else could you have handled the situation?
2. Danny wanted to stop the sale of computer games in order to increase the profits of his own business. But that's not what he told the crowd. Why not? What would have happened if he had told the crowd the truth?
3. Have there been any riots reported on the news recently? What was the cause of the riot? Were there any other reasons that may not have been obvious?
4. Read Acts 19:23-41. How are the characters of the skit and the people in this Bible event similar? When might someone like Demetrius exist in your school or community? What makes a mob so dangerous?

RIOT

CHARACTERS

DANNY
SHAWNA
MOB
AL
JOHN

DANNY: I can't understand it.

SHAWNA: What's wrong, Danny?

DANNY: I can't understand why business is so bad.

SHAWNA: I would have thought the reason was obvious.

DANNY: Well it's not obvious to me, Shawna. Explain it.

SHAWNA: What exactly do you sell?

DANNY: Video games. The best games in the world. Action-packed adventure. Excitement. All the thrills you can imagine.

SHAWNA: But sales are down.

DANNY: Yes. But why?

SHAWNA: Paul.

DANNY: Who's Paul?

SHAWNA: He's a computer game salesman. He's been going up and down the mall showing off his computer games.

DANNY: So what? Video games have been around a long time. What do I care about computer games?

SHAWNA: You had better care. He's selling them to all the computer outlets in the mall. He says they have better graphics, they're more intelligent. In short, he says they're better games.

DANNY: Nobody's going to believe that hype.

SHAWNA: Yeah? What's been happening to your sales?

DANNY: They've been dropping.

SHAWNA: But look at the crowds around the computer stores where the new computer games are being demonstrated.

DANNY: You're right! Paul's the cause of this. He has to be stopped.

SHAWNA: But how?

DANNY: How? How...how...I've GOT it. Watch genius at work.

SHAWNA: I'm almost afraid to look.

DANNY: People! People! People! Gather round!

MOB *(muttering)*: What's going on? What's happening?

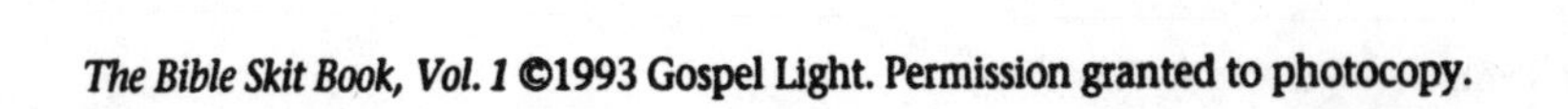

DANNY: People! We face a crisis and you're ignoring it!

MOB *(muttering)***:** What's he talking about?

DANNY: There's an evil in our midst! The computer game!

MOB *(muttering)***:** What?

DANNY: Don't you see the danger? Your children are out squandering your hard-earned money on expensive nonsense! Did you buy your child a computer to use as nothing more than a toy?

MOB *(muttering)***:** No. Not me. Did you?

DANNY: Of course you didn't! You're good parents! You bought your computer to help your child's education, so your children could learn how to compete in today's high-tech world!

MOB *(muttering)***:** He's right. That's why we bought ours.

DANNY: But what's happening? Not behind your backs but right out in the open! Paul has invaded your home through the computer stores! He's turning your good intentions into garbage! If he is allowed to continue, your computers will be nothing more than high-tech game boards.

MOB *(slightly louder)***:** He makes sense.

DANNY: Do you want your children to waste their minds and your computers?

MOB *(louder)***:** No!

DANNY: Well, it's happening! What are you going to do about it?

MOB *(confused)***:** I don't know. Do you? What do you think?

DANNY: I'll tell you what we'll do! We'll stop the computer game plot!

MOB *(shouting)***:** Right on!

DANNY: We'll end this travesty! Stop selling computer games!

MOB *(shouting)***:** Stop selling computer games! Stop selling computer games!

DANNY: March on the stores!

MOB: Stop selling computer games!

DANNY: Find Paul! Throw him out of the mall!

MOB: Stop selling computer games!

DANNY: Rid the mall of Paul! Rid the mall of Paul!

MOB: Stop selling computer games! Rid the mall of Paul!

AL: Ladies and gentlemen! Please! Control yourselves.

MOB *(quietly muttering)***:** Who's he? I don't know. Do you?

AL: We must behave in a civilized manner.

DANNY: Wait! He owns a computer store! He just wants your children's money! Stop selling computer games! Rid the mall of Paul!

MOB *(shouting)***:** Stop selling computer games! Rid the mall of Paul!

SHAWNA: What are you doing, Danny?

DANNY: I'm saving my business.

MOB: Stop selling computer games! Rid the mall of Paul!

SHAWNA: But you've started a riot! They'll tear the computer stores to pieces.

DANNY: I don't care. Let them look after their own businesses.

MOB: Stop selling computer games! Rid the mall of Paul!

JOHN: Ladies and gentlemen! Stop this noise right now!

MOB: Stop selling computer games! Rid the mall of Paul!

JOHN: People! Citizens! Silence, I beg of you!

MOB *(muttering)*: Who's he? I don't know? Does he sell computers, too?

JOHN: I am the manager of the mall! I must have your attention!

MOB: *(Mutters.)*

JOHN: Ladies and gentlemen. Everyone knows that you are good citizens, caring mothers and fathers. Since you are, you should not be reckless.

MOB *(muttering)*: He's right. Yes. He's right.

JOHN: You are marching against honest shopkeepers. And for what reason? If you don't like the merchandise they sell, then don't buy it. We have laws to protect everyone—not just the store owners, but you and your children. If these men are injuring Danny, let him bring a lawsuit against them.

MOB *(muttering)*: He makes sense.

JOHN: If you want to express yourselves, do it in a lawful assembly. A mob like this will only hurt people, the innocent and the guilty alike. If you persist, you will leave yourselves open to criminal charges.

MOB *(muttering)*: Why were we behaving that way? Do you know?

JOHN: Please. Go about your business and let this incident be a thing of the past. Help your fellow human beings, don't hurt them.

DANNY: Rats! He ruined my plan. Oh well, I'll just have to think of another.

THE BIBLE SKIT BOOK VOLUME ONE

FAREWELL

SCRIPTURE: Acts 20

SUGGESTED TOPICS: Early church; God's guidance

BIBLE BACKGROUND

Paul, persecutor of the Church, had become its greatest champion. He preached the Word from Palestine to Greece. He preached to Jews and Gentiles alike. Acts 20 records the latter part of his third missionary journey. For about three years, Paul had made Ephesus a center for evangelism into all of Asia Minor. He then traveled again through Macedonia and Greece. Paul was determined to return to Jerusalem, even though he had been warned repeatedly that imprisonment and other hardships awaited him there. Likely, he discussed the situation in Jerusalem with his friends and companions. Paul probably asked his friends to pray, to be certain that all were in agreement in the Spirit.

Knowing that he would not have another opportunity to minister in Ephesus, Paul wanted to meet with the Ephesian church leaders one more time. Paul wanted to prepare them for the trials he knew would come. He warned the Ephesian elders to be on the look out for wolves that would prey among their flock.

PERFORMANCE TIPS

1. Suggested props: Bible-time costumes.

2. The skit does not include the story of Eutychus (Acts 20:7-12). You may ask a member of your group to act the part of Luke and describe the event. Or, a group member may act the part of Eutychus and tell the story in the first person. In either case, allow the person time to prepare a script.

DISCUSSION QUESTIONS

1. Why was it so important to Paul to meet with the Ephesian church leaders again?

2. How did Paul show respect for the Ephesian leaders? (Read Acts 20:17-20,29-31,35.)

3. Romans 12:10 tells us to honor or respect others more highly than ourselves. What does it mean to honor someone? How can you honor a friend? A parent? A teammate?

FAREWELL

CHARACTERS

PAUL
LUKE
SILVANUS (SIL-vuh-nus)
DEMAS (DEE-mus)

PRONUNCIATION GUIDE

Demetrius (dih-MEE-tree-us)
Ephesus (EF-uh-sus)
Miletus (my-LEE-tus)
Troas (TROH-az)

SCENE ONE

PAUL: Luke, we need to change our plans.

LUKE: Why's that, Paul? Everything's ready for our return to Antioch. I've made all the arrangements with the ship's captain.

PAUL: I know, Luke. But our enemies have plotted to jump us as we board the ship.

LUKE: Don't those guys ever give up? What are we going to do instead?

PAUL: We'll go back through Macedonia. It'll take longer, but it will give us another chance to see the believers there.

LUKE: Imagine how those fellows who've been plotting will feel when they realize we're not getting on that boat.

PAUL: I wish I could be there to see it, but we'd better get started right away. I really want to get to Jerusalem before Pentecost.

LUKE: I don't get it, Paul. We change our plans here in Greece to avoid our enemies, but then we go back to Jerusalem where the city is full of even more people who hate you?

PAUL: But I must. The church in Jerusalem needs the offering we're carrying and I want to encourage the leaders there.

LUKE: How will it help the church in Jerusalem if you get arrested?

PAUL: You have a point. But I really feel God's Spirit is compelling me to go there. So let's hit the road before our enemies come looking for us.

(Skit continues on next page.)

SCENE TWO

LUKE: Paul. I thought you were in a hurry to get to Jerusalem.

PAUL: I am.

LUKE: So why did we stay in Philippi for a week?

PAUL: I just couldn't leave during the feast, Luke. Passover and the week of celebration afterwards are so important, I really wanted to spend it with the believers there.

LUKE: Fine, but why did we stay in Troas for a week?

PAUL: The believers here asked me to meet with them on the first day of the week to share the Lord's Supper. I couldn't say no.

LUKE: Paul, you're an old softie.

PAUL: I know, I know, but we still have time to get to Jerusalem by Pentecost. I just wish we had time to stop in Ephesus.

LUKE: Oh, right. And start another riot?

PAUL: Well, maybe there'll be time at Miletus to meet with the leaders from Ephesus. I've checked the boat schedules, and it just might work.

LUKE: If you don't preach any more all-night sermons.

PAUL: OK, I went on a little long. I'll keep it shorter next time.

SCENE THREE

PAUL: My good friends, thank you for coming. I trust the trip was pleasant.

SILVANUS: The sea was perfectly calm.

DEMAS: And the ship was trustworthy.

PAUL: I'm glad you arrived so quickly. Tomorrow I sail towards Jerusalem. I hope to be there in time for Pentecost.

SILVANUS: You can't!

DEMAS: You must not!

PAUL: I can and I must.

SILVANUS: But your enemies will be waiting for you.

DEMAS: You know how quickly news travels. You won't be safe in Jerusalem.

PAUL: Well, I wasn't too safe in Ephesus or Greece, or anywhere else. And, since the Holy Spirit has called me to Jerusalem, I must go.

SILVANUS: Is there nothing we can say...

DEMAS: Nothing we can do...

SILVANUS and DEMAS: ...to convince you to stay?

PAUL: Do you remember how I lived with you? I lived humbly and did nothing to cause you any shame.

SILVANUS: That's true.

PAUL: I always served the Lord, in spite of dangers and temptations around me.

DEMAS: You did indeed.

PAUL: I never held back anything from you. I taught the things of our Lord Jesus Christ, both on the street corners and in your homes.

SILVANUS: You certainly did. We are so grateful to you for that.

DEMAS: Before you came, some of us believed in the God of Abraham, but we had never heard of Jesus.

SILVANUS: And many others of us only believed in the goddess Artemis. A belief that couldn't help us at all.

DEMAS: But you came and showed us the truth—life, through Jesus Christ.

SILVANUS: And forgiveness through Him.

PAUL: I did not fear for myself then, and I am not afraid now. I must go to Jerusalem and finish the course laid out for me by the Lord Jesus.

DEMAS: But when will we see you again?

PAUL: To tell you the truth, you will never see me again. Prison and other trials await me in Jerusalem. But difficult trials await you, also.

SILVANUS: Trials? We're going to be arrested?

PAUL: Not that kind of trial. Listen! Danger will come to the flock.

DEMAS: Flock? Where did the sheep come from?

PAUL: Not sheep. The Holy Spirit has made you shepherds to feed the Church of God. That is the flock which Jesus Christ purchased with His own blood.

DEMAS: Oh! The Church.

PAUL: Be warned that after I leave, wolves shall enter among you.

DEMAS: I'm pretty good with a bow and arrow.

PAUL: Not four-legged wolves. I'm talking about people! Enemies of the Church!

SILVANUS: We'll be ready for them.

PAUL: Remember my warnings in the years to come.

DEMAS: But how can we shoulder such a responsibility?

PAUL: I entrust you to God. His grace will give you the strength to do all these things. Through His power, you will build up the Church.

SILVANUS: But what shall we do?

PAUL: Follow my example. Do not long for things owned by others, but earn your own living, as I did. Support those who are weak, remembering the words of our Lord Jesus Christ, "It's better to give than to receive."

DEMAS: All these things, we shall do.

SILVANUS: We'll protect the Church with our own lives.

PAUL: I know you will. But time grows short. We have time to pray, then I must be off to Jerusalem.

DEMAS: Farewell, Paul.

SILVANUS: We'll always remember what you've done for us.

The Scourge of Jerusalem

SCRIPTURE: Acts 21:27—22:30

SUGGESTED TOPICS: Responsibility for choices; wisdom; early church

BIBLE BACKGROUND

Rome's system of world domination differed from that of other conquerors. Instead of bringing in new rulers, the conquered leaders were often permitted to retain their leadership roles. Rome alone was permitted to sentence a man to death, but most other criminal matters could be settled before a local court overseen by local judges. However, Rome's presence in major cities was represented by a local garrison whose main purpose was to keep order. Under no circumstances was civil disobedience tolerated.

Paul returned to Jerusalem, during Roman rule, for the Feast of Pentecost. While in Jerusalem, he was spotted walking with a Gentile, Trophimus, by some of the Jews from the province of Asia. Apparently, they had not forgotten Paul and his preaching in their land. Seizing on the fact that Paul had been seen with a Gentile and that Paul was now in the Temple, they quickly spread the rumor that Paul had brought a Gentile into the Temple, thereby defiling the holy place.

Nothing more was required to stir the crowd into a frenzy and to change a peaceful group of worshipers into a murderous mob. Without the intervention of the Roman guard, Paul would have been murdered just outside of the Temple. To keep him safe from the mob, the commander of the Jerusalem garrison took soldiers and centurions (at least two hundred soldiers) to quell the riot and remove Paul to the adjacent Roman fortress for questioning. Considering Rome's high regard for order, the ruthlessness of the army in dealing with civil disobedience is understandable. Being in the army was considered one of the better jobs in Rome, offering excitement, adventure and many fringe benefits for the loyal soldier. Although the Roman army was one of the finest fighting machines the world has known, there must have been an occasional sadist or fool who made his way into its ranks. However, no matter what his rank or disposition, each soldier knew there were two sets of laws; one for Roman citizens and one for non-citizens.

PERFORMANCE TIPS

1. Suggested props: chair for the commander to sit in, rope or chain to tie Paul's hands.
2. Introduce the skit by saying, "The apostle Paul wanted to celebrate the Jewish Feast of Pentecost in Jerusalem. Many people warned him against traveling to Jerusalem because of his enemies. However, Paul was determined to meet with the Christians in Jerusalem. When he went to the Temple, a riot broke out. Roman soldiers were called and their commander questioned him. Listen to what happened."
3. After the skit, ask a member of your group to read Acts 21:27-29 to find out what caused the riot.

DISCUSSION QUESTIONS

1. Acts 22:29 tells us the commander was frightened when he learned Paul was a Roman citizen. Why was he frightened? (Roman citizens had special rights and privileges.)
2. As Christians, we are called by God to act responsibly. How did Paul act responsibly?
3. What are some ways someone your age can act responsibly?

THE SCOURGE OF JERUSALEM

CHARACTERS

COMMANDER
PAUL
SOLDIER
CENTURION (sen-CHUR-ee-un)

PRONUNCIATION GUIDE

Gamaliel (gah-MAY-lee-el)
scourge (SKURJ)

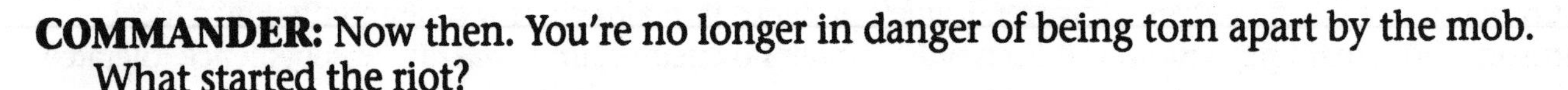

COMMANDER: Now then. You're no longer in danger of being torn apart by the mob. What started the riot?

PAUL: The hardness of the people's hearts, sir.

COMMANDER: A typical criminal response. Guard!

SOLDIER: Present and accounted for, O Supreme Commander!

COMMANDER: I need more information about this riot. Go down and find out what you can. Report back to me.

SOLDIER: But you were there. You heard it all.

COMMANDER: I heard shouting and screaming. But I heard nothing that made any sense. Maybe the mob has cooled down enough to give us some facts.

SOLDIER: With the speed of chariot and steed, I fly to obey your command. *(Exits.)*

COMMANDER: Now then, prisoner. Why are you in Jerusalem?

PAUL: I came to celebrate the Feast of Pentecost with my people.

COMMANDER: Another excuse for trouble. That's all these feasts are.

SOLDIER: *(Enters.)* Ahem.

COMMANDER: What did you learn?

SOLDIER: The people are still yelling a lot.

COMMANDER: I can hear that from here. What did you learn about the prisoner?

SOLDIER: As near as I can figure, he's some sort of Egyptian radical.

COMMANDER: Fool! Listen to the man. He spoke perfect Greek and Hebrew out there. And you think he's an Egyptian?

SOLDIER: Is that what he was speaking? I'm not a language specialist, myself. I only speak Latin.

COMMANDER: Well, go back and question the crowd.

SOLDIER: Your pleasure is my strictest order, my liege.

COMMANDER: I know that. Go! *(SOLDIER exits.)* Now then, prisoner, who are you?

PAUL: As I told you outside, my name is Paul. I am a citizen of Tarsus.

COMMANDER: Don't be insolent with me! Your fate is in my hands.

PAUL: Forgive me, sir. I meant no insult to you.

COMMANDER: Well, don't let it happen again.

SOLDIER: *(Enters.)* Ahem.

COMMANDER: Ah! You've returned. What did you learn this time?

SOLDIER: I've discovered this man's crime, Chief of Chiefs. It's so horrible as to be almost unmentionable.

COMMANDER: Well, what is it? We haven't got all day.

SOLDIER: This man, O Supreme One, is a...

COMMANDER: What?

SOLDIER: He's a...teacher.

COMMANDER: What?

SOLDIER: Well, you can understand why the crowd doesn't like him. He's a teacher.

COMMANDER: I find it difficult to believe that a riot started because the man is a teacher.

SOLDIER: Then you must not have gone to school.

COMMANDER: Insolent dog! Do you dare to criticize me?

SOLDIER: No, no, I just meant that every student hates teachers.

COMMANDER: Well in the future, watch your tongue. Riots don't start because men are teachers. What are you doing?

SOLDIER *(speaking with tongue sticking out)*: I'm trying to watch my tongue.

COMMANDER: I understand why you didn't get along with teachers. Put your tongue back into your mouth! Now, then. What did this teacher do?

SOLDIER: The most terrible of crimes. He tried to make people go to school on a holiday.

COMMANDER: Fool!

SOLDIER: Yes, he certainly is.

COMMANDER: Not him! You! Did that crowd look like a bunch of school children to you?

SOLDIER: Well, maybe they're all slow learners. I remember in my ancient history class...

COMMANDER: Go find out what happened or you will BE history!

SOLDIER: I leave with the greatest of haste. *(Exits.)*

COMMANDER: What's this army coming to? We used to be the best in the world. Now then, prisoner, are you a teacher?

PAUL: I am a Jew, born in Tarsus but raised in Jerusalem at the feet of the great scholar, Gamaliel. As such, I learned the Law and am well versed in the Prophets. I have gone to the Temple and discussed Scripture with the men gathered there.

COMMANDER: Another teacher of Jewish law. You claim they tried to kill you for teaching their own law?

SOLDIER: *(Enters.)* Ahem.

COMMANDER: Ah! You must know the reason for the riot now.

SOLDIER: I have learned all there is to know, O Mighty Commander.

COMMANDER: Good. What is this man's crime?

SOLDIER: He invited someone to the Temple.

COMMANDER: What?

SOLDIER: I know it sounds impossible that this man could be such a villain, but that's what he did. I got it straight from the horse's mouth.

COMMANDER: You talk to animals, do you? That's the first thing you've said that I find believable. Apparently we'll learn nothing from this buffoon.

SOLDIER: Dragoon, Commander, Sir. I'm a dragoon, not a buffoon. Sounds like someone in charge of shining sandals.

COMMANDER: He's in charge of driving his commander crazy! Leave!

SOLDIER: Oh, thank you, Commander.

COMMANDER: What?

SOLDIER: I've only been on the job two days and already you're giving me leave. I told my mother I'd be the best soldier she's ever seen. How much leave are you giving me, Sir?

COMMANDER: *(Hides his face in his hands.)* The rest of your life. Which, if I have my way, will not be long. Now go.

SOLDIER: With haste, before you change your mind, I go.

COMMANDER: Has he gone?

PAUL: Yes.

COMMANDER: Good. *(Looks up.)* Now then, we can't seem to learn anything from the crowd. We'll have to examine you more thoroughly. Centurion!

CENTURION: Yes, Commander.

COMMANDER: Take this man away and question him.

CENTURION: Come along. *(Leads Paul away.)*

PAUL: What's going to happen next?

CENTURION: Nothing too bad. You see these leather thongs? We use them to bind your hands. You see that whip? We use it to scourge you until you tell us the truth. Don't worry. A year from now, your wounds will be healed.

PAUL: Is it lawful to scourge an uncondemned Roman?

CENTURION: Of course not. But...you're Jewish, right?

PAUL: Yes.

CENTURION: Good.

PAUL: And a Roman citizen.

CENTURION: Not good. Come with me. Commander!

COMMANDER: What? Has he confessed already?

CENTURION: We must be careful. This man is a Roman citizen.

COMMANDER: What? Are you a Roman citizen?

PAUL: I am.

COMMANDER: I am, too. My freedom cost me a great deal of money. How much did you pay?

PAUL: I am a Roman citizen from birth. Free born in the city of Tarsus.

COMMANDER: Centurion! Why is this man bound? Release him! Citizen.

PAUL: Commander?

COMMANDER: Citizen, come. We'll have a little supper, a little wine. We can discuss this unfortunate incident. I don't think we need report it to Rome, do you?

PAUL: It's up to you.

COMMANDER: Good. Then, after a good night's sleep, we'll bring in the high priest and the Jewish council tomorrow and hear what they have to say.

The Plot Thickens

SCRIPTURE: Acts 22:30—23:15

SUGGESTED TOPICS: Responsibility; courage; early church

BIBLE BACKGROUND

Paul had been accused of one of the most serious crimes under Roman law, civil disobedience. The Roman government was not concerned about defiling holy places (the charge brought against Paul by the Jewish leaders), but they were concerned about the consequences that could arise from this action. Paul had to stand trial. However, he had all the benefits available under two legal systems. At least, he should have.

Jewish law could not find a man guilty of any crime unless two witnesses would agree upon every element of their testimony. However, given the experience of the Lord at His trial, and Stephen at his, Paul could not expect the Jewish council to follow the letter of the law. But Paul had an ace in the hole. The Roman government might not care very much about what happened to the local residents in disputes, but it cared very much that justice should be properly meted out to Roman citizens. Paul was not only a Roman citizen—he had been born a free man.

The Jewish council was the civil ruling body in Judea, having been permitted to retain its position by the Roman governor. But it would only be allowed to keep its authority if it could keep the peace. The council also had to oversee the religious affairs of the Jewish people. Balancing these two duties—civil authority and religious authority—was not easy in a country which hated its Roman overseers and believed that God wanted Rome to be destroyed. The zealots were forever hatching plots to throw off Rome's yoke and, because the council was the religious authority, it had to secretly, though not overtly, approve of any action which would give Judea its independence.

Jesus had not criticized the religious leaders for their lack of courage in not standing up to the Roman government. He attacked them for their lack of spiritual leadership. Fearing that His criticism could damage their standing with the people and ultimately with Rome, the council conspired to have Him crucified, thereby preserving their secular and religious authority and position. Unfortunately, for them, Jesus' followers were not daunted by the threat of beatings and death. Not only were the original apostles preaching, but the council's staunchest ally, Saul of Tarsus, had become one of the leading proponents of the teachings of Jesus.

PERFORMANCE TIPS

1. Prior to the skit, introduce the class to the differences between the Pharisees and Sadducees. Briefly tell the class about the Jewish council and its diversity of religious opinion before the skit begins.

2. Give the class a brief synopsis of last week's adventure. "Last week, Paul was almost killed by a mob in Jerusalem." Have the class quickly update Paul's current location (in a Roman jail, awaiting his appearance before the council).

3. Depending on the maturity of your class, either tell the story of the trial and then begin the skit or, do the skit and ask your class to tell you what happened at the trial. Read Acts 23:1-5 and Acts 23:11 with the class.

4. After the skit, have the class tell what they think happened to Paul the next day. Then, finish the story with Paul's appearance before Felix.

DISCUSSION QUESTIONS

1. Paul acted responsibly during his trials. In what ways did he act responsibly?

2. Does acting responsibly always make you comfortable? Why or why not?

3. What would have happened if Paul told the council he would never talk about Jesus again?

4. Sometimes it feels easier to lie than to tell the truth. What should you do when you are tempted to lie?

5. If you tell the truth, will everybody like you? Why or why not?

THE PLOT THICKENS

CHARACTERS

TERTULLUS (tur-TUL-us)
ANNAS (ah-NAHS)
ALEXANDER

PRONUNCIATION GUIDE

Pharisee (FARE-uh-see)
Sadducee (SAD-you-see)

TERTULLUS: OK. We all know why we're here. It's time to stop Paul for good.

ANNAS: Have you got a plan?

TERTULLUS: I have.

ANNAS: Well? Tell us.

TERTULLUS: Come closer. We'll need as many men as possible.

ANNAS: That should be no problem. We already have forty men here.

ALEXANDER: Correction. Forty-one. I'm here.

TERTULLUS: Where have you been? You should have been here an hour ago.

ALEXANDER: Well, it was supper time. So I went to see that old guy with the white beard and hair. You know, he wears a white suit. He makes the best chicken...

ANNAS: We don't want to hear about it.

ALEXANDER: I think it must be the combination of herbs and spices...

ANNAS: We don't want to hear about it.

ALEXANDER: Or maybe it's the oil he cooks it in...

ANNAS *(yelling)***:** We don't want to hear about it!

ALEXANDER: You don't have to yell. I'm not deaf, you know.

TERTULLUS: If you two have finished...

ANNAS: We're listening.

TERTULLUS: Now then, here's what we do about Paul.

ALEXANDER: Why do we have to do anything about Paul?

TERTULLUS: Are you insane? The man's a menace to society.

ANNAS: A wreaker of havoc among honest people.

ALEXANDER: Well of course he is. Everyone knows that.

TERTULLUS: That's why we have to get rid of him.

ALEXANDER: But he's a prisoner of the Romans. Nobody lives too long in a Roman prison. Let THEM get rid of him.

ANNAS: They may not kill him.

ALEXANDER: I don't see why not. The Romans don't like Jews.

TERTULLUS: But he's more than a Jew.

ALEXANDER: OK, so he's a member of the Pharisees. They don't like Pharisees very much, either.

ANNAS: He's more than a Jew and a Pharisee. He's a Roman citizen.

ALEXANDER: So they'll speak to him nicely when they torture and kill him.

TERTULLUS: No, they'll give him a fair trial.

ALEXANDER: You mean...

ANNAS: That's right. They might acquit him.

ALEXANDER: We can't have that! What's the plan?

TERTULLUS: Come close. We don't want this overheard by any curious ears.

(ALEXANDER covers his ears.)

ANNAS: Why are you covering your ears?

ALEXANDER: Because I'm curious about the plan. And Tertullus doesn't want it over heard by any curious ears.

ANNAS: He doesn't mean people here. He means anyone who might be sympathetic to Paul.

ALEXANDER: Well, he should make himself clear. Go ahead, Tertullus.

TERTULLUS: We must stand together to fight this common enemy. You know what happened this morning?

ALEXANDER: Yeah. That sure was funny.

TERTULLUS: Funny?

ALEXANDER: Yeah, the way he got the Pharisees and the Sadducees fighting among themselves. *(Imitating Sadducee.)* "There is no resurrection. The man's a blasphemer." *(Imitating Pharisee.)* "Of course there's a resurrection. You Sadducees are just too stupid for words."

TERTULLUS: You thought that was funny?

ALEXANDER: Well sure. All those holier-than-thou types just about punching each others' lights out.

ANNAS: That's why Paul is so dangerous. He encourages disputes among good people. Even so, we almost got to him during the minor disagreement between the Pharisees and Sadducees.

TERTULLUS: Yes, but the Roman captain interfered before we could dispose of Paul during the riot—I mean, discussion. But here's how we get rid of him for good.

ANNAS: Go ahead. We're all ears.

ALEXANDER: No we're not. We have eyes and mouths and fingers and...

ANNAS: We're all listening attentively.

ALEXANDER: Oh.

TERTULLUS: We will have the council tell the Roman captain that they wish to question Paul more about certain aspects of his testimony.

ALEXANDER: I thought he made himself very clear this morning.

TERTULLUS: Of course he did. This is just an excuse to get him away from his Roman guards. We will position ourselves throughout the council hall. When Paul is brought down, he will have to pass one of us. When he comes near, we strike. Paul is dead, no problems.

ANNAS: Brilliant! It can't fail.

ALEXANDER: Unless the Pharisees and Sadducees start fighting again.

TERTULLUS: I've thought of that. For the plan to succeed, we must be of one mind. We must put aside our petty differences for the common good.

ANNAS: How will we do that?

TERTULLUS: We swear a common oath. Now. All of us.

ALEXANDER: How exciting. What kind of an oath? Like, "If Paul lives, may maggots eat me when I die." Something like that?

TERTULLUS: Something a little more forceful. Repeat after me. I hereby swear...

ANNAS and ALEXANDER: I hereby swear...

TERTULLUS: ...that until Paul is dead...

ANNAS and ALEXANDER: ...that until Paul is dead...

TERTULLUS: ...I shall neither...

ANNAS and ALEXANDER: ...I shall neither...

TERTULLUS: ...eat nor drink anything.

ANNAS: ...eat nor drink anything.

ALEXANDER: Time out! Time out!

TERTULLUS: What?

ALEXANDER: Let me get this straight. We're going to kill Paul...

TERTULLUS: Of course.

ALEXANDER: On an empty stomach? Is that wise? I mean, what happens if Paul comes down to the council hall and just as I'm ready to strike, I faint from hunger.

ANNAS: Paul will be brought down to the council hall tomorrow morning. You're only going to miss breakfast.

ALEXANDER: But breakfast is the most important meal of the day.

TERTULLUS: Are you with us or against us, Alexander?

ALEXANDER: I'm in complete sympathy with your cause. It's your oath that concerns me. But wait—I'll go home and have breakfast tonight. Then I'll make the vow in the morning. Am I brilliant or what?

TERTULLUS and ANNAS: You're what.

TERTULLUS: The oath is made now. From this moment, none of us will eat or drink until Paul is dead.

ALEXANDER: Of course, a small snack wouldn't count as a meal...

ANNAS: None of us will eat ANYTHING...

ALEXANDER: A nice big glass of goat's milk. That wouldn't be eating...

TERTULLUS: Or DRINK anything...

ALEXANDER: Maybe a...

ANNAS: Nothing.

TERTULLUS: Until Paul is dead.

ALEXANDER: Which will be...

ANNAS: Tomorrow morning.

ALEXANDER: Oh, all right. I swear not to eat or drink anything until Paul is dead.

TERTULLUS: Good. I'll go see the council and have them get in touch with the Roman captain. Annas!

ANNAS: Yes?

TERTULLUS: Tomorrow, make certain you're stationed beside Alexander. We don't want any slipups.

SCRIPTURE: Acts 27

SUGGESTED TOPICS: Choices; responsibility; wisdom; courage; trust; early church

BIBLE BACKGROUND

Paul had been placed on trial before the governor, Felix. Although Felix found no reason to keep Paul in custody, Paul was kept under a loose house arrest for two years. Paul was in the custody of a centurion, but the centurion had orders not to deny any visit to Paul by any of his friends. Apparently, Felix was hoping for some monetary gain from Paul (see Acts 24:26). However, then as now, political appointments are not for life, and Felix's place as governor was taken over by Porcius Festus.

The Jewish leaders tried again to have Paul assassinated by requesting that Festus send Paul to trial in Jerusalem. Instead, Festus arranged the trial in Caesarea. During the trial, Paul, being a Roman citizen, exercised his right to have his case heard before Caesar. He also pled his case before King Herod Agrippa II, who, although he found Paul innocent of wrongdoing, could not release him because of the appeal to Rome. On the trip to Rome, disaster struck.

What sort of people did Paul meet along the way? Julius, the centurion, was courteous to Paul from the start (see Acts 27:3). Was this a result of Paul impressing Julius, or merely the courtesy that Julius would have shown to any citizen who had not yet been convicted of a crime? Whatever the centurion's attitude at the beginning, it was definitely one of great respect by the time of the shipwreck (see Acts 27:31,32,43). On the other hand, the hardened sailors had no trust in Paul, preferring to risk their lives in a lifeboat rather than stay with the ship.

PERFORMANCE TIPS

1. Suggested props: sailor hats, binoculars.

2. Introduce the skit by explaining, "Because Paul was a Roman citizen, he had the right to appeal his case before Caesar in Rome. Julius, a Roman centurion, was assigned to escort Paul to Rome. Their trip was anything but smooth. Listen to what happened."

3. Display a map which traces Paul's trip to Rome. Locate these places on the map: Caesarea, Antioch, Tarsus, Myra, Cnidus, Fair Havens, Phoenix, Malta.

4. The captain obviously does not respect Paul. Suggest the person playing this role speak sarcastically whenever he addresses Paul.

DISCUSSION QUESTIONS

1. Who acted in a responsible way during the storm? How?

2. What sort of emergencies might you face in your life? How could you act responsibly in the midst of an emergency?

3. How can you prepare yourself ahead of time to handle those emergencies?

EMERGENCY

CHARACTERS

JULIUS
CAPTAIN
PAUL

SCENE ONE

JULIUS: Will we soon be ready to sail, Captain?

CAPTAIN: Aye, soon enough. Ship's nearly loaded.

PAUL: If I may speak freely, Julius, I think it would be best to wait.

CAPTAIN: Oh? And would you be a sailor, laddie?

PAUL: No, I am a tentmaker by trade. But I have traveled a great deal.

CAPTAIN: No doubt you have, laddie. No doubt you have great wisdom of the ways of the sea. Forbid it that I, a mere sea captain, should know as much as yourself.

JULIUS: Why do you think it unwise to sail, Paul?

PAUL: This voyage will be perilous. I see danger and damage, not only to the ship and cargo, but also to everyone aboard.

JULIUS: What do you say, Captain?

CAPTAIN: Oh, would you stoop to seek the unworthy opinion of your humble seagoing servant? Late in the season it might be, but I've sailed worse seas and am alive to tell my adventures. Of course, I can understand how one having to face trial in Rome might want to wait.

PAUL: I am not afraid of what might await me in Rome. But this voyage is ill-advised.

CAPTAIN: Is the poor tentmaker not afraid of Rome? Then he's a fool. But, sail we must. This is no place to winter a ship. If you be afraid to sail for Rome, then we must sail to Phoenix and lay over there.

JULIUS: Paul, you know I respect your opinion. But I must believe that the captain knows his business. We'll sail to Phoenix and from there we'll decide whether or not to continue to Rome.

CAPTAIN: There's a man who knows how to be a leader. That's why he's a centurion. Tentmakers! Pah!

JULIUS: Alright, men! Load the prisoners on board! We set sail.

(Skit continues on next page.)

SCENE TWO

CAPTAIN: Oh, they let tentmakers have their free roam of the ship, do they?

PAUL: Julius knows I have no intention of attempting an escape.

CAPTAIN: Truly, you are the strangest man I've met. But no sailor.

PAUL: What do you mean?

CAPTAIN: Oh, you haven't noticed the gentle south breeze under which we're sailing, have you? Makes you fear for your life, don't it? A few more days, we'll be in Phoenix, safe and sound.

PAUL: I don't want to alarm you, but hasn't the wind shifted direction? And isn't it blowing stronger?

CAPTAIN: Oh, I'm so frightened. Ha! Haven't you seen the wind change before? Sometimes it swirls a bit. Sometimes it changes speed. But then, being a tentmaker, you must live all your life indoors. Wouldn't know about the wind inside, would you?

PAUL: I know you don't believe me. But the wind is considerably stronger and has shifted direction.

CAPTAIN: You needn't tell me my job, laddie. C'mon sailors. Look alive. Let's show these landlubbers how real men face the weather.

SCENE THREE

JULIUS: Captain, we've been tossed about in this storm for days without seeing the sun or the stars. Have you any idea where we are?

CAPTAIN: Aye. We're in the middle of the Great Sea in a tempest. And we're headed for Sheol, every man jack of us. Make your peace with your god.

PAUL: Gentlemen, I hate to say I told you so...

JULIUS: But you told us so. Paul, before we all perish, let me say it has truly been a plea sure to know you.

PAUL: Thank you, Julius. But do not fear. Even though we should have stayed at Crete, all is not lost. True, the ship and its cargo have been damaged, but no man aboard shall lose his life.

CAPTAIN: So you're a fortune-teller now, are you?

PAUL: No. But this very night, an angel of the God I serve stood before me and told me not to be afraid. He told me I must go to Rome to face Caesar and that God will spare all who are with me on this ship. I believe God. However, before we're through, we'll be cast ashore on an island.

CAPTAIN: Well excuse me for livin', but I'll believe the wisdom of the sea. Not your angels.

JULIUS: Paul, you've shown much wisdom in the past. I believe you.

CAPTAIN: Look alive men! What's over starboard? Land ho!

JULIUS: Can we make it to the island?

CAPTAIN: We're sounding fifteen fathoms. There's rocks all about and it's the middle of the night. Throw four anchors from the stern! We'll have to weather the night here and sail tomorrow in daylight!

JULIUS: Whatever you say. You're the captain.

CAPTAIN: Aye. And we'll want to be setting anchors in the fore. Let down the boat!

PAUL: Julius, the captain is not planning to use the small boat to set anchors in the fore of the ship. He and the crew are planning to abandon the ship. But if they do not stay with the ship, we'll all perish.

JULIUS: Paul, I failed to listen to you in the past and I regret it. I won't ask you how you know the crew's intentions, I'll just believe you do. Soldiers, cut the ropes and let that boat fall into the sea.

CAPTAIN: Think you're smart, don't you, tentmaker! See you in Sheol.

PAUL: Not likely, Captain. Not likely. Certainly not this night. Men! All of you, soldiers, sailors, prisoners—for fourteen days we've battled the storm, and we haven't had time or stomach to eat. Take food now and eat. You'll need all your strength in the morning.

CAPTAIN: Now that's the first decent idea you've had this trip.

PAUL: But first, let's give thanks to God.

JULIUS: Would you lead us in prayer to your God, Paul?

SCENE FOUR

CAPTAIN: Well, tentmaker, we've lightened the ship as best we could, but the storm still blows.

PAUL: But at least it's day, and we can see a little better.

CAPTAIN: Wonderful. We'll be able to see the wave that drowns us all.

JULIUS: Look! Up ahead! A beach!

CAPTAIN: We just might be able to sail onto it. Look lively, lads! We're headed for shore! If that's alright with you, tentmaker.

PAUL: You're the captain.

CAPTAIN: Weigh the anchors! Look lively, lads! You know what to do!

(All stagger from the jolt.)

JULIUS: What was that?

CAPTAIN: We've run aground! Must be a sandbar. We're stuck fast.

JULIUS: Will we be safe here?

CAPTAIN: Not likely! The aft is breaking up!

JULIUS: We'll have to swim for it. Spare the prisoners! Paul said we would all land safely! Those who can swim, dive in and make for land. Those who can't, find a board or a piece of the ship. Don't be afraid. We'll all make it.

Unfair

SCRIPTURE: Philippians 4:11,13

SUGGESTED TOPICS: Response to injustice; choosing wisdom

BIBLE BACKGROUND

God never promised us a fair world. Sin has changed the perfect to the imperfect. Again and again in this lifetime we will experience disappointment, heartache and pain. The way we handle these setbacks will show the world around us our true faith.

PERFORMANCE TIPS

1. Suggested props: hat and clipboard for coach.

2. Before the skit ask, "Have you ever been judged unfairly in a competition or other situation? What happened? What did you do?" Then introduce the skit by saying, "Let's see how someone else handles an unfair situation."

DISCUSSION QUESTIONS

1. How did Julie respond when her score was lower than she and her coach believed she deserved?

2. Who could have helped her? How?

3. Why do you think unfair things happen?

4. It's easy to recognize times when we feel we are treated unfairly. It's harder to recognize the times when we may have treated someone else unfairly. When might you have been unfair to someone?

5. When you have been treated unfairly, what should you do? When you have treated someone else unfairly, what should you do?

UNFAIR

CHARACTERS

COACH
JULIE
TRAINER

COACH: Great routine, Julie! Great!

JULIE: It felt good. I think it's the best I've done.

COACH: It wasn't just good, it was great! The gold is ours for sure!

JULIE: What about the wobble on the second back flip?

COACH: Nothing to worry about. And you nailed the landing on your dismount.

JULIE: Look! They're posting the marks.

COACH: Nine-point-six-five? What are they talking about? It was worth at least a nine-point-nine!

JULIE: Nine-point-six-five isn't even good enough for bronze.

COACH: What's the matter with you judges? Are you totally blind?

JULIE: I worked so hard. For nothing.

COACH: Never mind, Julie. Don't let it bother you. Get ready for the floor exercises.

JULIE: But I was good. I did my best routine ever. It's not fair.

COACH: It sure isn't. You judges are blind! Did you know that? You can't see your noses in front of your faces!

JULIE: How can I face people back home? They all expected me to win.

COACH: You're going to have to put it behind you. Let's go over your floor routine.

JULIE: I start...I start with...oh, I can't remember!

COACH: C'mon. You can do it. Step-by-step, the first tumbling pass.

JULIE: I start on the northeast corner of the mat and...front hand spring...

(TRAINER enters.)

COACH: Joe! Can you believe those judges?

TRAINER: Unbelievable! We were robbed blind!

COACH: If you judges need new glasses, why didn't you buy them before you came?

TRAINER: Things like that shouldn't be allowed. The whole bunch should be replaced.

COACH: Learn the sport before you sit in judgment!

JULIE: Front hand spring...I can't remember!

COACH: C'mon now, Julie. You can't let one disappointment get you down.

JULIE: I know, but I can't remember.

COACH: You stupid judges! You're trying to destroy the whole competition, aren't you? Well it won't work! Do you hear me? It won't work!

JULIE: Why was I ever born? I'll make a fool out of myself. I don't want to go on. I can't remember my routine. It's not fair. It's just not fair.

There's Fruit and There's Fruit

SCRIPTURE: Galatians 5:22,23

SUGGESTED TOPICS: Fruit of the Spirit; wise choices; Christian life

BIBLE BACKGROUND

Paul, in writing to the Galatians, tried to warn them against trying to please God through the works of the flesh. He exhorted them to accept the "fruit of the Spirit" which is freely given from God through Christ's sacrifice on the cross. "Against such things there is no law" (Galatians 5:23).

Many people think of farming and raising crops as being some sort of easy work. You plant the seed and wait for the harvest. Nothing could be further from the truth. The land must be prepared carefully, the seed must be planted at the right depth, the correct fertilizer must be employed to achieve the greatest yield, the proper amount of moisture must be applied and the field must be weeded. Similarly, the fruit of the Spirit does not automatically grow in a person's life, but must be carefully nurtured.

PERFORMANCE TIPS

1. Suggested props: overalls and shovel for Joe.
2. If you know a farmer (or someone who used to live on a farm), ask him or her to come to your group and describe the steps in growing a crop.
3. Introduce the skit by saying, "In the book of Galatians, Paul used a word picture to describe the kinds of attitudes and actions the Holy Spirit helps a Christian to demonstrate. Paul called these attitudes and actions the fruit of the Spirit. Listen to this skit to find out what it takes to produce the fruit of the Spirit."

DISCUSSION QUESTIONS

1. Do you think Joe will harvest a large crop from his apple tree? Why or why not?
2. Paul talks about fruit of the Spirit in his letter to the Galatians. Why might he have chosen fruit as a comparison for love, joy, peace, patience, kindness, goodness, faithfulness, gentleness and self-control?
3. How can you help this fruit to grow in your life? What do you think would happen if you try to grow it alone, without God? Why?

There's Fruit and There's Fruit

CHARACTERS

JOHN
JOE

JOHN: Hi, Joe. Hey, that's some hole you've dug. What's it for?

JOE: It's going to make me rich.

JOHN: What, you got buried treasure down there?

JOE: Better than that. If it were treasure, somebody else would want a piece of it.

JOHN: The dirt—is it some kind of special dirt? Is it full of uranium or oil or something?

JOE: Nope.

JOHN: Well if the dirt isn't special and there's no buried treasure, what's so special about this hole?

JOE: Fruit.

JOHN: Where? I don't see any fruit.

JOE: It's not there yet. But I'm going to plant an orchard, starting with one apple tree. Right here in this hole.

JOHN: That's your big money-making scheme? Planting an apple tree?

JOE: Sure. Everybody's health conscious these days. And what's healthier than apples? You know, an apple a day keeps the doctor away. So I'll grow apples, sell them, buy more trees, sell the fruit from them and become rich.

JOHN: I guess it could work. But I didn't know you could grow apples here.

JOE: Of course you can. There's no law against it.

JOHN: I was talking about the climate. Is this the right climate for apples?

JOE: Are you kidding? Apples grow anywhere.

JOHN: Are you sure?

JOE: Pretty sure. Anyway, they'll grow here for sure. Because if they wouldn't, the nursery wouldn't sell apple trees, would it?

JOHN: I guess not. How about this soil? It looks like it has a lot of sand in it. Is that good for growing apples?

JOE: Dirt is dirt. You plant the tree in dirt and it grows.

JOHN: I thought different kinds of trees grew best in different kinds of soil.

JOE: That's too much trouble. I say, just plant the trees and let them grow.

JOHN: If you say so. Where's your tree?

JOE: Over there. Leaning against the house.

JOHN: But that's just a little sapling. Should you have dug this deep of a hole for such a little tree?

JOE: Sure. Its roots need to get down real deep. That'll make it grow faster.

JOHN: I sure never knew all this before. What kind of apples are you growing?

JOE: APPLE apples. The kind you eat.

JOHN: But don't different kinds of apples need different kinds of fertilizer?

JOE: Fertilizer? Who's got money for fertilizer? That would cut into my profit. All trees need to grow is dirt and water. Man, will I be raking in the dough this year.

JOHN: This year? From that little tree? I don't think it will grow apples for a few years.

JOE: It's an apple tree. That means it will grow apples. You don't know anything about fruit, do you?

JOHN: I guess I don't know anything about the kind of fruit you're planning to grow. But I know lots about fruit of a different kind.

JOE: Oh? Is it any good?

JOHN: It's the fruit of the Spirit, the best kind of all.

JOE: Never heard of it. Where do you grow it?

JOHN: Inside yourself.

JOE: Right. This better be good.

JOHN: First you have to prepare the ground.

JOE: You mean like digging a hole.

JOHN: Well, for this kind of fruit, you start by accepting Jesus as your Savior. Then God's Spirit grows His fruit inside you.

JOE: Fruit can't grow inside of people.

JOHN: This kind can. If it's properly nurtured.

JOE: What does that mean—nurtured?

JOHN: It's like watering and fertilizing plants. But the water and plant food I use is the Bible and prayer.

JOE: Reading books and talking with your eyes closed doesn't grow fruit.

JOHN: It does with this kind of fruit. And do you know what the best part is?

JOE: I haven't a clue.

JOHN: The fruit begins to grow right away. You don't have to wait a long time for it. As long as you continue nurturing God's Spirit within you, He produces fruit.

JOE: You don't have to wait for the fruit?

JOHN: Nope.

JOE: I could make a lot of money from this. What kind of fruit are we talking about here? And how do you get it out of your body?

JOHN: The fruit of the Spirit is love, joy, peace, patience, kindness, goodness, faithfulness, gentleness and self-control. And you don't have to pick it. You give it away.

JOE: Man, I never know what you're talking about. But I don't think I could sell that any way. So you can keep it. I'll stick with apples.

JOHN: Well, if you ever need the fruit of the Spirit, you'll know where to find it. Lot's of luck with your apples. I think you'll need it.

JOE: Luck? Ha! Just old-fashioned hard work. That's all it needs. Now let's see. Which end of this thing goes up?

Love, Love, Love

SCRIPTURE: 1 Corinthians 13

SUGGESTED TOPICS: Love; Christian life

BIBLE BACKGROUND

Love is easily the most misunderstood word in the English language. Most people hear the word and associate it with tender feelings, soft music and soft lights, walks on warm summer nights, moods and situations that change. It has been used to mean so many different things that it now means almost nothing. Paul's letter to the Corinthians gives the correct perception of love as an active verb, not a passive noun.

Children and teenagers—and many adults—tend to view the world around them on an emotional level. If something feels right, it is right. Stopping to analyze a situation intellectually does not come naturally. One way to break through the emotional barrier is to present a situation as a caricature, to make it so obvious and ludicrous that it is laughable. Although learners may not see themselves clearly, they do catch a glimpse of themselves.

PERFORMANCE TIPS

1. Suggested props: backpacks for girls to wear.

2. Ask group members to suggest a popular singer and a favorite store for the script.

3. In preparing to use this skit, explain that you need two people to pretend to be silly teenagers. If you are using the skit with young people, they may be reluctant to play these parts for fear of being laughed at. Consider playing one part yourself, even if you are male. Your participation will encourage a student's willingness to participate.

DISCUSSION QUESTIONS

1. The two girls in the skit used the word love many times. How would you define love?

2. Does your definition include feelings, actions, or both?

3. Read 1 Corinthians 13:4-7. Compare your definition with Paul's definition. Does his definition of love include feelings or actions?

4. In Matthew 5:44 Jesus tells us to "love your enemies." How can you show love to an enemy?

5. If you show love to your enemies, will they always show love to you? Why does Jesus tell us to show love to them?

6. Paul's letter to the Romans explains that God loved us when we were His enemies (see Romans 5:6-11). How can we respond to God's love?

LOVE, LOVE, LOVE

CHARACTERS

BUFFY
MUFFY

BUFFY: Hi, Muffy. Where are you going in such a hurry?

MUFFY: Hi, Buffy. I have to get down to the record store, like NOW.

BUFFY: Why?

MUFFY: Why? Are you kidding? *(Insert name)*'s new CD comes out today, and I just HAVE to be the first to get it.

BUFFY: Today! I thought it came out tomorrow. I'll go with you. I just LOVE him so much. I'll just DIE if I don't get ALL his CDs.

MUFFY: What's your favorite song?

BUFFY: Favorite? How can anyone have a favorite? ALL of his songs are just SO-O-O wonderful. I love them all!

MUFFY: Me, too! But I especially love his love songs. They're SO romantic, they send goose bumps up my arms. I LOVE it when he sings about how much he loves me.

BUFFY: I love that, too. I just KNOW he's singing to me. Oh, I love him!

MUFFY: Are you going to his concert next month?

BUFFY: How can you even ask? When the tickets go on sale, I'll be first in line.

MUFFY: Right behind me. He's so wonderful on CD, I just know I'll love him a HUNDRED times more in person.

BUFFY: Me, too. But I have to decide what to wear. It has to be special, to show him how much I love him.

MUFFY: I already have my outfit picked out.

BUFFY: No! What? Tell me.

MUFFY: I just bought these electric blue pants at *(insert store name)*.

BUFFY: Oh, I've seen them—I LOVE those. They're so cool. I'd love to have some just like them.

MUFFY: Well, they'll be absolutely perfect with a T-shirt I saw yesterday. I'm buying it right after the CD.

BUFFY: Wait a minute. Don't tell me. It's white.

MUFFY: That's right.

BUFFY: With blue lettering on the back?

MUFFY: Right again.

BUFFY: And on the front...

MUFFY and BUFFY: His picture!

BUFFY: Oh, I LOVE that shirt!

MUFFY: Me, too. I fell in love with it as soon as I saw it.

BUFFY: We're here. I've got an idea. We'll buy the CDs, then we'll go to my house. We'll play them over and over and over, and you can help me pick out what I'll wear to the concert.

MUFFY: I LOVE it. What a great idea! We'll have such a wonderful afternoon.

Knight Without Armor

SCRIPTURE: Ephesians 6:10-18

SUGGESTED TOPICS: Armor of God; choosing wisely; Christian life

BIBLE BACKGROUND

Paul wanted the early church to realize that it was engaged in warfare. To accomplish this end, he illustrated God's protection for His warriors by describing a common sight in the Roman Empire—a Roman soldier's armor.

PERFORMANCE TIPS

1. Suggested props: camouflage jackets.

2. Most of your group members will probably not be familiar with the armor referred to in Ephesians 6:10-18. This skit can help your group understand how each piece of armor was used by soldiers in the first century. Introduce the skit by asking, "What kinds of weapons do soldiers use today?" After group suggests answers say, "In Bible times a soldier's armor was very different. Listen to find out what he used."

DISCUSSION QUESTIONS

1. In Ephesians 6 Paul talks about Christians fighting battles. Who is the enemy we fight against? (See Ephesians 6:11-12.) What evidence of this enemy do you see in our world?

2. What might happen to an army that is not prepared for battle? What armor has God given His followers so they may be prepared for battle?

3. For each part of God's armor, what specific action can you take to put on or use the armor?

4. Satan is an intelligent enemy who will attack our weak points—the places in our lives where we have difficulty obeying God. What are your weak points? How can putting on God's armor protect you against this attack? Prepare yourself for battle. Put on God's armor everyday and ask for His protection.

KNIGHT WITHOUT ARMOR

CHARACTERS

SERGEANT
SOLDIER

SERGEANT: Alright, men. I have a dangerous mission and need a volunteer.

SOLDIER: I'm ready, Sarge! What do you want me to do?

SERGEANT: As you know, the main attack will come from the north side. I need you to approach from the south and allow yourself to be seen.

SOLDIER: But if they see me, they're going to shoot at me.

SERGEANT: That's the idea. While you're diverting their fire, we'll catch them unawares.

SOLDIER: I don't want to seem squeamish, Sarge, but I could be killed.

SERGEANT: I said it was a dangerous mission. What did you think that meant?

SOLDIER: Oh, yeah. I forgot. OK! I'm ready! When do we start?

SERGEANT: As soon as you're ready.

SOLDIER: I'm ready now, Sarge! I'm off.

SERGEANT: Hold it!

SOLDIER: Changed your mind, Sarge? Decided I was too important to risk?

SERGEANT: No. I have a question.

SOLDIER: Fire away, Sarge!

SERGEANT: You've got a lot of equipment to carry. You'll be on your own. How will you carry your equipment?

SOLDIER: No problem! All my equipment fits onto my belt. Not only that, my belt protects the old stomach. Didn't you take basic training, Sarge?

SERGEANT: I taught it. Where's your belt?

SOLDIER: It's here, around my—oh. No it isn't...oh, I remember. I took it off in the tent while I was resting. Half a minute. I'll just run and get it.

SERGEANT: And he wonders if he's expendable. OK, men. Listen up. When he comes back, he'll be heading south. Now, we'll split up into three sections...

SOLDIER: Ready now, Sarge! I'm off! Wish me luck?

SERGEANT: Wait a minute! I have another question.

SOLDIER: Questions, questions, questions. I thought we were supposed to fight.

SERGEANT: We are. But we're also supposed to be prepared. Now. What's going to happen when the enemy spots you?

SOLDIER: They'll be so overcome with fear, they'll all run away?

SERGEANT: Guess again.

SOLDIER: They'll shoot at me?

SERGEANT: Right! And what will happen if an arrow strikes you on the chest?

SOLDIER: Nothing, Sarge.

SERGEANT: Why not?

SOLDIER: Because it will bounce harmlessly off of my breastplate.

SERGEANT: What breastplate?

SOLDIER: The one that I'm wearing. *(Looks.)* The one I'm not wearing. Where did I leave it? I remember. When we stopped to make camp, I saw some blueberries and decided they would be good for dessert. But I didn't have a bucket to collect them, so I used my breastplate. It's over at the mess hall. Wait here. I'll be right back.

SERGEANT: OK, men. Let's go over the plan one more time. James and John, you'll command the other two sections. If anything happens to me, Peter, you'll take over the third section...

SOLDIER: I'm back. And I'm off.

SERGEANT: I was afraid of that. But before you go...

SOLDIER: Yes, Sarge?

SERGEANT: What sort of terrain will you be going through?

SOLDIER: Train? I'm not taking the train. I'm walking. Besides, trains haven't been invented yet.

SERGEANT: Not "train." I said terrain. That's the territory, the ground, the land. What will it be like?

SOLDIER: Didn't you read the reconnaissance reports, Sarge?

SERGEANT: Yes, I did. Did you?

SOLDIER: Of course I did. There's rocks and thistles and thorns...

SERGEANT: And how will you get across that terrain without hurting your feet?

SOLDIER: Are you kidding? These army sandals are the finest made. Nothing can penetrate their soles. Made to withstand all the rigors of battle and hiking.

SERGEANT: Which sandals are you talking about?

SOLDIER: The ones I have...where? What did I do with my sandals? Wait! I remember! When we stopped, my feet were tired and sore. So I took off my sandals and swished my feet in the river. I must have left them by the river. Don't go away. I'll be back.

SERGEANT: That's what I'm afraid of. OK, men. Now, James and John, you'll have to select an alternate from your section to replace you as leader in case something happens...

SOLDIER: Ta da! I found them. Right there by the river, just like I said.

SERGEANT: So now you're ready to go?

SOLDIER: You got that right!

SERGEANT: One question about basic combat. Suppose you stumble on an enemy sentry and he strikes at you with his sword? What will you do?

SOLDIER: Easy. I ward off his blow with my...

SERGEANT: Bare arm?

SOLDIER: Shield. I know I had one when I left. What did I do with it?

SERGEANT: Why me? What did I do to deserve him?

SOLDIER: Umbrella!

SERGEANT: What?

SOLDIER: My tent doesn't have any shade around it. So I took two poles and stuck them in the ground. Then, I strung a rope between the two poles and through my shield. Pretty clever, huh? I made my own shade tree. I'll just run, quick like a bunny, and get it.

SERGEANT: I don't think this attack will ever happen.

SOLDIER: OK, Sarge. Ready for inspection.

SERGEANT: Another basic element of combat. You'll be traveling through the trees. Suppose you're fighting and your head strikes a large tree branch?

SOLDIER: Bwonggggg! Right off the old helmet. No damage...

SERGEANT: If you're wearing a helmet. Where's your helmet, soldier?

SOLDIER: Heh, heh, heh. You're not going to believe this, Sarge...

SERGEANT: Try me. I'm ready to believe anything.

SOLDIER: When I was down at the river, I got to thinking...

SERGEANT: Thinking? You're right. I don't believe it.

SOLDIER: I'm going to need hot water in the morning. To shave with. So I took my helmet and filled it with water. Then I took it to my tent. See. I'm prepared.

SERGEANT: Go and get it! He's driving me crazy. Two more like him and we'll lose the war.

SOLDIER: Okey-dokey, Sarge. Ready when you are.

SERGEANT: You can't believe how relieved I am to hear that. Now, is your sword sharp?

SOLDIER: You bet. See...what do you suppose happened to my sword?

SERGEANT: I couldn't even hazard a guess.

SOLDIER: Ohhhhh! Sure! When I tried to push the poles into the ground, they wouldn't go. So I used my sword to sharpen their ends. You wouldn't believe how much simpler it is to push pointed sticks into the ground than rounded ones.

SERGEANT: I believe it.

SOLDIER: I've got it. Now I'm ready to go.

SERGEANT: I don't think there's any need.

SOLDIER: You just realized how important I am to this army, right?

SERGEANT: No. While we were waiting for you, the enemy snuck up and surrounded us. Don't shoot. We surrender.

SCRIPTURE: 2 Corinthians 8; 9

SUGGESTED TOPICS: Serving others; stewardship; responsibility to body of believers

BIBLE BACKGROUND

Paul's second letter to the Corinthian church has a great deal to say about giving. The church at Corinth was materially well-to-do, but suffered from spiritual poverty. Those who had wealth were reluctant to share with those less fortunate (see 1 Corinthians 11:17-34). Paul, seeing their lack of charity, commended the Macedonian church to the Corinthians and recommended that they examine their ways.

"Our desire is not that others might be relieved while you are hard pressed, but that there might be equality. At the present time your plenty will supply what they need, so that in turn their plenty will supply what you need" (2 Corinthians 8:13,14). Some condemn the above statement as communism. Indeed, it sounds similar to the writings of Karl Marx. But there is a major difference. Communism uses the power of government to force people to share with those around them. Christianity commends charity toward one another on the basis of Christ's gift to us (see 2 Corinthians 8:9).

PERFORMANCE TIPS

1. Suggested props: real or pretend money.

2. After the skit, present opportunities for group members to respond by donating time or money to someone in need.

DISCUSSION QUESTIONS

1. Compare the two attitudes described in 2 Corinthians 9:6. Which is better? To give a lot, grudgingly, or to give a little, cheerfully? Why? (In your discussion emphasize that the Bible does not teach that the purpose of giving is to gain more money. The Bible teaches that our generous giving is a response to the generous love God has shown us.)

2. What does 2 Corinthians 8:14 say will be the result when people give as they are able?

3. Some people are not able to give money. What are examples of other ways to share with people in need?

4. What can you give this week?

Mine, Mine, Mine

CHARACTERS

VINNIE
ZACK

VINNIE: *(Counting money.)* Nineteen, nineteen twenty-five, nineteen fifty, sixty, seventy, eighty, ninety, twenty dollars. Alright!

ZACK: Hi, Vinnie. What are you doing?

VINNIE: *(Quickly hides money.)* Nothing, nothing, nothing. What about you?

ZACK: I'm going over to Mrs. Green's.

VINNIE: Why? She's an old woman.

ZACK: That's one reason why I'm going.

VINNIE: Sometimes you don't make much sense, Zack.

ZACK: Well, she lives in that old house. And you've seen her fence.

VINNIE: Yeah. The thing's an eyesore. The city should make her tear it down.

ZACK: There's nothing wrong with her fence that a little paint won't cure. I looked at it yesterday. The wood's all OK. Only the paint is flaking off.

VINNIE: Well, she should do something about it. It's a disgrace to the whole neighborhood!

ZACK: Something is being done about it. I'm going over to paint it today.

VINNIE: That explains the can of paint you're carrying. Hey! That's a good idea. Painting a fence. How long would that take?

ZACK: Well, there's more than just painting. First, you have to scrape off the old paint. Then you prime the wood, because it's awfully dry right now. Then, you can paint it. It should take most of the day. Maybe even longer. I might have to finish tomorrow.

VINNIE: OK. Let's see now. All of today...say, eight hours?

ZACK: At least.

VINNIE: At five dollars an hour, that would be forty dollars. But that's pretty cheap, because you're supplying materials as well as labor. And you want to make a decent profit so, say, sixty dollars. Hey, you're going to do alright out of this.

ZACK: What do you mean?

VINNIE: Money! You know, the thing that makes the world go around.

ZACK: I thought love made the world go around.

VINNIE: Boy, have you got a lot to learn. Now, about that paint.

ZACK: What about it?

VINNIE: It's too good. Use cheaper paint. Less money spent, more profit.

ZACK: You don't understand at all. Mrs. Green hasn't painted her fence herself because of her arthritis. And she hasn't hired someone to do it because she can't afford it. I'm going over to paint it for free.

VINNIE: You've been out in the sun without a hat for too long. You've lost your marbles.

ZACK: No I haven't. They're on top of my dresser.

VINNIE: Think, boy. If you ain't got money, you ain't got nothin'. Don't do things for free. It's...it's un-American.

ZACK: No wonder you failed history. It's a hundred percent American. Not only that, it's Christian. People have always helped each other.

VINNIE: Yeah, right. Nobody does anything for nothing anymore.

ZACK: You don't believe that.

VINNIE: I sure do. Everybody looks out for Number One. You have to look out for yourself, because nobody else will.

ZACK: You not only don't know history, you don't even remember your own life.

VINNIE: What are you talking about?

ZACK: Five years ago.

VINNIE: What about it? I was a kid.

ZACK: Do you remember when your Mom was sick in the hospital?

VINNIE: Yeah, vaguely. She was there for a few days.

ZACK: And then?

VINNIE: She had to stay in bed for a few more days. What a drag. We all had to be quiet so we wouldn't disturb her.

ZACK: So who looked after your family?

VINNIE: Dad did. He went to work and then came home. Every day.

ZACK: So, who made lunch for you?

VINNIE: I don't know. I guess Dad must have.

ZACK: But he was at work.

VINNIE: Well, maybe it just materialized out of nowhere. What does it matter?

ZACK: I'll tell you who did it. Mrs. Green. And Mrs. Alverez. And Mrs. Vincetti. The older ladies in the church. They all got together and made sure your house was cleaned and all you kids had lunches.

VINNIE: So they made a few extra bucks helping us out. What's the big deal?

ZACK: They didn't make a few bucks. They did it out of love. For free.

VINNIE: Ah, who cares? That's ancient history.

ZACK: No it isn't. It's everyday life. People need other people. That's why all those ladies helped your family, and that's why I'm going to paint Mrs. Green's fence. Everybody needs help sometime. That's one reason people get together to be the church. To help other people. It's called giving.

VINNIE: I thought giving is when you put money in the offering plate.

ZACK: That's a part of giving. But even when you have no money, you can give. You can give your time and your talents.

VINNIE: It still doesn't make sense. Why should I give anything to anybody? I work hard to make what I do.

ZACK: Why are you able to work hard?

VINNIE: What is this? Some kind of game show? Answer the question and win a hundred bucks?

ZACK: No. I'm serious. Why can you work hard?

VINNIE: Because I'm healthy.

ZACK: And who made you healthy?

VINNIE: Nobody. I just am.

ZACK: Wrong. God made you healthy. He's given you good health. Not everybody is as fortunate. So what do we do with our good health? We thank God for it by using it to help others.

VINNIE: Why should we?

ZACK: Because it's right.

VINNIE *(pauses)***:** And what do I get out of it?

ZACK: Maybe nothing. That is, nothing you can see. But it makes you a better person, and that's something you can't buy with all the money in the world.

VINNIE: Look, I'm not doing anything right now anyway. If we stop at my house, I could change into some old clothes and maybe come and help you.

ZACK: Great! I could use the help.

VINNIE: Not that I'm saying you're right. But Mrs. Green did help us....

I Am Content

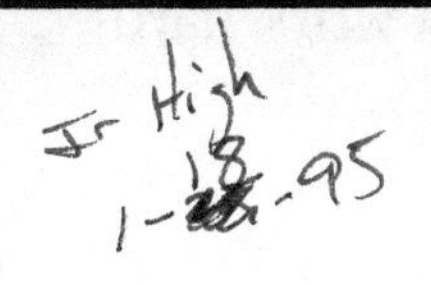

SCRIPTURE: Philippians 4:12

SUGGESTED TOPIC: Contentment

BIBLE BACKGROUND

Paul criticized the Corinthian church for timidity, lack of contentment and selfishness, among other failings evident in that early group of Christians. Similar shortcomings continue to be prevalent within the Church.

Rodeo is one of the strangest sports and attracts some of the most unusual competitors. Making one's living by trying to stay on the back of a raging bull for eight seconds, risking life and limb, is not for the faint-hearted. Huge monetary rewards are not their guiding principle. The few elite make large dollars, but most barely make enough to pay their travel expenses. And yet, they are among the most contented athletes in the world. Rarely does one hear complaints from them about any aspect of the life they have chosen.

PERFORMANCE TIPS

1. Suggested props: western clothes and hats.
2. Suggest that Johnny Jay speak loudly and excitedly. Jim Bob should show calmness by his relaxed tone of voice.
3. Just for fun, announce the rodeo to your group ahead of time. Ask group members to wear western clothes. Provide popcorn, peanuts and other snacks for a group party.

DISCUSSION QUESTIONS

1. How would you describe Jim Bob's attitude? Why was he so calm even in the middle of a difficult situation?
2. What might make someone discontent or unhappy with his or her life circumstances? When are some times you feel discontent? Why?
3. Read Philippians 4:11,12. How would you describe Paul's attitude? What key to Paul's contentment do you find in verse 13?
4. What is a difficult situation you are in? If you can't change the situation, what can you do to be contented?

I Am Content

CHARACTERS

GABBY

JIM BOB

JOHNNY

GABBY: Hello, rodeo fans! This is Gabby Day welcoming you to another edition of all-pro rodeo. We've got lots of excitement lined up for you today, all the events you know and love. And today, we have a special guest. Last year's world champion bull rider, Jim Bob James. Jim Bob, welcome to the show.

JIM BOB: Thank you, Gabby. Always a pleasure.

GABBY: Jim Bob, you've drawn a tough ride for tonight. Your old nemesis, Twisted Mister.

JIM BOB: Beg pardon there, Gabby?

GABBY: A bull that's given you lots of trouble in the past. Your nemesis.

JIM BOB: Yeah. Well now, Twisted Mister is one rank bull, that's for certain. Don't hardly never get rode by nobody.

GABBY: How do you feel about drawing such a tough bull?

JIM BOB: Well, that's just the way things happen. Sometimes you draw a rockin' chair that won't give no trouble at all, and other times you get a bad one that's liable to kick you clear to Oklahoma. Ain't no use frettin' about it.

GABBY: So, how are you planning to ride him tonight?

JIM BOB: Well now, I been ponderin' this for some time. He tends to go left, so I gotta ride him outta the chute and plan on a tough left spin. Ride that boy right tonight, could be I'll be at the pay window before the night's out.

GABBY: Last year, you had your best year ever. World Champion at the National Finals Rodeo.

JIM BOB: Well now, feller couldn't hardly plan on having a better year than I had last. Won lots of cash. Traveled the country, meetin' lots of fine folks. Enjoyed that year mighty well.

GABBY: This year has been something of a disappointment, however.

JIM BOB: Ain't been as fine as others. But can't say as I got anything particular to complain about.

GABBY: But it started out with a broken leg in your first rodeo of the year.

JIM BOB: That's true, yeah. But broken legs heal up and I'm ridin' again, so I guess it ain't all bad.

GABBY: Speaking of injuries, you also had three concussions, two broken ribs and a broken jaw.

JIM BOB: I suppose it ain't been the best season a cowboy could hope for, but everything's healing up just fine. And I'm sure glad I'm riding these days. Few years back, some of them little nicks coulda put you out of action for a whole year. Now, things is different.

GABBY: In what way?

JIM BOB: Oh, they's got these new braces and mouth shield things. Shucks, a fella's pretty near indestructible with all this here equipment.

GABBY: It's been great talking to you, Jim Bob. We'll be looking forward to seeing your ride tonight.

JIM BOB: Always a pleasure. See you at the pay window.

GABBY: We're ready for the first section of bull riders. This is always an exciting event, a crowd favorite. Joining me now is former bull riding great, Johnny Jay.

JOHNNY: Hey there, Gabby! We got us some excitement here tonight! Ol' Jim Bob, he's got his hands full with that big Brahma, Twisted Mister. But that bull's capable of getting a cowboy to the pay window, that's for sure.

GABBY: Speaking of Jim Bob, he'll be the first rider tonight.

JOHNNY: He sure will be. Get ready! The clowns are coming out! Old Ray Coutts, the grand old man of bull fighters, is rolling out the barrel, and Billy Ayers and Mickey Jones will be protecting those riders who get thrown.

GABBY: The clowns are ready, the judges are ready. Looking into chute number six, we see Jim Bob wrapping the bull rope around his right hand. Looks like he's ready. He nods his head.

JOHNNY: Whoowee! Look at that bull come outta that chute! Oh, oh! Looks like Jim Bob's in trouble! Bail outta there, boy! He's down! Come on, Billy Ayers! Get in there! Protect that cowboy!

GABBY: Ouch! Looks like Twisted Mister stepped right on old Jim Bob.

JOHNNY: Let's check out that replay. You can see how Jim Bob figured Twisted Mister was gonna spin left. But that ol' bull outright fooled him, that's for sure. Jim Bob was leaning and the big Brahma went the other way. He was out of there right from the start.

GABBY: Right here, at the end. Look at that. Twisted Mister stepped right on Jim Bob's boot. Looks like he got him right on the ankle.

JOHNNY: He sure did. That boy's in a lotta pain. But he's a tough old boy. You know he'll be back.

GABBY: They're helping him out of the arena now. I'm going back to try to get a word with him, see how he is.

JOHNNY: While Gabby's gettin' down there, let's take one last look at the replay. Yeah, he definitely didn't have a chance of staying with that bull, right from the get-go.

GABBY: Jim Bob. Tough break on the ride. Tell us what happened.

JIM BOB: Well, he just downright kinda fooled me. I was expecting the left spin, but he went right.

GABBY: Right at the end, just before Billy Ayers got in there, it looked like Twisted Mister stepped on you.

JIM BOB: Well, he did that, right enough.

GABBY: What's the condition of your leg?

JIM BOB: Oh, she's hurtin' a might. But she's been hurt before. Can't waste time complainin' about what's happened in the past. Feels like she might be broke, but we won't know for sure 'til the X rays get took.

GABBY: It looked like Billy Ayers may have been a bit late getting in to distract the bull. What can you tell us about that?

JIM BOB: Oh, Billy's a good ol' boy. Does a fine job. Couldn't have done much better than he did. Hadn't been for him, I mighta been hurt a lot worse. Plumb thankful he was quick as he was.

GABBY: I see the ambulance is ready to leave...

JIM BOB: It's been right nice talking to you again. And all you folks out there, I wanna thank you for all them prayers you been saying for me and all them cards you been sending. Don't you worry. Ol' Jim Bob'll be back soon.

GABBY: An amazing display of courage. Back to you, Johnny, for the next ride.

Gospel Light's Junior Curriculum Index

The skits in this book are based on scriptural material studied in Gospel Light's Junior Curriculum, Year A.

FALL: GOD IS MY GUIDE

WINTER: JESUS IS MY SAVIOR

SPRING: THE CHURCH IS MY FAMILY

SUMMER: GOD'S PLAN IS FOR ME

Biblical Character Index

CHARACTER	SCRIPTURE	SKIT TITLE	PAGE NUMBER
Jesus			
Teachings	Matthew 6:5-15	"To Trap a Teacher"	98
	Matthew 6:25-34; 7:7-11; Luke 12:6,7, 22-31	"Don't Worry"	81
	Matthew 18:21-35	"Forgive and Forget"	87
	Matthew 25:14-30	"The Talents"	91
	Matthew 26:6-13; Mark 14:3-9; John 12:1-8	"Waste Nard, Want Nard"	102
	Luke 6:46-49	"Ocean Front Property"	16
	Luke 15:1-10	"Lost and Found"	84
	John 3:1-21	"Nicodemus"	95
	John 13:1-17; 21:3-8	"Going Fishing"	104
John	Matthew 28:1-10; Luke 24:1-12; John 20:1-18	"He's Alive!	124
	Acts 3:1—4:22	"Crippled"	132
	Acts 8:1-25	"Samaria Today"	145
John the Baptist	Luke 1:5-45,57-66; Matthew 1:18-25	"The Birth of John"	70
Joshua	Joshua 3; 4	"Problems, Problems, Problems"	26
	Joshua 6:1-21	"Such Sound"	30
	Joshua 6:19; 7:1-4	"Ai!"	34
Josiah	Deuteronomy 30:11—31:13; 2 Kings 22:1—23:3; 2 Chronicles 34:1-15	"This Is the Law"	9
Luke	Acts 1; 2	"Acts"	129
	Acts 20	"Farewell"	181
Nicodemus	John 3:1-21	"Nicodemus"	95
Paul	Acts 13:1-12	"Paphos by Night"	165
	Acts 17	"Troublemakers"	171
	Acts 20	"Farewell"	181
	Acts 21:27—22:30	"The Scourgeof Jerusalem"	185
	Acts 22:30—23:15	"The Plot Thickens"	190

SCRIPTURE INDEX

Topical Index